DECONSTRUCTING CORRUPTION IN AFRICA

This book investigates corruption and anti-corruption efforts in Africa, emphasising the regional and thematic differences across the continent, whilst also exploring key patterns and trends.

Combatting the ethnocentrism of Western corruption research, this book highlights the importance of a home-generated and contextualised approach to understanding corruption in Africa. Bringing together a rich array of qualitative, quantitative, and mixed methods research, the book considers how corruption manifests in a range of selected countries across the political, economic, and social spheres. The book adopts a strong comparative approach, exploring patterns, dynamics, and mechanisms in African societies. It assesses the historical underpinnings of corruption, emerging trends, and socio-economic realities before suggesting realistic contemporary solutions to the challenges of corruption in Africa. Bringing together academics and practitioners, readers will encounter intellectual discussion face-to-face with realities on the ground.

As such, the book will be useful for scholars, politicians, public officials, and civil society organizations, as well as for students and researchers across the fields of political science, public administration, economy and corruption studies.

Ina Kubbe is a professor at the University of Tel Aviv, at the School of Political International Relations, where she mainly researches and teaches on corruption, migration, gender politics, and conflict resolution. Ina is also a professor at the International Anti-Corruption Academy (IACA) in Austria. She specialises in social science methodology and comparative research on empirical democracy, corruption and governance research. Ina has published several books, special issues, and articles in the field and is one of the founding members of the Interdisciplinary Corruption Research Network (ICRN) as well as the Chair of the ECPR Standing Group on (Anti)Corruption and Integrity.

Emmanuel Saffa Abdulai is a barrister and solicitor of the High Courts of Sierra Leone, and lecturer in the Department of Legal Studies, Faculty of Law, University of Sierra Leone. He is deputy editor of the *Institute of Advanced Legal Studies' Law Review*, and founder and editor-in-chief of the *Journal of Law* in the Faculty of Law, Fourah Bay College, Sierra Leone. Over the last two decades, Abdulai has been a leading campaigner for the passing and implementation of freedom of information law in Sierra Leone and Africa as a civil society practitioner working for the Society for Democratic Initiatives. Abdulai was chair of the Governing Council of the African Freedom of Information Council, and is also chairperson of the Political Affairs Cluster of the African Union's Economic Social and Cultural Council.

Michael Johnston is a Charles A. Dana Professor of Political Science Emeritus at Colgate University in Hamilton, New York, USA. He retired from Colgate in 2015, but since 2012 has offered lectures and seminars at the International Anti-Corruption Academy near Vienna. He now lives in suburban Texas in the USA, and continues his research projects.

Routledge Corruption and Anti-Corruption Studies

The series features innovative and original research on the subject of corruption from scholars around the world. As well as documenting and analysing corruption, the series aims to discuss anti-corruption initiatives and endeavours, in an attempt to demonstrate ways forward for countries and institutions where the problem is widespread. The series particularly promotes comparative and interdisciplinary research targeted at a global readership.

In terms of theory and method, rather than basing itself on any one orthodoxy, the series draws broadly on the toolkit of the social sciences in general, emphasizing comparison, the analysis of the structure and processes, and the application of qualitative and quantitative methods.

Corruption Proofing in Africa
A Systems Thinking Approach
Edited by Dan Kuwali

Corruption, Ethics, and Governance in South Africa
Issues, Cases, and Interventions
Edited by Modimowabarwa Kanyane

Deconstructing Corruption in Africa
Edited by Ina Kubbe, Emmanuel Saffa Abdulai and Michael Johnston

For more information about this series, please visit: www.routledge.com/Routledge-Corruption-and-Anti-Corruption-Studies/book-series/RCACS

DECONSTRUCTING CORRUPTION IN AFRICA

Edited by Ina Kubbe, Emmanuel Saffa Abdulai and Michael Johnston

LONDON AND NEW YORK

Designed cover image: Getty Images / VPanteon

First published 2025
by Routledge
4 Park Square, Milton Park, Abingdon, Oxon OX14 4RN

and by Routledge
605 Third Avenue, New York, NY 10158

Routledge is an imprint of the Taylor & Francis Group, an informa business

© 2025 selection and editorial matter, Ina Kubbe, Emmanuel Saffa Abdulai and Michael Johnston; individual chapters, the contributors

The right of Ina Kubbe, Emmanuel Saffa Abdulai and Michael Johnston to be identified as the authors of the editorial material, and of the authors for their individual chapters, has been asserted in accordance with sections 77 and 78 of the Copyright, Designs and Patents Act 1988.

All rights reserved. No part of this book may be reprinted or reproduced or utilised in any form or by any electronic, mechanical, or other means, now known or hereafter invented, including photocopying and recording, or in any information storage or retrieval system, without permission in writing from the publishers.

Trademark notice: Product or corporate names may be trademarks or registered trademarks, and are used only for identification and explanation without intent to infringe.

British Library Cataloguing-in-Publication Data
A catalogue record for this book is available from the British Library

ISBN: 9781032743004 (hbk)
ISBN: 9781032742908 (pbk)
ISBN: 9781003468608 (ebk)

DOI: 10.4324/9781003468608

Typeset in Sabon
by Newgen Publishing UK

CONTENTS

List of Contributors   *x*
Acknowledgements   *xiv*

    Introduction: The Many Faces of Corruption in Africa   1
    Emmanuel Saffa Abdulai, Ina Kubbe and
    Michael Johnston

PART I
Corruption in the Political Sector   11

1   The Politics of State Capture in South Africa:
      A New Variant of Corruption?   13
      Thomas A. Koelble

2   Domains of Corruption in Nigeria: A Four-Part
      Taxonomy and Nigeria's Anti-corruption Paradox   31
      Aruna Kallon

3   Recounting How Electoral Corruption Manifests in
      Sierra Leone: Stories and Lessons from the Field   50
      Marcella Samba-Sesay née Macauley

4 Understanding Political Corruption in Uganda through the Lens of Complexity Thinking and Historical Institutionalism 70
Clare Cheromoi, Asiimwe Godfrey, Charlotte Karungi Mafumbo and Richard Sebaggala

5 Unravelling the Complexities: Identifying Persistent Factors Hindering Anti-corruption Efforts in Cameroon 88
Kwei Haliday Nyingchia

6 Lobbying in Tunisia: Developing a Transparency Regime to Tackle Perceptions of Corruption 104
Barry Solaiman

PART II
Corruption in the Economic and Social Sector **129**

7 Corruption as an Investment Risk: A Case Study on Anti-corruption Strategies in Djibouti 131
Wael Saghir

8 Debunking the Demand-Driven Myth of Corruption: The Case of the Saint Louis Scandal in Mauritius 150
Sanjeev Narrainen

9 Charismatic Churches and Corruption in Ghana: Feeding the Beast? 180
Riccardo D'Emidio

10 The Causes and Consequences of Corruption in Zambia 197
Arthur Chisanga, Steven Daka, Victor Kaonga and Tambulani Chayima Nyirenda

Conclusion: The Way Forward – Deconstructing the
Many Faces of Corruption in Africa   214
*Ina Kubbe, Emmanuel Saffa Abdulai and
Michael Johnston*

Index   224

CONTRIBUTORS

Tambulani Chayima Nyirenda is a lecturer and researcher in the Department of Government and Management Studies at the University of Zambia. He holds a Bachelor's degree in Public Administration and a Master of Public Administration degree from the University of Zambia. He specialises in Governance, Health Policy and Public Procurement. His recent publications have appeared/will appear in the *Sexual & Reproductive Healthcare* journal, *Clinics in Mother and Child Health*, *BMJ Open* and Sage publications.

Clare Cheromoi, PhD is a fellow at the College of Humanities and Social Sciences, Makerere University. Her research interests focus on political corruption in post-independent Uganda, from a historical perspective. She holds a Master's Degree from Erasmus University, International Institute of Social Studies, The Hague in the Netherlands and a Master's in Anti-Corruption Studies from Austria.

Arthur Chisanga has a Master of Science Degree with a specialisation in International Administration and Global Governance obtained in 2016 from the University of Gothenburg. He previously received his Bachelor of Arts Degree with a minor in Development Studies obtained in 2012 from the University of Zambia. He has worked as an undergraduate teaching assistant for Public Administration (UNZA) and a research assistant at the Varieties of Democracy Institute at the University of Gothenburg, Department of Political Science. He currently works as a full-time lecturer at the Lusaka Apex Medical University in Zambia. His main research interests include governance of the commons, local governance and development, quality of government, gender equality, human resource management, public policy and industrial relations.

Steven Daka is a Public Management expert, mainly specialising in Public Management, Public Policy and E-government. He has recently published a paper titled "A critical analysis of the guarantee mechanism of the Australian and UK's health sector on open data". He is also a holder of a Master of Science in Public Management from the University of Electronic Science and Technology in China and an undergraduate degree in Public Administration from the University of Zambia.

Riccardo D'Emidio is a doctoral candidate at the Centre for the Study of Corruption, University of Sussex (UK). His research explores the nexus of social norms and corruption.

Asiimwe Godfrey, PhD is an ISS (Erasmus) Assoc. Professor, Lecturer Makerere University College of Humanities Social Sciences Department of Development Studies/ Department of History. He holds a BA/Educ (Hons) from Makerere University.

Kwei Haliday Nyingchia is a judge and examining magistrate, an assistant lecturer at the Bamenda University of Science and Technology and a part-time lecturer at the Higher Technical Teachers' Training College-Kumba in the University of Buea, Cameroon.

Aruna Kallon is a doctoral candidate and teaching assistant at the University of Wisconsin-Madison, USA. He holds a master's degree in Sustainable Peacebuilding, a Bachelor of Laws (LLB), and a Bachelor of Arts in English. Aruna worked for over three years in the non-profit sector in Sierra Leone, advocating for civil and political rights, gender justice, and judicial accountability, principally with the Center for Accountability and the Rule of Law in Freetown.

Victor Kaonga is a Development expert, currently specialising in Public Health Research, Sustainable Development Policy and climate change. He has an MSc in Sustainable International Development from the University of Bradford in the UK and an undergraduate degree in Development Studies from the University of Zambia.

Charlotte Karungi Mafumbo is the current head of the Department of History and a lecturer at Makerere University. She is also an academic director of the SIT Study Abroad semester-long program, Uganda: Development Studies, as well as academic director of the SIT Study Abroad summer program, Uganda and Rwanda: Peace and Conflict Studies in the Lake Victoria Basin (Summer) Charlotte obtained her PhD from the University of Cape Town, South Africa. She also holds an MA in international studies from the University of Sydney, Australia; a postgraduate certificate in gender and conflict studies from Hannover University, Germany; a postgraduate diploma in social conditions and policies from Copenhagen University; and a BA of history and international organisation from Makerere University in Kampala. She completed a fellowship as a 2012 Global South Scholar at the Graduate Institute of International and Development Studies in Geneva.

Thomas A. Koelble is a professor of Business Administration in Political Science at the Graduate School of Business, University of Cape Town, South Africa. He is the author of several books and has published in journals such as *New Political Economy*, *Democratization*, *Public Culture*, *Governance*, *Comparative Politics*, *Politics and Society* amongst others.

Sanjeev Narrainen holds a doctorate in Criminology/ Criminal Justice from the University of Portsmouth, an LLM in ICT Law from the University of Strathclyde, and a Bachelor's degree in Mechanical Engineering from the University of Mauritius. He is now the Integrity and Compliance Manager at the Green Climate Fund leading the Prevention Unit on the development of Integrity policies, prevention strategies, due diligence and assessment of the anti-money laundering and counter-financing of terrorism.

Wael Saghir is a senior lecturer in Innovation at LSBU, co-director for the Digital Culture, Finance and Ecological Sustainability Think Tank Programme at the Global Research Network, an international consultant and consulting professor to US academic institutions, and an expert in international business risks, innovation, and financial law.

Marcella Samba-Sesay nee Macauley is a democracy-building practitioner of 17 years standing and heads the Campaign for Good Governance (CGG), a civic participation organisation, and is also chairperson of the National Election Watch (NEW), a coalition of over 400 organisations observing, monitoring and promoting credible elections in Sierra Leone. She has observed a number of elections across the world and trained thousands of domestic election observers. Marcella holds a Master of Arts Degree in Democracy, Politics and Governance from the Royal Holloway University of London.

Richard Sebaggala, PhD is a fellow at the School of Business, University of Agder, Norway. He has been a lecturer of economics at Uganda Christian University, School of Business since 2007. Richard completed his Master of

Science degree in Quantitative Economics and a Bachelor of Arts Degree with Education majoring in Economics from Makerere University. His research interests lie in the areas of development economics, health, disability and welfare, corruption, inequality and poverty, and behavioural economics. Richard is also an associate research fellow with the Policy Analysis and Development Research Institute (PADRI). Between 2011 and 2012, Richard worked with the Program for Accessible Health, Communication and Education (PACE) as a research manager. Over the years, Richard has independently designed both quantitative and qualitative research studies for program evaluation, managed large fieldwork data collection activities, data management and analysis.

Barry Solaiman is an assistant professor of Law at Hamad Bin Khalifa University (HBKU), College of Law. He holds a PhD in Law from the University of Cambridge.

ACKNOWLEDGEMENTS

Corruption in Africa is a pressing and far-reaching concern that affects every facet of society, from governance and development to social justice and individual well-being. It has implications that extend beyond national borders and create challenges at all levels of society. Writing and editing a comprehensive book on this pervasive issue would not have been possible without the support, contributions, and dedication of many individuals and organisations. We want to express our heartfelt gratitude to all who contributed to bringing this project to fruition.

First and foremost, we extend our gratitude to the esteemed authors who contributed their expertise, research, and insights to this book. Your dedication to shedding light on the complex dimensions of corruption in Africa is deeply appreciated.

We thank the tireless efforts of the reviewers and editors who meticulously reviewed and refined each chapter, ensuring the highest academic rigour and clarity.

We are also indebted to the organisations and institutions that provided research grants, data, and resources that supported the research and writing process. Your commitment to advancing our understanding of corruption in Africa is commendable.

Special thanks go to our colleagues and friends who offered valuable feedback, encouragement, and moral support throughout this endeavour. Your insights and encouragement were invaluable.

Lastly, we would like to acknowledge the readers of this book, on whom the ultimate significance and impact of our work will depend. We hope that the information and insights presented here will contribute to a deeper understanding of corruption in Africa and inspire meaningful action towards combating this pervasive issue.

Thank you all for your unwavering support and commitment to addressing corruption in Africa. Together, we can make a difference.

This book is dedicated to all the people affected by corruption and enduring its detrimental impacts on their daily lives. It is also committed to those individuals who courageously stand up and fight against corruption, working tirelessly to bring about positive change.

We acknowledge the hardships and injustices corruption inflicts upon individuals, communities, and societies. We sincerely hope that the research presented in this book will promote equality and justice around the globe.

May the knowledge and insights shared within these pages inspire individuals, organisations, and governments to take action against corruption. Let us strive for a world where integrity, transparency, and accountability prevail, creating a brighter and more equitable future for all.

Ina Kubbe (*Tel Aviv University*)
Emmanuel Saffa Abdulai (*University of Sierra Leone*)
Michael Johnston (*Colgate University, Hamilton, New York*)

INTRODUCTION

The Many Faces of Corruption in Africa

Emmanuel Saffa Abdulai, Ina Kubbe and Michael Johnston

Much of the research literature on corruption in Africa is driven by the agenda of the international anti-corruption industry and, as a result, is empty in essential respects of the experiences of Africa and Africans. Those are the points of departure of this book.

Corruption is often considered a side-effect of development, poverty and instability within fragile states, particularly in the African region (Momoh, 2015; Asongu, 2013; Okorie, 2018; Agang et al., 2019). However, it also does much to perpetuate underdevelopment (Agbiboa, 2013). That general outlook has led to misleading conceptualisations of corruption in the continent, to unsustainable anti-corruption measures quickly abandoned because they are not homegrown, or to reforms that have failed outright due to a lack of proper diagnosis (Kubbe & Engelbert, 2018; Kubbe & Varraich, 2019). For instance, most accounts of corruption in Nigeria have ignored culturally ingrained ways of life that, even if they go against internationally sanctioned strategies, might help reduce corruption (EgoAlowes, 2017). South Africa, by contrast, reveals a unique corruption case of a cabal capturing the machinery of the state with brilliant and almost undetectable cover-ups (Madonsela, 2018). Such patients present us with corruption threats and reform opportunities and require new thinking.

Historically, Africa was one of the regions that attracted corruption analysts' attention earliest, going back as far back as 1963 (Wraith & Simpkins, 1963). However, ironically, it is now the region most needing fresh concepts and practical applications. To that end, this book avoids repeating the frequent mistake of clustering different countries into blanket categories such as "Africa" or "Sub-Saharan Africa". African countries represent widely divergent societies and themes, deserving more than the monolithic misdescriptions that pervade the research on an over-generalised continent. African states, institutions and their contrasts matter; their internal dynamics and differences are worth our attention.

Compounding these problems requires more detailed empirical literature on the causes, effects and consequences of corruption in Africa. Typically, the debate has been dominated by researchers from non-governmental organisations with an agenda of problem identification for project development using the paradigms of Western diagnosis based on a conception of affluent nations' histories and experiences that have severe shortcomings in their own right. The resulting lack of research grounded in African social realities provides an excellent opportunity for this book to bring together African-oriented researchers and experts seeking an enriched understanding of their respective societies, political institutions, cultures and norms.

Further, the existing corruption literature continues to inform national and international anti-corruption interventions and measures despite continuing changes in Africa and our understanding of corruption. The international community is still locked into fighting corruption for people rather than with them, much fewer helping people fight it themselves (EgoAlowes, 2017; Abdulai, 2022; Johnston & Fritzen, 2021).

The Book's Guiding Questions

Accordingly, this book aims to answer the following main research questions:

1. What are the specific corruption issues facing ten selected African countries?
2. How do those issues resemble and differ from each other and those assumed in the mainstream anti-corruption literature and reform playbooks?
3. What broader lessons can be learned from a detailed study of those cases?

Our book aims to avoid treating Africa as a monolith, depicting it instead as containing diverse countries, regions and a vast range of communal identities and divisions – in short, analysing it just as we would other continents. Offering a range of African voices, we also hope to develop a solid comparative perspective illuminating the diverse patterns, dynamics and mechanisms found among Africa's societies. We study the historical underpinnings and emerging trends of systemic corruption, searching for cultural bedrock to support the reinvigorated resistance to corrosion rather than falling back upon theories crafted in and shaped by the experiences of other parts of the world. In the end, we hope to encourage further innovative research that will unravel emerging issues, conceptualise socio-economic realities and proffer realistic and contemporary solutions to the scourge of corruption in the continent. We have convened a diverse group of mid-career academicians and

Introduction: The Many Faces of Corruption in Africa   **3**

practitioners to connect intellectual discussion with realities on the ground. Additionally, we hope to create a vibrant and lasting network of corruption and anti-corruption analysts and activists who will continue the debate long after the book has been published.

Plan of Attack

The book consists of two significant parts focusing on corruption's political and socio-economic aspects and reform challenges. Part one, with six chapters, deals with corruption in the political sphere in South Africa, Nigeria, Sierra Leone, Uganda, Cameroon and Tunisia. Part two includes five chapters that cover economic and social activities that have attracted corruption to Djibouti, Mauritius, Ghana and Zambia.

Part I: Corruption in the Political Sector

Chapter 1 presents "*The Politics of State Capture in South Africa: A New Variant of Corruption?*" Thomas Koelble explains that since the election of Cyril Ramaphosa as President of the ANC in 2017 and South Africa in 2019, there has been a marked shift in the government's tolerance toward corruption, particularly toward "state capture". The former State President, Jacob Zuma, was widely regarded to have encouraged multiple networks of ANC-connected individuals to take advantage of state funds to enrich themselves. Since Ramaphosa's rise to power, several investigations, including a Commission of Inquiry headed by Judge Raymond Zondo, have uncovered the extensive nature of corruption. Several books, articles and investigative newspaper accounts further reveal the extent of the damage. Several high-ranking members of the ANC, including the former president, are now awaiting court proceedings on corruption-related matters. The chapter reveals that what might appear to be a straightforward case of the "corrupt" facing off with the "incorruptible" is unclear. First, the coalition of forces supporting Zuma remains powerful, and Ramaphosa's hold over the ANC is precarious. Second, there is a widespread view in South Africa that "corruption" is justifiable because the "rules of the game" are neo-liberal, imposed by the West. While there is a good portion of self-serving ideology about Zuma's claim that "there is no corruption" in Africa and that it is a Western term designed to reinforce negative images of African politics while forgetting its colonial history of exploitation, the argument resonates with large sections of the population and within the ANC. The chapter considers the implications of the unfolding situation for South Africa.

Nigeria presents an intriguing case in Chapter 2, "*Domains of Corruption in Nigeria: A Four-Part Taxonomy and Nigeria's Anti-corruption Paradox*". Aruna Kallon argues that corruption has devastating consequences for many African economies. It is a significant impediment to economic development, not only for the continent but especially in most low-income countries. Kallon argues that corruption is a product of individual attributes of greed and dishonesty enabled by structural, bureaucratic and political inefficiencies. These factors frustrate – even render unachievable – national development policy objectives and ultimately weaken the Nigerian economy. Corruption adversely affects social welfare, mobility, social justice and socio-economic livelihoods as a small but privileged segment of the population illegally accumulates massive wealth at the expense of a powerless majority. The chapter recommends policy reforms and actions to ensure that scarce governmental resources are allocated to fight against corruption in Nigeria.

Chapter 3, by Marcella Samba, brings a unique and often overlooked theme to the discussion of corruption. "*Recounting How Electoral Corruption Manifests in Sierra Leone: Stories and Lessons from the Field*" provides a detailed field report and argues that corruption has become a binding constraint on the agenda-setting of Sierra Leone's public policy. The electoral system suffers from vote-buying, vote-rigging, violation of procedures and outright violence. Samba shows that while little literature exists on this topic, such flagrant abuses are becoming commonplace. In the case of Sierra Leone, she shows that in the 2018 General elections, political party operatives were filmed publicly distributing cash to supporters while chanting political songs with sentiments supporting vote-buying. In a 2019 by-election, civil society observed for the first time evidence of ballot-box stuffing. Evidence of "turnout" buying exists where influential chiefs and party functionaries pledge to hand over whole tribes, chiefdoms or districts to a political party of their choice rather than leaving voters to make individual choices. As the country's electoral laws are primarily silent on money politics, it becomes difficult to pursue further actions. Conversely, political parties and stakeholders are less inclined to unearth electoral corruption. The chapter identifies the sources of political campaign finance using a practitioner's approach, archives of election observation reports, and interviews conducted with stakeholders. It explains why the politics of reward bedevil democracy in Sierra Leone.

Chapter 4 deals with "*Understanding Political Corruption in Uganda through the Lens of Complexity Thinking and Historical Institutionalism*". Clare Cheromoi, Asiimwe Godfrey, Charlotte Karungi Mafumbo and Richard Sebaggala show that political corruption has become endemic in many African countries, including Uganda. Unlike bureaucratic corruption, which might be checked by the effective implementation of regulatory and anti-corruption reforms, political corruption appears to be an extractive and power-preserving corrupt activity. Therefore, reform has proved difficult because few political actors have a stake in fighting electoral corruption. The implication of that argument is the suggestion that those opposed to corruption must become more determined and persistent to be successful. However, is it also possible that the Crusaders are using the wrong ideas? Or what if those interested in corruption are too entrenched to be challenged by other political actors? The authors argue that while political corruption is a complex problem with historical roots, previous researchers have not used historical institutionalism to interrogate political corruption in the continent. Historical institutionalism conceptualises institutions as arenas for power-distributional conflicts. It focuses on how institutions develop over time and affect actors' positions in ways that may have been unintended or undesired by their creators. African traditions that allow significant family problems and responsibilities to fall upon one member who works in a public office are just one case in point.

Chapter 5, "*Unravelling the Complexities: Identifying Persistent Factors Hindering Anti-corruption Efforts in Cameroon*", by Kwei Haliday Nyingchia, notes how, in 1998 and 1999, Cameroon was the absolute cellar-dweller in Transparency International's corruption perception index. Since then, the country has continued to be classified as one of the most corrupt in the world. Since 2000, several legal and institutional mechanisms have been put in place in response, but unfortunately, the level of corruption and whether it is systematic raise different questions. This chapter holds that Cameroon's alarming level of crime can be attributed to many causes. The first cause concerns how extraordinary powers accorded to the President of the Republic, subject to little or no accountability, have weakened control organs. The absence of a strong opposition and a legislature that the ruling party has captured further amplifies corruption. There is also a weak and inefficient judiciary and prosecution service. Furthermore, anti-corruption institutions lack independence. An inefficient system of accountability and the non-criminalisation of conduct, such as illicit enrichment and non-declaration of assets, continue to serve as incentives for corruption. The situation is made worse by the derisory implementation of multilateral anti-corruption conventions. Other historical and socio-economic causes like meagre salaries, favouritism, nepotism, and a culture of irresponsibility and systematic impunity have remained among the severe causes of corruption in Cameroon. The main objective of this chapter is to investigate why the incentives for bribery have remained endemic despite enacting several anti-corruption measures.

Chapter 6 by Barry Solaiman discusses "*Lobbying in Tunisia: Developing a Transparency Regime to Tackle Perceptions of Corruption*". In the last two decades, there has been a proliferation of legislation around the globe, including in Tunisia, New Zealand and Singapore, to tackle concerns surrounding political lobbying. Laws have been enacted to promote transparent registers detailing meetings, donations and events between lobbyists and politicians. Transparency is seen as a prerequisite to accountability and restoring public trust. However, as D'Angelo and others argue, sometimes transparency strengthens the hand of contributors by enabling them to monitor recipients' actions and ensure they get value for money. African countries lag far behind in these developments, with a distinct omission of regulations surrounding political lobbying. Even the African Union lacks the institutional transparency register that would be the norm in other supranational institutions. This gap must be remedied carefully, paying particular attention to the overarching framework that guides anti-corruption initiatives. In that regard, this chapter analyses Tunisia as a case study to develop an analytical framework that can be used to identify concerns about political corruption and suggest regulatory solutions. Tunisia is the only democracy in North Africa, following the revolution of 2010–2011 and the significant constitutional changes it brought. It must implement lobbying transparency regulations, the first in Africa. Concerns about the control of the media by lobbyists, the links between government ministers and industry, and the flow of "corrupt money" in parliament to influence legislation threaten to derail its progress.

Part II: Corruption in the Socio-economic Sector

In Chapter 7, "*Corruption as an Investment Risk: A Case Study on Anti-corruption Strategies in Djibouti*", Wael Saghir deals with the risks foreign direct investors (FDIs) and multinational corporations (MNCs) encounter in the international arena – in particular, political risks. Those risks come in different forms, causing investors and MNCs different levels of unease and threatening their property rights. Corruption is a political risk since it is closely related to the quality of the host state's political institutions. This becomes particularly evident when the host state's officials demand personal benefits. Such threats are likely to discourage FDI. However, corruption is not only a problem for investors and MNCs; it threatens the host states and their ability to protect their environments, labour forces and natural resources. Foreign state-owned enterprises have bribed host state officials to secure unearned business advantages, as witnessed in the case of China's investments in Zambia and other African states. Finally, this chapter elaborates on the role played by Export Credit Agencies and home-state laws like the US Foreign Corrupt Practices Act and the Anti-Bribery Act of the UK in combating bribery and corruption and how they could discourage corrupt practices by other foreign investors.

Chapter 8, "*Debunking the Demand-Driven Myth of Corruption: The Case of the Saint Louis Scandal in Mauritius*", by Sanjeev Narrainen, introduces corruption in multilateral institutions and the energy sector. International development projects present a fertile ground for corporate crime, a set of abuses that have become pervasive and entrenched in the corporate world.

Bribery to win contracts and post-contract assessment is a widespread problem. In recent years, international financial institutions have sanctioned many corporations for participating in corruption schemes in Africa. A case study shows how and why contractors in an energy project in Mauritius engaged in corrupt systems. The chapter identifies the main determinants that encourage corporate corruption in development projects, emphasising institutional corruption as a leading cause. The research provides a macro-level analysis of corporations through a supply-side lens and contributes to a better understanding of the dynamics of corporate crime.

Chapter 9, "*Charismatic Churches and Corruption in Ghana: Feeding the Beast?*", by Riccardo D'Emidio, offers a novel perspective on a sector whose corruption deserves much more analysis than it has received. In the past thirty years, Ghana has emerged as one of the centres of Neo-Pentecostal (or Charismatic) Christianity. This new doctrine has permeated the Ghanaian public sphere, emphasising acquiring financial wealth and prosperity. Using Critical Discourse Analysis, this chapter explores the complex relationships between the discourses on wealth and prosperity as preached in the Ghanaian Charismatic movements and the overall "corruption complex" in the country. Through an analysis of semi-structured interviews with representatives of the Ghanaian anti-corruption sector and a set of sermons delivered in leading charismatic churches, D'Emidio contends that charismatic churches sometimes develop and reinforce discourses, norms, and practices that feed into the "corruption complex". There is a significant relationship between the charismatic quest for wealth and the banalisation or, as some call it, "the cultural legitimation" of corruption in Ghana. These findings have significant implications for anti-corruption theory and practice, reaching further into question liberal expectations – often underpinning many anti-corruption campaigns and awareness-raising initiatives in Africa and elsewhere – that citizens need more information or an increased level of awareness in order not to engage in corrupt behaviour. Instead, this research indicates that even in the religious sector, discourses and norms embedded in relationships of power and patronage constrain citizens' engagement and action against corruption.

Chapter 10, titled "*The Causes and Consequences of Corruption in Zambia*" by Arthur Chisanga, Steven Daka, Victor Kaonga and Tambulani Chayima Nyirenda, considers corruption as a major hindrance towards the realisation of development goals by governments in societies the world over. In Zambia, corruption remains a significant challenge despite the existence of watchdog institutions and institutional and legal reforms spearheaded by successive governments since independence. The public sector in Zambia has been heavily affected by systemic corruption, and misappropriation of public resources is still widespread in government institutions. Following the country's transition from a one-party rule to participatory democracy in the early 1990s, corruption has increased. The corruption mechanism in Zambia involves high-level abuses perpetrated by public servants and private entities. Some contributing factors include a lack of political will to eradicate the scourge, a lack of transparency and accountability, and a culture of patronage among political government leaders. Despite the longstanding prevalence of corruption in Zambia, previous studies have mainly focused on confirming its existence rather than spelling out its causes and consequences. This chapter relies on secondary qualitative data from published reports by the Anti-corruption Commission of Zambia and information posted by non-governmental organisations like Transparency International Zambia and civil society organisations operating in Zambia.

The book concludes with an outline of its central themes and findings. We emphasise the importance of studying corruption, its sources and its consequences in detail and from the ground up – rather than just falling back on concepts and conclusions that may reflect a broad international outlook but can be misleading regarding Africa. It spells out what we have learned, identifies patterns and paradoxes, similarities and differences between regions and countries, and sets forth questions and themes for future research. It also provides challenging governance recommendations to guide analysis and reform in the case study counties and other countries with similar histories, current trends and governance challenges. The result will not be any simple "toolkit" for dealing with African corruption but rather a set of perspectives essential to encourage fresh thinking about fighting crime with, rather than for, African countries and their people.

References

Abdulai, Emmanuel Saffa. 2022. Political Corruption in Africa: Extraction and Power Preservation. *Canadian Journal of African Studies / Revue Canadienne des études africaines*, DOI: 10.1080/00083968.2021.2004650

Agang, Sunday Bobai; Pillay, Pregala and Jones, Chris. 2019. *A Multidimensional Perspective on Corruption in Africa. Wealth, Power, Religion and Democracy*, Cambridge Scholars Publishing.

Agbiboa, Daniel Egiegba. 2013. Between Corruption and Development: The Political Economy of State Robbery in Nigeria. *Journal of Business Ethics* 108(3):325–345.

Asongu, Simplice. 2013. Fighting Corruption in Africa: Do Existing Corruption-control Levels Matter? *International Journal of Development Issues* 12(1):36–52.

EgoAlowes, Jimanze. 2017. *Corruption in Africa: Resolution through New Diagnosis*. Ibadan: Safari Books Ltd.

Johnston, Michael and Fritzen, Scott. 2021. *The Conundrum of Corruption: Reform for Social Justice*. Routledge.

Kubbe, Ina and Engelbert, Annika. 2018. *Corruption and Norms: Why Informal Rules Matter*. (Eds.), Palgrave Macmillan. Political Corruption and Governance Series.

Kubbe, Ina and Varraich, Aiysha. 2019. *Corruption and Informal Practices in the Middle East and North Africa* (Eds.), Routledge. Corruption and Anti-Corruption Studies.

Madonsela, Sanet. 2018. Critical Reflections on State Capture in South Africa. *African Studies* 11(1):113–130.

Momoh, Zekeri. 2015. *Corruption and Governance in Africa*. Proceedings of The International Academic Conference for Sub-Sahara African Transformation & Development Vol. 3 No. 6 March, 12-13 2015-University of Ilorin, Nigeria.

Okorie, Hagler. 2018. Evaluation of the Effects of Corruption in the Armed Conflict in the Northeast and Other Violent Situations in Nigeria. *Beijing Law Review* 9(5), 623–660.

Wraith, Ronald and Edga Simpkins. 1963. *Corruption in Developing Countries*. Routledge.

PART I
Corruption in the Political Sector

1
THE POLITICS OF STATE CAPTURE IN SOUTH AFRICA

A New Variant of Corruption?

Thomas A. Koelble

Introduction: The Politics of "State Capture"

The story of the African National Congress (ANC) since 1990 is one of immense hope and grave disappointment. For decades, the ANC embodied the global struggle against colonialism, systematic racism and injustice perpetuated by South Africa's apartheid regime. The liberation movement finally triumphed, and the ANC formed the first democratically elected government. The iconic images of Nelson Mandela walking out of prison and the long lines of voters waiting to cast their ballot in 1994 symbolized the hope that South Africa would become not only a democratic but also a more equitable society.

Yet, after nearly 30 years of continuous ANC rule, the country remains the most unequal society on the planet.[1] Its economy is burdened with over 34% unemployed.[2] Over 46% of South African youths have never held a job.[3] Some 50% of the population lives on or below the poverty line and another 30% are in imminent danger of dropping into poverty as soon as they lose their income (Schotte, Zizzamia and Leibbrandt 2018). Inequality has increased since the end of apartheid, rather than decreased (Soudien, Reddy, and Woolard 2019).

And, most of all, the ethical and moral principles of the ANC are questioned by the fact that South Africa has experienced a looting spree spearheaded by its former president and other leading political figures that is unparalleled in the country's already far too long history of exploitation and impoverishment (e.g. Rossouw 2020, Myburgh 2019, van Rensburg 2020). The reign of Jacob Zuma, often described as "the politics of state capture", is only the tip of an iceberg of corruption that winds its way through the public and private sectors.[4] Some researchers put the cost of corruption under the Zuma regime at over a trillion Rand (or 68 billion US dollars based on the exchange rate in July 2021) lost to the public sector from 2011 to 2017 (Wilson 2019; Davis 2021).[5] Many of the social and economic ills the country faces today could have been addressed had the state's funds not been misappropriated.

The following chapter argues that corruption in South Africa is far more serious than individuals in powerful public and private sector positions abusing their power to benefit themselves at the expense of the public. Corruption in South Africa is systemic and rooted in public institutions that were taken over from the colonial/apartheid era without a great deal of thought given to their democratization. The state apparatus remained an instrument of the ruling party (only this time dominated by the ANC) and while the constitutional framework requires an impartial state, in practice the lines between the ruling party and the state bureaucracy remain heavily blurred (Koelble 2022). The idea that concerned citizens can fight corruption through collective legal and civil action is hopelessly inadequate given the nature of "state capture". Only a fundamental structural reform of the public sector that ensures appointments based on merit rather than political affiliation and impartiality in terms of service delivery, coupled with legal consequences for those breaking these formal and informal rules of conduct, will bring about a situation where corruption is contained. South Africa provides an example of how systemic corruption develops despite a vibrant civil society effort to contain it. And how corruption thrives in a political economy characterized by gross economic and social inequality that feeds particularistic interests rather than universal ones.

Research Question: What is "State Capture"?

The term "state capture" emerged as a way of distinguishing between corruption, defined as a form of opportunistic self-enrichment through illicit means, and a concerted attempt to undermine the state's institutions to enable a small set of individuals to funnel public funds to themselves. In 2018 Ivor Chipkin, Mark Swilling and others published *Shadow State: the Politics of State Capture* in which they outlined a vast network of organized and institutionalized corruption (Chipkin et al. 2018). They suggested that state capture is a systematic attempt to subvert the formal and informal rules of constitutional democracy. Capturing the state requires central planning and coordination, high degrees of loyalty among its participants, and the cooperation of legal and other state institutions ranging from the police to the courts. It fosters fear and intimidation among civil servants. State capture differs from corruption in terms of its scale, being a systematic process of undermining the authority of almost all state institutions.

Zuma, with the assistance of a group of Indian businessmen headed by brothers Ajay and Atul Gupta, established a network of operations spanning across the public sector designed to channel funds through public procurement tenders and kickbacks paid to shell companies functioning as money-laundering units in and outside of South Africa (Holden 2021a,b,c).[6] A state inquiry into "state capture" known as the Zondo Commission is currently hearing evidence on how these networks operated to defraud the South African state, revealing that the Gupta-Zuma network was only one of several such entities (e.g. Basson 2019).[7] Much of the Gupta/Zuma money was channelled to banks in Dubai and Hong Kong (Holden 2021a; Holden 2021b). There is evidence to suggest that the Guptas used the same money-laundering network as Al-Qaeda. State capture involved fraudulent contracts and tenders involving the parastatal electricity monopoly ESKOM, the Passenger Rail Agency of South Africa (PRASA), the state-owned entity Transnet responsible for ports, harbors, freight haulage, South African Airways (SAA) and its subsidiaries, the social security and pensions system, and most other government service departments. Supplier companies involved and benefitting from these deals include the Chinese Rolling Stock Corporation, the German telecommunications company Deutsche Telekom T-Systems, Neotel, and Tegeta (a Gupta-owned mining company) (Holden 2021c). In order to cover their tracks, the Zuma/Gupta enterprise used the services of companies such as McKinsey, Bain and Co., SAP and Deloitte, all of which have admitted to participating in this gigantic corruption matter (Snapp 2019; Williams 2021).[8]

The project of state capture was ideologically justified through a political campaign designed to convince voters that while South Africa might have achieved democracy, its underlying power structure had not shifted (Poplak 2020). "White Monopoly Capitalism" not only survived the end of apartheid, it thrived under the rule of Thabo Mbeki and Nelson Mandela Segal, 2018).[9] The current global "rules of the game" and their local by-products continue to disadvantage black South Africans. In order to bring about fundamental changes, the current constitutional order needs to be dismantled as it cemented apartheid-based structures of ownership and control into the new dispensation. The stated aim of the Zuma regime was to bring about "radical economic transformation" designed to produce a class of black entrepreneurs and a middle class of black South Africans, largely through the expansion of the public sector (Gerber 2021).[10] In order to challenge the stranglehold of white monopoly capitalism, the institutions of the state, particularly the law enforcement institutions and the judicial system, needed to be fundamentally transformed.

While the rhetoric of "radical economic transformation" may be a smokescreen for the corruption that took place under Zuma, the political project his faction in the ANC addressed is a powerful one (Thamm 2021). It rests on the ideological foundations of anti-imperialism, anti-colonialism and rejects Western notions of capitalism and constitutional democracy. The ideas expressed by the Zuma faction are also found in the student protest movements such as #FeesMustFall and #RhodesMustFall, or the land protest movement "Black First Land First" and, indeed, the ideological position of the Economic Freedom Fighters (EFF) (Shivambu 2014). All of these ideological groups argue that the transformation that took place in the 1990s did not bring about the kind of socio-economic change required to liberate the black majority of citizens but left the socio-economic conditions of apartheid untouched (Bond 2002).

Zuma failed to institute any specific policy that could be interpreted as part of the "radical economic transformation" platform in the decade of his rule, yet he engineered a systematic weakening of the oversight institutions of the state ranging from the National Prosecuting Authority (NPA), the judiciary, police force, security apparatus, Public Protector's office and many other institutions aimed at furthering transparency and accountability in government (Wiener 2018). Through a policy of appointments of his political allies to ministerial and bureaucratic positions, Zuma disabled many of the oversight mechanisms within the civil service. This campaign affected almost every department at the national and provincial levels of government.[11] And it undermined the functionality of South Africa's extensive network of state-owned enterprises, most of which are currently bankrupt.

During the period from 2011 to 2017, Zuma appeared to be untouchable and, except for a long-standing feud with the then Public Protector, Thuli Madonsela, largely unquestioned by his political party and the state institutions. His modus operandi allowed the ANC to use the resources of the state to finance its operations and offered its functionaries a wide range of opportunities for self-enrichment.[12] The tide only turned when Cyril Ramaphosa narrowly won the presidency of the ANC in 2017 and replaced Zuma as President of the Republic in 2018, shortly before the 2019 general elections. A Commission of Inquiry, the Zondo Commission, has collected testimony from thousands of witnesses on the issue of "state capture". Zuma has steadfastly refused to give evidence to the commission and was finally sentenced to a 15-month prison term (of which he served less than a month in prison) for contempt of the Constitutional Court's ruling that he should give evidence (Ferreira 2021). But even today, there are many within the ANC and in the larger society, as the riots in July of 2021 against Zuma's incarceration illustrate, that are willing to support and defend him in his never-ending attempts to evade the courts (Camaren 2021).

Theorizing Corruption in a Post-colonial State

Since the literature on explaining corruption is vast, I will focus on the approach used by Bo Rothstein to help unravel the current South African situation (Rothstein 2011). His analysis begins with an obvious point, drawn from Dani Rodrik, for anyone working in non-Western and post-colonial societies. Many of the assumptions made by Western economists and social scientists presuppose the existence of:

> A moderately cohesive society exhibiting trust and social cooperation, social and political institutions that mitigate risk and manage social conflicts, the rule of law and clean government – these are social arrangements that economists usually take for granted, but which are conspicuous by their absence in poor countries.
> *(Rothstein 2011, quoting Rodrik, p. 7)*

The South African apartheid and colonial state made no attempt to create trust or social cooperation except amongst white citizens. The "rule of law" was a racially segregationist enterprise designed to humiliate, exploit, disenfranchise, impoverish and dehumanize black South Africans. Clean government consisted of nothing but an attempt to hoist one race's economic, cultural and social interests over another. Given this history, it should be clear that governing institutions in South Africa did not acquire legitimacy purely because there was a democratic election in 1994. While the new political leadership enjoyed legitimacy, state institutions and its officials did not. And, as Rothstein suggests, democracy may be vastly overrated in terms of creating legitimacy for a state and its administrative apparatus.

Rothstein argues that legitimacy for a state arises from the quality of government rather than whether elections are fair and effective (Rothstein 2011, p. 80). As citizens are far more likely to come into contact with the output side of a political system – the bureaucracies of the state and its policy implementation – than its input side, the quality of what they receive from that state largely determines their view of the legitimacy and value of the existing state. What the majority of South Africans received from the state up to 1994 was based on racial discrimination and for most completely illegitimate. And changing that situation, even after political liberation, is full of difficulty as Rothstein remarks:

> First, corruption is driven by the workings of a large set of historically rooted formal and informal institutions in a society. Second, neither the formal nor the informal institutions are easily changed since they constitute "self-reinforcing equilibriums."
> *(Rothstein 2011, p. 110)*

On taking power, the ANC attempted to transform the bureaucracy through a retirement policy and replaced white bureaucrats with ANC operatives. Yet, the culture of these institutions, their formal and informal rules and procedures, remained largely intact. A transformation of an institution requires more than just the replacement of one set of bureaucrats with another. It requires a complete remake of the procedures, the rules of engagement, the informal and formal processes of operation and its ethos. If this kind of organizational and institutional reform is not undertaken, then the institution remains true to its original state. In the chapter entitled The Low Trust-Corruption-Inequality Trap, Rothstein writes:

> Poor countries may thus find themselves trapped in continuing inequality and mistrust. High levels of inequality contribute to lower levels of trust, lessening the political and societal support for the state to collect resources for launching and implementing universal welfare programs in an incorrupt and non-discriminatory way. Highly corrupt societies find themselves trapped in a continuous cycle of inequality and low trust in others and the government and with policies that do little to reduce the gap between the rich and the poor and thus create a sense of equal opportunity. Demands for radical redistribution, as we see in many transitional countries, are likely to exacerbate social tensions rather than relieve them.
> *(Rothstein 2011, p. 162)*

Rothstein's analysis is, from a South African perspective, depressing since all of the criteria he raises are present in the current quagmire. By the 1994 elections, the South African state was completely delegitimized. It lacked any authority outside of a narrow base of white beneficiaries of the now-defunct system. It became subject to pent-up demands by a black majority that had little faith in the institutions and its bureaucrats, viewed the police and courts with utmost suspicion, paid little attention to the instructions of the state in terms of formal economic and social rules, and demanded resources from that state that were either unavailable or not expansive enough for a much larger population than the 5 million privileged whites it had previously served.

But there is a way forward and Rothstein points to the Swedish example where a country successfully moved from relatively high levels to low levels of corruption and from low levels to high levels of quality of government. He refers to the development as a "big bang" approach and posits that countries can move in a positive direction (Rothstein 2011, p. 111–119). The key to the change lies in the realization by its political elites that a change in orientation is necessary for the survival of the country. Rothstein writes:

> In a "stateless", Robert Nozick society, where everything should be arranged by individual, freely entered contracts, markets will deteriorate into organized crime and corruption. The conclusion is, again, that there can be a market for anything as long as there is not a market for everything. In other words, if everything is for sale, markets will not come close to what should count as economic efficiency, and poor people in poor countries will remain in poverty.
> *(Rothstein 2011, p. 225)*

Self-interested actors have to realize that pure self-interest leads to suboptimal outcomes. Corrupt systems of administration are an expression of unrestrained self-interest. There are formal and informal systems that encourage non-market logic of action. However, to obtain these systems requires a full-scale reform of the civil service and the implementation of "impartiality" by its civil servants who need to view every citizen that approaches them equally and without prejudice or discrimination. Rothstein's point is summarized thus:

> "If public officials in a society are known for being corrupt, partial, or untrustworthy, citizens will believe that even people who are required by law to act in the service of the public cannot be trusted. From this they make the inference that most other people cannot be trusted either."
> *(Rothstein 2011, p. 173)*

A vicious cycle evolves from this inference that is difficult to break. The opposite is true in societies where public officials are trustworthy and impartial. In that case, citizens will make the inference that all people in the society are trustworthy resulting in a virtuous cycle (Rothstein 2011, p. 109).[13]

Zuma and his acolytes exploited the fact that the South African state, its civil service, lacked legitimacy and authority. After years of struggle to delegitimize the apartheid state, these efforts successfully ended the regime. However, instead of embarking on Rothstein's "big bang" approach to bring about impartiality and trustworthiness within the state, it served the interests of at least a part of the ANC's leadership to continue the subversion of the state and access its resources. Given its composition of largely white civil servants in 1994, the lack of legitimacy made it simple to rid the state of its leading administrators, to replace them with ANC cadres who were willing to embark on this quest and leave its ethos of partiality intact. Added to this is the fact that many of these ANC cadres were themselves impoverished by the policies of the apartheid state and the personal justifications for acting in a self-interested manner would not have been difficult to reach.[14]

Perhaps the constitutional negotiations of 1990 to 1994 were not fundamental enough in re-imagining what a governmental system appropriate for a decolonized society should look like. Hence, for most South African citizens the new democratic state is not fundamentally different from the old apartheid state. Zuma and his faction, and that includes the EFF as well, are questioning the legitimacy of the Western constitution, the Western conception of governance and the capitalist structure of the underlying economy that has exploited black labor for close to 400 years and continues to do so. Ramaphosa was a key negotiator of the transition to democracy and brought into the Black Economic Empowerment (BEE) policies that became the primary vehicle for the transformation of the economy. BEE represented a compromise with capital that encompassed the black elite through its redistribution program of providing shares to a small group of beneficiaries. Far from becoming the means by which a new black entrepreneurial class would emerge to drive socio-economic transformation as Mandela had hoped, BEE ensured the opposite – the emergence of a small class of asset-rich ANC-affiliated capitalists (Mbeki 2009, p. 61). And it is an important aspect of the current political situation that Ramaphosa, and his ANC cohort, benefited massively from BEE.[15]

For the average South African citizen, however, many of the legacies of the apartheid regime were left unchallenged. The property clauses of the constitution cemented the injustices of the past into the present and future and the promised provision of a "better life for all" has not eventuated. While the BEE and affirmative action policies have paved the way for a "black middle class" to emerge, it is highly dependent on the growth of the public sector where many of the new black middle class have found employment (Southall 2016). In that way, the South African state has replicated its role of creating opportunities for upward mobility since 1994 as the apartheid state did for Afrikaners in the 1920s and '30s.[16] The problem is that the state has again become an instrument in racial and ethnic advancement and not a site of impartiality, as Rothstein would recommend. Like the colonial/apartheid state before it, it is a means to ensure the upward mobility of a class of citizens rather than a redistributive state that operates on principles of impartiality and equality.

Moreover, while Western observers see the local constitution as a model of good governance principles, in South Africa there are many who question its appropriateness. Is this a constitution that is really appropriate for an African state, economy and society? The fact that Jacob Zuma raises these questions may be seen by some Western observers as anti-democratic or anti-constitutional but is welcomed by many ordinary South African citizens as a relevant question.[17] And it is part of a much larger questioning about decolonization that is, on the one hand, expressed in the post-colonial literature of authors such as Achille Mbembe (2021) and, on the other hand, social protest movements such as the #RhodesMustFall campaign.

Potential Anti-Corruption Strategies: The Legal Route and the Civil Society Route

There are two obvious strategies to combat corruption. One relies on the capacities of the state's institutions to detect corrupt individuals and prosecute them via the law courts. The other is to uncover corruption via civil society groups and wage a public campaign against corruption by illustrating the damage it does to affected citizens. While the civil society route will also include prosecution via the state law enforcement agencies, it is qualitatively a different strategy to one that focuses on the capacity of the prosecutorial agencies of the legal system. Both strategies are, however, limited. They are both reactive and do not address the larger issue Rothstein raises, namely the fundamental change in formal and informal institutions and rules that is necessary to bring about the expectation that all citizens will abide by those rules and not engage in corrupt behavior.

The Legal Route

In this strategy, corrupt behavior is identified, investigated by the police or other forensic units trained to deal with such crimes, and then prosecuted through the institutional channels of the court system. This strategy relies on a whistleblower to draw attention to a particular process and provide the investigation units with information that can be used in a court of law to prosecute the case. This initial process can be derailed at several points. A potential whistleblower might be discouraged from any action through intimidation, threats, or bribes. The current wave of court cases speak to these issues and Mandy Wiener's book on *Whistleblowers* provides a plethora of cases and examples of intimidation, threats to family and friends, or attempts to bribe (Wiener 2020).

Even if a whistleblower exposes a corruption case, it is far from guaranteed that the case will get attention.[18] There are several individuals who drew attention to various aspects of the Guptas' activities very early on in the development of the Gupta corruption network who were simply ignored and suffered the consequences of retaliation. Whistleblowers pay a high price, which hardly ever gets rewarded (Mlambo 2020). Similarly, employees in several SOEs drew attention to illegal activities at SAA, ESKOM, and PRASA/Transnet that were ignored by the state authorities, even after they went to the press. And these cases are particularly worrisome because they point to the observation by Rothstein that corruption will grow ever larger if the ethos of both formal and informal institutions is to not just tolerate corrupt activity but to normalize it. In such a scenario, every individual faces the reality that all others may be corrupt and therefore being a law-abiding citizen is, in fact, impossible and undesirable.[19]

Having a whistleblower is, however, only the beginning of the process. Once a case has been identified as worthy of investigation, the investigation teams require resources to uncover the relevant evidence. The investigation may be hindered if a president or a government minister or even a head of department in one of the prosecutor's offices sanctions the corruption. The unit may not get the resources necessary to do a proper investigation; it may not get the go-ahead to devote resources to the case. The withholding of funds may actively or passively hinder information gathering; the unit may receive information that is incorrect or misleading; it may not receive information at all. There are all sorts of ways in which an investigation can be derailed from within the state apparatus if it is deemed to be a threat to a corrupt individual in a position of power.

It is not surprising that the Zuma/Gupta group devoted a good deal of its time and efforts in appointing pliable ministers, heads of departments, and lower-level bureaucrats into positions where they could undermine any investigation of their various activities. All of this was done to avoid a case actually reaching the stage of a prosecution. Efforts by law enforcement agencies were systematically undermined, their agents weakened in order to avoid first detection, and, if detected, prosecution. Mandy Wiener's book *Ministry of Crime* outlines in some detail how the NPA and various other law enforcement agencies were systematically undermined in order to protect criminal organizations and individuals (Wiener 2018).

And things may become even more problematic at the prosecution level because it is incumbent on the prosecution to prove that wrongdoing has taken place. To do so, the prosecution needs strong *prima facie* evidence for its case. If the prosecution team is so overwhelmed and/or understaffed, as the NPA became under Zuma, then it is very difficult to actually successfully prosecute a well-insulated and officially protected individual. Not only the NPA may be overwhelmed by caseloads but what if the courts are completely overworked in terms of a shortage of judges and prosecutors? In such a scenario it is likely that court cases are postponed and drawn out over many years. The accused may be able to "dodge and dive" and avoid any punitive action.[20] Zuma's tactics of delaying court processes have become telling examples of what is sometimes called a "Stalingrad" defense. The defense mounts objection after objection, asks for postponements to formulate its arguments and calls into question every single piece of evidence. If these tactics fail, the defense demands more time to consider its response further delaying the process.

Should the prosecution of a corrupt individual fail, the damage is by far greater to the prosecution than it is to the corruption network. In such a case, the corruption network will invariably portray the prosecution as political persecution of a perfectly honest public servant and citizen. Should the prosecution succeed it still faces the problem of linking the prosecuted individual to the larger network through detailed evidence. In other words, the legal route is largely a reactive and complicated one; it is not a proactive strategy to bring about change in informal and formal institutions that mitigate and prevent corruption in the first place.[21]

The Civil Society Route

The second route to fighting corruption is the mobilization of civil society organizations (CSOs) to identify possible cases of wrongdoing and the damage done to citizens. While the two strategies are inter-connected, they rely on different platforms of organization – one based almost entirely within the state apparatus, the other in the broader civil society space. There are several high-profile CSOs involved in the fight against corruption. For instance, the Public Service Accountability Monitor (PSAM) at Rhodes University is one such organization.[22] Its primary aim is to uncover failures in public service delivery in the Eastern Cape Province. There are other civil society organizations ranging from the Council of Churches to organizations such as Corruption Watch, Accountability Now, the Organization Undoing Tax Abuse (OUTA), the Desmond Tutu Foundation, and the Nelson Mandela Foundation, to name just a few. An important mechanism is the independent media where several news outlets, such as the *Daily Maverick* or the *Mail and Guardian*, have developed investigative teams devoted purely to corruption issues.

These CSOs are at the frontline of the struggle against corruption and that represents a potential problem in post-colonial settings. The work by Partha Chatterjee illustrates that there is a gulf between such CSOs and many citizens who find themselves outside of the purview of civil society (Chatterjee 2020). Chatterjee draws attention to "political society" that consists mainly of subaltern groups in post-colonial settings. He argues that India emerged with a democratic constitution, universal suffrage, and competitive electoral representation in 1947 but lacked a transformed agrarian sector or a developed industrial/ commercial society until recently. In other words, the kind of assumed but totally absent preconditions for good governance and functional democracy that Rodrik pointed to at the outset of Rothstein's analysis becomes of importance. Chatterjee states:

> The space of politics became effectively split between a narrow domain of civil society where citizens related to the state through the mutual recognition of legally enforceable rights and a wider domain of political society where governmental agencies dealt not with citizens but with populations to deliver specific benefits of services through a process of political negotiation.
>
> *(Chatterjee, 2011, p. 13–14)*

What Chatterjee describes are the negotiations between a vast array of communities and governmental agencies. The following extract resonates with any observer in South Africa:

> Take the familiar example of squatter settlements of the poor in numerous cities of the post-colonial world. These urban populations occupy land that does not belong to them and often use water, electricity, public transport, and other services without paying for them. But governmental authorities do not necessarily try to punish or to put a stop to such illegalities

because of the political recognition that these populations serve certain functions in the urban economy and that to forcibly remove them would involve huge political costs. On the other hand, they cannot be treated as legitimate members of civil society who abide by the law. As a result, municipal authorities or the police deal with these people not as rights-bearing citizens but as urban populations who have specific characteristics and needs and who must be appropriately governed. On their side, these groups of the urban poor negotiate with the authorities through political mobilization and alliances with other groups.

Chatterjee (2011, p. 14) suggests that these "rules of exception" are usually cloaked in justifications by the authorities that it is less costly to provide services to such illegal communities than it would be to remove them and house them elsewhere. In other words, the specter of urban violence, protest, resistance, and resulting upheaval is never far from the politics of governing such populations. However, given the size of the population that is governed in this manner, post-colonial governmental praxis implies an enormous number of exceptions. And for the population groups seeking such exceptions, the case they make is that they have a right to live in urban spaces, that they seek employment and a better life, that they are the victims of the apartheid/colonial past, and that they (not privileged whites who now own land that actually belongs to Africans) have a general right to land ownership anywhere in South Africa. Those are precisely the voters Jacob Zuma appeals to and is popular with.

A key component of Chatterjee's analysis is that post-colonial government plays out at two very different levels – civil society and political society. The civil society level encompasses the middle class and the prevailing formal capitalist system. It is embedded in terms of production, the concept of property rights, civil rights accruing to the individual and encompassment in the formal economy. Political society is a much more fragmented, contested, and anarchic space encompassing a large part of the population that acts largely on the fringes of capitalism and in the interstices of the informal and formal economy. However, groups operating in political society utilize the democratic system to place pressure on political parties to obtain access to state resources. Chatterjee notes that often the "rich" and propertied class in civil society will justify their transgressions against the law by claiming that politicians are corrupt and that exceptions are granted to the poor on a regular basis. Some even flaunt their transgressions with impunity, but they do not manage to mobilize the kind of moral justification that the poor can muster. Chatterjee remarks:

> It could even be said that the activities of political society in post-colonial countries represent a continuing critique of the paradoxical reality in all

capitalist democracies of equal citizenship and majority rule, on the one hand, and the dominance of property and privilege, on the other.
(Chatterjee 2011, p. 17)

Chatterjee argues that the normative principles of Western political theory have an enormous influence on post-colonial politics but that the actual praxis of governance has resulted not in the abandonment of those principles but a piling up of exceptions and improvisations in the course of administering the law. And the task of theorizing an adequate analysis of the post-colonial political praxis is to come to grips with this mountain of improvisation.

The politics around the "rules of exception" are directly linked to the politics of corruption. If a state allows for the preferential treatment of some of its citizens over others, the notion of impartiality highlighted in Rothstein's work is violated, not just occasionally but as a matter of routine and expediency. And the politics of exception also invite those in positions of power to abuse their positions to create exceptions for themselves, their families, friends and business associates. If Chatterjee's observations and theoretical arguments are correct, and I believe that they are empirically accurate and theoretically sustainable, the problem for post-colonial democracies with large political societies comes into sharp focus. Not only does a political figure like Jacob Zuma raise the question of the suitability of a Western constitutional arrangement for a country like South Africa, but he also taps into the energies of political society to mount a credible challenge to the idea of impartiality in the civil service. In summary, this double negation of both the adequacy of Western constitutionalism and impartiality in the public sector raises a profound challenge to the notion of corruption-free public administration. And, if taken to its logical conclusion, challenges the notion of "corruption" itself.

Challenges and Future Prospects

I have tried to provide a realistic assessment of the chances of a successful challenge to corruption in South Africa. The problem is considerably larger than the self-interested behavior of a few politicians, their business associates, friends and family members. The problem is systemic and directly implicates the methods of the ruling party in its efforts to raise finance and unify its internal and highly fragmented coalition, and in its attempts to create a black bourgeoisie. Corruption is pervasive throughout the state involving state-owned enterprises as well as most, if not all, parts of the public sector. And it goes to the heart of the matter of what a post-colonial democracy should look like; how it should govern; and whether the Western norms, models and assumptions upon which many post-colonial constitutions are based are even appropriate for the task.

Trying to deal with corruption through the state's legal capabilities and the mobilization of civil society are reactive responses to a systemic problem. The legal route is complicated as it requires courageous whistleblowers, meticulous investigators and adequate resources to conduct lengthy court procedures. Further, it demands committed prosecutors as well as judges capable of independently assessing the case material. Lastly, success is not guaranteed, and setbacks are costly precisely because they indicate that corruption pays.

There exists a broad coalition of political forces mobilizing political society in opposition to civil society and the constitutional state. By running against "the elite" in a move reminiscent of populists across the globe, the "neo-liberals" in the Treasury, the white minority that is supposedly in control of the economy, this political grouping is able to mobilize significant electoral support amongst the population groups most likely to suffer from their ascension to power. And it legitimizes their demand to be treated as groups of claimants on government resources rather than as individual rights-bearing citizens thereby furthering a system of exceptions that plays right into the hands of a corrupt political elite. This is, in essence, the conundrum facing post-colonial democracies in regard to corrupt elites.

Conclusion: Democracy and the Fight against Corruption in Africa

The conclusions reached in the previous section bring us back to Rothstein's ideas about the role of formal and informal institutions. While the legal and political battles against corrupt individuals are necessary to stem the corruption tide, they can only do so much in the effort to bring about changes in both formal and informal rules of governance in the post-colony. South Africa had a "big bang" moment in 1994 but in the attempt to create a functional post-apartheid democracy, some fundamentals were simply overlooked. Little attention was given to the reorganization of the state and the legitimization of its civil service. It was assumed that the apartheid state was a powerful unit that could be used to transform the underlying economy and society. Taking over the state was not viewed as a "problem" but a welcome means to a new end, not unlike the intentions of the nationalist Afrikaner elite that captured the state in the aftermath of the Anglo-Boer war. The ANC turned the post-apartheid state into a mechanism of advancement for its political cadres under the guise of black empowerment. ANC activists were appointed to administrative positions from which they controlled resources. These were routinely used to both enrich individuals as well as pay for ANC activities designed to assist politicians to win and maintain political power. And now, a generation after the transition from apartheid to democracy, the socio-economic profile of the country has not changed greatly but the state is virtually bankrupt.

Without being able to bridge the gap between civil and political society and without fundamental changes in the everyday experiences of the majority of citizens, there will be no improvement in citizens' attitudes towards non-functional "democratic" systems. Such a change will require the building of adequate infrastructure accessible to all citizens and residents. Simultaneously, the regime will have to build a civil service that is impartial and that provides adequate public goods in an impartial manner. Without a commitment to an impartial civil service decoupled from the self-enrichment strategies of politicians, it will be difficult, if not impossible, to develop a development trajectory that is transformative. Until that point is reached, there will be actors for whom the idea that everything is for sale is attractive and personally beneficial.

Notes

1 See the World Bank report on the GINI Index measuring economic inequality. It places South Africa at the top of its inequality scale with a score of 63.3 ahead of countries such as Brazil. See https://data.worldbank.org/indicator/SI.POV.GINI.
2 The official unemployment rate (August 2021) according to Statistics South Africa is 34.4%. However, a wider definition of unemployment that includes those discouraged from seeking employment is 42%. See Reuters Staff, "Update: South Africa's unemployment rate reaches new record high in first quarter", *Reuters: Economic News*, 1 Jun 2021.
3 See "South African Youth Unemployment Rate", *Trading Economics*, 1 August 2021.
4 A superficial library search of academic and media coverage of corruption in South Africa revealed over 10,000 articles were published on this topic since 2017.
5 Tom Wilson, "Corruption under Zuma Cost Rand 500 Billion, Says Ramaphosa", *Business Live*, 14 October 2019. Rebecca Davis, "The total(ish) cost of Gupta state capture: Rand 49,157,323,233.68", *Daily Maverick*, 24 May 2021. Both estimates are only focused on the Zuma/Gupta enterprise and do not include all other corruption networks in national, provincial or local government.
6 Paul Holden's testimony to the Zondo Commission of Inquiry into State Capture was conducted in his role as forensic accountant to the inquiry.
7 While Zuma was not involved in some of the other corruption networks, he certainly would have known about them as they involved leading ANC officials. In the Eastern Cape, for instance, the BOSASA scandal took center-stage for several months at the Zondo Commission hearings (Basson 2019).
8 See also the deeply personal account by Williams (2021). Williams was a South African partner at Bain and Co. and blew the whistle on the machinations of the local Bain office that worked closely with Zuma and the Guptas to enable their corrupt activities. Williams has since fled South Africa fearing for his life after receiving multiple death threats.

9 Bell Pottinger coined the term "white monopoly capitalism" in its media campaign organized to assist the Zuma/Gupta group.
10 Zuma's defense has been consistent – his political enemies have captured the state's institutions, the judicial system, and, above all, the Constitutional Court in order to prevent his plans to radically transform South African society.
11 While the book by Chipkin and Swilling (2018) cited above covers these issues, there is a judicial inquiry under way, the Zondo Commission, which has heard evidence regarding corruption. The commission began its hearings in August of 2018 and continued its work until the latter half of 2021. The South African media has been privy to public testimony by several highly placed witnesses and informants on the mechanisms of corruption in both the private and public sectors. Moreover, there are several high-profile court cases currently under way in this regard as well.
12 The Zondo Commission has heard evidence to the effect that many of the kickbacks to ANC politicians also involved payments to the ANC's various offices that were then used for campaigning purposes. See Thamm (2021), cited above.
13 Rothstein (2011), p. 109 points to the deep division between "personal-particularistic" and "impersonal-universalistic" policy-making systems. While the former will encourage corruption, the latter is likely to be intolerant of such practices.
14 In 2004, during a parliamentary debate about the sale of a Rand 6.6 billion stake in the telecommunications SOE Telkom, Smuts Ngonyama, the ANC's then national spokesperson and a personal beneficiary of this deal to the tune of Rand 160 million, expressed the view that "I did not join the struggle to be poor". Ngonyama's statement has become symbolic for an attitude among the ANC's leadership that there is nothing wrong with the enrichment of its political elite.
15 Ramaphosa's net wealth is estimated at US$ 460 million by Forbes, making him one of the richest individuals in South Africa and on the continent. His extended family also benefitted massively from various BEE deals.
16 See, for instance, the findings of Imraan Buccus that the Department of Public Service and Administration conceded that of the 9,477 senior public servants, 3,301 did not have the required qualifications for their position and that most of these individuals hold the position purely because of their political affiliations. Middle managers in the public sector earn between R 779,000 and R 922,750 while their superiors earn between R 1,078,267 and R 1,974,067. This compares to an average salary for wage earners of R 140,000. See Buccus (2021).
17 Zuma has on many occasions argued that he believes that the ANC is more important than the constitution. He did so consistently at ANC rallies and other public speeches over more than a decade and his position was largely unchallenged by anyone from within the ANC.
18 See the text by Williams (2021). Williams drew attention to the scandalous relationship between Bain's local office in Johannesburg and the Zuma/Gupta corruption network, yet Bain's head office largely ignored his warnings. His book outlines in great detail the difficulties that a whistleblower might encounter.
19 The murder of Babita Deokaran, the chief financial officer of the Gauteng Department of Health, on 23 August 2021 is a terrible case in point. Deokaran acted as a whistleblower to corruption taking place in regard to COVID-related PPE equipment in the provincial department. She was gunned down by a group

of assassins, five of whom are now facing murder charges. The killing is subject to an extensive investigation to uncover those who ordered her murder, as it would appear that it was intimately connected to the PPE misappropriation of funds. See Cruywagen and Heywood (2021).
20 In an interview with the news outlet News 24, the former Public Protector, Thuli Madonsela, outlined the tactics employed by the former president to avoid legal prosecution. See du Toit (2019).
21 It is, for instance, remarkable that many of the payments by the SOEs to the Gupta money laundering companies continued in 2016 and 2017 despite several legal opinions by the SOE's own legal departments that these transactions had to cease. See Davis (2021), "The total(ish) cost of the Gupta's State Capture", *Daily Maverick*, 24 May 2021, where Paul Holden is quoted as making that point to the Zondo Commission.
22 The Public Service Accountability Monitor (PSAM) hosts a website https://psam.org.za.

References

Basson, Darian (2019), *Blessed by BOSASA*, Johannesburg: Jonathan Ball.
Bond, Patrick (2002), *Unsustainable South Africa: Environment, Development and Social Protest*, Durban: University of Natal Press.
Buccus, Imraan (2021), "Do we Need Government: Let Alone the Lesser Spotted Public Servant?", *Daily Maverick*, 25 May 2021.
Chatterjee, Partha (2011), *Lineages of Political Society: Studies in Postcolonial Democracy*, New York: Columbia University Press.
Chatterjee, Partha (2020), *I Am the People: Reflections on Popular Sovereignty Today*, New York: Columbia University Press, pp. 111–122.
Chipkin, Ivor and Mark Swilling, with Haroon Bhorat, Mbongiseni Buthelezi, Sikhulekile Duma, Nicky Prins, Lumkile Mondi, Camaren Peter, Mzukisi Qobo, and Hannah Friedenstein (2018), *Shadow State: The Politics of State Capture*, Johannesburg: Wits University Press.
Cruywagen, Vincent and Heywood, Mark (2021), "Murder of Gauteng Health Official Babita Deokaran: Investigators Probe Link to her PPE Whistle-Blowing", *Daily Maverick*, 24 August 2021.
Davis, Rebecca (2021), "The Total(ish) Cost of Gupta State Capture: Rand 49,157,323,233.68", *Daily Maverick*, 24 May 2021.
du Toit, Pieter (2019),"The Madonsela Manoeuvre: how Zuma will try to Dodge Zondo", *News 24*, 27 June 2019.
Ferreira, Emsie (2021), "In depth: Constitutional Court sentences Zuma to 15 months in Jail, gives him Five Days to Report", *Mail and Guardian*, 29 June 2021.
Gerber, Jan (2021), "Revealed: What Jacob Zuma told ANC's Top Six", *News 24*, 5 April 2021.
Holden, Paul (2021a), "Part Three: The Local and International Laundries used by the Gupta Enterprise and Its Associates", *Daily Maverick*, 29 June 2021a.
Holden, Paul (2021b), "Part Five: How the Guptas used their Loot", *Daily Maverick*, 11 July 2021b.
Holden, Paul (2021c), "Part One: What the Gupta Enterprise Corruption Cost South Africa, *Daily Maverick*, 27 June 2021c.

Koelble, Thomas A (2022), "Poverty, Corruption and Democracy: The Role of 'Political Society' in Post-colonial South Africa", *Globalizations*, 19, pp. 1137–1149. DOI: 10.1080/14747731.2022.2035054.

Mbeki, Moeletsi (2009), *The Architects of Poverty*, Johannesburg: Picador Press.

Mbembe, Achille (2021), *Out of the Dark Night: Essays on decolonization*, Johannesburg: Wits University Press.

Mlambo, Sihle (2020), "Former Trillian CEO Bianca Goodson Challenges Lawmakers to Compensate Whistleblowers", *IOL News*, 21 October 2020.

Myburgh, Peter-Louis (2019), *Gangster State: Unravelling Ace Magashule's Web of Capture*, London: Penguin Books.

Peter, Camaren (2021), "The Imprisonment of Jacob Zuma is a Failure of our Politics, not our Institutions", *Daily Maverick*, 11 July 2021.

Poplak, Richard (2020), "Radical Economic Transformation is Upon us – but it is not what you thought it is", *Daily Maverick*, 3 April 2020.

Rossouw, Rehana (2020), *Predator Politics: Mabuza, Fred Daniel and the Great Land Scam*, Johannesburg: Jacana Press.

Rothstein, Bo (2011), *The Quality of Government: Corruption, Social Trust, and Inequality in International Perspective*, Chicago: University of Chicago Press.

Schotte, Simone, Rocco Zizzamia, and Murray Leibbrandt (2018), "A Poverty Dynamics Approach to Social Stratification: the South Africa case", *World Development*, 110, pp. 88–103.

Segal, David (2018), "How Bell Pottinger, PR Firm for Depots and Rogues, Met Its End in South Africa", *New York Times*, 4 February 2018.

Shivambu, Floyd (2014), *The Coming Revolution: Julius Malema and the Fight for Economic Freedom*, Johannesburg: Jacana Press.

Snapp, Shaun (2019), "How Deloitte, McKinsey, the Guptas and SAP Ripped Off ESKOM", *Brightwater Research and Analysis*, 5 November 2019.

Soudien, Crain, Vasu Reddy, and Ingrid Woolard (eds.) (2019), *Poverty and Inequality: Diagnosis, Prognosis and Response*, Pretoria: Human Sciences Research Council.

Southall, Roger (2016), *The New Black Middle Class in South Africa*, Johannesburg: Jacana Press.

Thamm, Marianne (2021), "ANC's Milking of State Coffers has become a way of Life, Explosive Report Reveals", *Daily Maverick*, 4 May 2021.

van Rensburg, Dewald (2020), *VBS: A Dream Defrauded*, Cape Town: Penguin Books.

Wiener, Mandy (2018), *Ministry of Crime: An Underworld Explored*, Johannesburg: MacMillan Press.

Wiener, Mandy (2020), *The Whistleblowers*, Johannesburg: MacMillan Press.

Williams, Athol (2021), *Deep Collusion: Bain and the Capture of South Africa*, Cape Town: Tafelberg.

Wilson, Tom (2019), "Corruption under Zuma Cost Rand 500 Billion, Says Ramaphosa", *Business Live* 14 October 2019.

2
DOMAINS OF CORRUPTION IN NIGERIA

A Four-Part Taxonomy and Nigeria's Anti-corruption Paradox

Aruna Kallon

Introduction

It is now clichéd that corruption is endemic in Africa and has detrimental effects on economic growth and development. Development strategies, agendas and visions for prosperity across Africa have often promulgated control of corruption – with its attendant buzzwords of transparency and accountability – as an imperative. The bane of sin has, for a long time, had devastating consequences for many African economies. While corruption may be more evident or rifer in certain African economies than others, its negative impact constitutes a significant impediment to economic development, especially in countries considered low-income, like most African countries, where the persistence of corruption is an essential concern in the development of African economies (d'Agostino et al., 2016).

Corruption can result from individual attributes of greed, selfishness and dishonesty, enabled by structural and bureaucratic inefficiencies (Alatas, 1990). It can also be need-corruption, such as when people must give a bribe to access the health care system. The term "need-corruption" was developed by Monika Bauhr. While theorising about what she refers to as the primary motivations for corruption in her article: Need or Greed? Conditions for Collective Action against Corruption, Bauhr (2017) describes the distinction between "need and greed corruption", which transcends many traditional conceptualisations. According to Bauhr, the need for corruption arises from a desire to gain access to fair treatment by citizens who perceive themselves as victims of corruption and are, therefore, likely to enact or support a "direct and obtrusive transgression of government power". In contrast, greed corruption is based on the desire to gain access to particular illicit advantages and is somewhat surreptitious (Bauer, 2017, p. 562).

The connivance of these factors produces negative consequences that derail and frustrate – even render unachievable – national development policy objectives and ultimately weaken a country's economy. Corruption adversely affects social welfare, mobility, justice and socio-economic livelihoods. In contrast, a tiny and tyrannical percentage of the population can illegally accumulate massive wealth at the expense of a powerless majority. This chapter will increase knowledge and understanding of the differences between Nigeria's distinct but interactive corruption apparatuses. It seeks to identify the areas where corruption occurs, examples and the different, often evasive methods crooks use. This paper addresses the nature, locale and impact of Nigeria's most detrimental forms of corruption.

This chapter argues that corruption renders reform more difficult – even impossible. Institutional change is more likely to succeed, and the social benefits of reform are more realistic with practical and productive changes in corruption and its prosecution over time. In Nigeria, like in many African countries, while corruption at all levels and in all forms remains the bane of the economic growth of developing nations, political corruption – that which takes place at the highest levels of government and political authority – is more detrimental to the modern-day democratic dispensation of developing economies. I also argue that the Nigerian government's partisan approach to the fight against corruption presents a paradox that gravely hinders the successful implementation of the federal government's anti-corruption strategy and contributes immensely to the persistence of corruption.

The chapter is limited to the forms of corruption in Nigeria. It does not attempt to delve into the other intricate aspects of the subject, doing justice to which would require ample space and more in-depth analysis. The chapter, therefore, paints a crowded canvas of phenomena describing and illustrating public sector corruption in Nigeria without attempting to dabble into other aspects of the subject. In other words, while this chapter predictably mentions corruption embedded in social relations, including practices at the individual and societal levels that facilitate and legitimise corruption, it needs to provide an exhaustive account or analysis of these forms of corruption.

Methodology

A review informs this chapter of secondary data from qualitative research on corruption in sub-Saharan Africa. The secondary data sources include research material published in journal articles, books, and official reports of international organisations, and the primary databases used include Google Scholar and other university-based digital library collections and catalogues. The primary focus of the analysis is Nigeria, and the chapter's main objective is to understand the nature, locale and impact of the most detrimental forms of political corruption in Nigeria. I have limited my discussion of the conditions of corruption in Nigeria to only four domains which I consider the most encompassing and most impactful to the modern-day democratic dispensation of the federal republic, namely, Political and Institutional Corruption, Economic Sector Corruption, Corruption in the Social Sector, and Political Party Corruption.

Conceptual Analysis

There are countless and varied definitions of corruption, and not one clear standard definition has been adopted. Nevertheless, many famous and widely used descriptions of corruption abound in textbooks and other scholarly literature. Corruption is a deviant behaviour driven by the desire for private gain and exacted at public expense (Hope & Chikulo, 2000). Corruption is the abuse of public office in exchange for personal benefits (Wei, 2001). In a chapter on conceptualising political corruption, Mark Philp describes political corruption as the abuse of office by public officials. Philp's characterisation provides the conceptual foundation of this chapter, as it succinctly presents the antecedent to the chapter's central preoccupation, as posited in Philp's own words:

> Most commonly, politics is understood as providing publicly endorsed practices, institutions and rules which affect an ordered resolution to a conflicting individual or group interests. Corruption subverts this process in favour of a rule to promote the interests of a single individual or group.
> *(Philp, 2002, p. 41)*

A common thread that plaits these definitions together is their reference to the behaviour of public office holders, misuse of authority and shared resources, deviation from rules and roles, and a penchant for private gain.

According to Hope and Chikulo (2000), there is a connivance between "corrupt actors in both the public and private sectors . . . to undermine public institutions" (p. 74). Hope and Chikulo (2000) argue that corruption in Nigeria is exacerbated by the country's massive petroleum deposits, exports from which provide most of the government's revenue. State control of the enormous oil reserves provides opportunities for pillaging by state officials with trusteeship of the oil wealth and their political buddies (p. 75).

Some scholars have acknowledged the agency of ordinary citizens in the fight against corruption in many African countries, including Nigeria, by pointing out that government scandals have led to the downfall of several regimes (Hope & Chikulo, 2000). While this may partly explain why Nigeria has had many military coups, the removal of a political leader in any manner in Nigeria has not produced a meaningful change to date. Even though many coup plotters cited corruption as justification for their rebellion (Ani, 2018), none of their leaders could prevent corruption within their government or the rank and file of their regimes. They instead resorted to sharing the benefits of their political power with their 'allies' (Hope & Chikulo, 2000: p. 76). Thus, Ani (2018) argues that the military rule in Nigeria was always politically and economically disastrous, as corruption only blossomed and gained a firm root under military rule.

Hope and Chikulo (2000) argue that countries whose policies are more distorted and give more control rights to politicians and bureaucrats may be more corrupt. Corruption thrives when the regulatory regimes and procedures are laden with distortions and where institutions for restraint are weak and permeable. Weak administration of justice also reinforces corruption by encouraging reoffending. It also allows for corrupt public officials to be recycled by their parties even after they may have been accused or previously been found wanting in their positions of trust. Often, public officials convicted of financial crimes are too quickly let off the hook or receive lighter sentences than are required for the nature of their offence. In many African countries, there is hardly any chance that lawmakers will be punished for their corruption-related offences, and even where they are, their penalty may be disproportionately lower compared to the benefits they gained from the said corrupt practices they engaged in (Hope & Chikulo, 2000).

Corruption has had several ruinous effects on the countries of Africa. It severely impedes social and political development, good governance, and fundamental freedoms and rights, including the right to work and education. More importantly, corruption is a significant impediment to economic growth and vitality, and it has deleterious effects on the well-being of individuals, families and communities (Transparency International, 2019). Corruption causes and exacerbates inequalities, as it benefits the few who have power and control over state resources and who misappropriate them at the expense of the many who lack such ability and are the neediest. Corruption derails and delays economic development, diverts resources from essential services, and forestalls fundamental citizen rights and due process (Johnston, 2005). Corruption in Nigeria has a debilitating effect on all the key sectors of public and political administration, including the judiciary, the legislature, the economic sector, health, infrastructure and agriculture, to name but a few. Corrupt state and local officials' abuse of authority in granting occupancy rights stifles opportunities for mechanised, well-irrigated, industrial-scale farms, in the same way as corrupt officials have derailed countless projects for the development of roads, railways, ports, electrical power, schools, hospitals, and universities (Page, 2018, p. 3).

Moreover, corruption seriously threatens the integrity of public services and draws negative evaluations from Nigerian citizens, who lose faith in the administration and the government (UNODC, 2019, p. 13). This latter point deserves attention because it is essential, particularly for policymakers and development partners, to understand the dynamics of citizens' perceptions of and public participation or the lack thereof, in the fight against corruption in any African country, not least in Nigeria. To this end, I ask: What should Western reform movements understand about African politics and the fight against corruption? Western reforms, peddled mainly by international donors and Western development partners to the African government, have not yielded many desired outcomes because of the failure to understand fundamental features of African politics. Western reforms quickly identify the state as the problem and liberalisation and democratisation, including increased accountability and public participation, as the solution (Glaeser & Goldin, 2006). For example, to remedy the numerous failures of anti-corruption reforms, international organisations, scholars and policymakers often tout and support measures to enhance democratic accountability. These measures are often based on assumptions of citizens' keenness to be engaged and protest corruption (Bauer, 2017, p. 561). However, citizen participation is not a given. Citizens and civil society organisations in Nigeria who have tried to expose and fight corruption have found themselves exposed to risks and dangers, including those which Ngozi Okonjo-Iweala describes as "physical and reputational threats and the bullying and harassment from the corrupt and politically motivated" (Okonjo-Iweala, 2018: xi.). Part of the problem is that Western reforms, illustrated above, lack systems and strategies for addressing nepotism, partisanship and cronyism, all of which are features of African, not least Nigerian, politics that abet sustains corruption.

The illegal and unscrupulous distribution of state resources is an example of what Johnston (2005) regards as resource diversion. Nepotism and favouritism have a deleterious effect on public service delivery and the fair distribution of public resources by downgrading the quality of the public service and creating room for public help to be wantonly concentrated in certain places or allocated to specific sections of the population more than others. These practices also adversely affect the fair administration of justice, including exempting one's relatives and friends "from the application of certain punitive laws or regulations, and this may disrupt esprit de corps and trust" (Ijewereme, 2015, p. 3). Corruption can also divert resources from the persons most in need, such as the poor and vulnerable, the unemployed and small business owners who could benefit from government support through welfare programs, support to households, grants-in-aid and other welfare systems. For example, tens of millions of Nigerians are prone to life-or-death risks because Nigeria's public health infrastructure is inadequate and incapacitated by mismanagement and corruption in the health ministry (Page, 2018).

I have limited my discussion of the forms of corruption in Nigeria to only four domains which I consider the most encompassing and most impactful to the modern-day democratic dispensation of the federal republic, namely, Political and Institutional Corruption, Economic Sector Corruption, Corruption in the Social Sector, and Political Party Corruption. Political and institutional corruption is a form of systemic influence "legal, or even currently ethical". It emasculates the efficacy of governmental institutions and weakens their capacities to achieve their goals, thereby diminishing public trust in those institutions (Lessig, 2013, p. 2). Economic sector corruption refers to corruption that upends the economic determinants of growth both at the individual and national levels, such as financial freedom, international integration (globalisation), education, infrastructural development, and resources (income) distribution (Ghabbir & Anwar, 2007, p. 752). Political party corruption, also known as electoral corruption, mostly takes place in Nigeria in the form of direct sabotage of the electoral system and process by individuals to affect electoral success through mendacious activities meant to misrepresent or falsify the outcome of the electoral process (Olarinmoye, 2009). The social domain of corruption in Nigeria has a cultural basis. It depends on and abetted by some cultural elements prevalent in Nigeria's diverse cultures, including "family, clan, community and tribe . . . " (Chinweuba, 2018, p. 112). In other words, social-level corruption is produced by cultural norms, rules of behaviour, beliefs and practices inherent in diverse cultures and expressed in daily interactions. For example, the customary exchange of gifts is as prevalent in Nigerian culture as in most African cultures. Sadly, this culture of gifting too quickly relapses into bribery and favouritism (Chinweuba, 2018). Chinweuba puts it succinctly:

> The traditional "exchange of gifts" and "recognition" prevalent in most Nigerian cultures expose the thin line, create a sharp link between "appreciation and anticipation" and convey an undue advantage on the giver, which eventually leads to corruption.
>
> *(Chinweuba, 2018, p. 177)*

The Nigeria example demonstrates that strategies for curbing corruption in Africa should invariably include a holistic understanding of the local political dynamics. Nigeria is Africa's largest economy, with its Gross Domestic Product (GDP) amounting to 441.5 billion US Dollars in 2021, making it the highest in Africa (Arimoro, 2023). Due to Nigeria's size and economic importance in West Africa, Africa and the world, the Nigerian situation is relevant to our understanding of the fundamental features of African politics, primarily political and economic governance. Also, the Nigerian problem is a pertinent illustration of the universality of Africa's most potent corruption curse – deterrence to economic growth and stability. In other words, corruption continues obstructing economic, political and social development across Africa. It will remain a significant barrier to economic growth, needing more effective and more informed prevention and intervention strategies.

The Many Faces of Corruption in Nigeria: A Snowballing Tale of Impropriety

Transparency International's 2020 Corruption Perceptions Index ranked Nigeria 149/180, scoring 25/100. The 2019 (most recent) Global Corruption Barometer reported the percentage of Nigerians who thought corruption in Nigeria increased over the previous 12 months at 43 per cent and the rate of public service users who paid a bribe in the last 12 months at 44 per cent. In 2020, the federal government of Nigeria, in its request to the International Monetary Fund (IMF) for assistance, committed to implementing several transparency and accountability measures to forestall malfeasance in financial dealings relating to all emergency-response activities. The government's actions in its request to the IMF included, *among other things*, conducting an independent audit of crisis-mitigation spending and related procurement processes.

Corruption in Nigeria takes many forms and spans many sectors, from complex racketeering and money laundering schemes involving vast sums of money in high places in government finance, public service and administration, and from the ministries of education, health, and defence to the National Assembly public commissions, and the judiciary; street level corruption involving to petty bribery, fraud and sin as seen in day-to-day encounters and interactions of citizens with public officials. Also, crime encompasses a wide range of behaviours across all sectors of public administration and government (Akinwotu & Olukoya, 2017).

Citing Matthew Page, the former United States intelligence community's leading expert on Nigeria, Akinwotu Olukoya argues that there is an apparent overlap between political and economic power in Nigeria. Politicians often connive with businesses to pilfer state coffers. In contrast, business associates benefit from handouts from their politician friends in the form of government contracts or policies that look out for them, says Page (Akinwotu & Olukoya, 2017).

Ijewereme (2015, p. 1) argues that "corruption in Nigeria manifests in the form of misappropriation, kickback, over-invoicing, bribery, embezzlement, tribalism, nepotism, money laundering, outright looting of the treasuring, and so on". Top bureaucrats use elected and appointive public office to illegally and unfairly obtain personal gain, which is commonplace in Nigeria's public sector. Corruption is rife in Nigeria's security sectors. Police and defence sector corruption have seriously weakened and haunted the security sector so severely that responding to internal conflicts and rising domestic terror has become arduous and is now feared to be impossible. Corruption is cited among Nigeria's top challenges to insecurity and is regarded as a significant cause of the insurgency. Research and empirical evidence suggest that the pervasiveness of corruption in the rank and file of the military affected the effectiveness and capacity of military responses to defeat Boko Haram (Banini, 2019). Boko Haram is a Nigeria-based Islamic sect group that seeks to overthrow the current Nigerian government and create what they believe would be a "pure" Islamic state based on Islamic 'Sharia' law. The term "Boko Haram" means Western or non-Islamic education is forbidden. The group has existed in various forms since the late 1990s and has since carried out several attacks on police stations and military bases; local, state and national level politicians; religious leaders; ordinary civilians and children (Adelaja & George, 2019), including the globally condemned kidnapping of 276 schoolgirls in the remote Nigerian town of Chibok. This act alarmed the world and prompted the "Bring Back Our Girls" campaign (Seay, 2021).

Mukolu and Ogodor (2018, p. 494) analogise corruption and insurgency by "encouraging capital flight as many foreign investors are reluctant to invest in Nigeria for fear of losing their money to swindlers and fraudsters". According to Suleiman and Karim (2015), curtailing the activities of Boko Haram requires addressing pervasive corruption. Why do some perceive corruption to have as bad an effect on Nigeria's economic growth as insurgency does? Insurgency creates instability and disrupts the smooth flow of business, movement of capital and distribution of services, in much the same way as corruption binds the hands of the federal government by slashing off or misallocating state funds needed for developmental projects and discouraging foreign direct investment in the country, thereby stifling economic activity (Suleiman & Karim, 2015). Thus, the federal government's determination to win the war against insurgency should be matched by efforts to purge the military of corrupt elements and curb corruption at all levels and forms of state government and politics. Moreover, the pervasiveness of corruption in Nigeria's judicial system not only stands in the way of much-needed judicial accountability and independence but also hinders the fight against corruption, undermining the country's already weak accountability structures (Page, 2018).

Page (2018) believes corruption is the greatest obstacle preventing Nigeria from achieving its enormous potential. Corruption, according to Page (2018, p. 1), "drains billions of dollars a year from the country's economy, stymies development, and weakens the social contract between the government and its people". Corruption is complex and ubiquitous in Nigeria, permeating all government and economic sectors. The contexts in which the manifold forms of corruption exist span all domains of public management at the national, state and local levels.

Political and Institutional Corruption

Public officials are supposed to be trustees and custodians of the communal wealth, which, according to proclaimed national aspirations, should be used only to convert into the common good. Sadly, Nigeria's political and institutional structures are in the firm grip of political party systems that prepare the ground for exploitation and abuse of office through electoral corruption (Page, 2018). Political corruption in Nigeria takes several forms, prominent among which are election rigging, bribery, bid rigging; inducement and undue influence, embezzlement; nepotism, falsification of financial records, judicial interference; and conflict of interests, evident in the award of contracts by public officials to their associates, family members and personal businesses (Ijewereme, 2015). Once the foundations are laid and parties bribe their way into legislative and executive domains of power, the opportunities for exploitation lay bare. Often, there is collusion between these two branches of government, as one doles out fake contracts and phoney projects to cronies and their fake companies, whilst the other approves them with reckless alacrity at the detriment of real projects that would otherwise alleviate the country's widespread privation (Page, 2018). This is an enterprise where a handful of power-laden party stalwarts who make up a tiny proportion of the country's population can defraud the system and burrow their way out with massive loot that would otherwise benefit most of the country. In this enterprise, an inordinate portion of government expenditures is funnelled into spurious "development" projects and pretentious government initiatives that only benefit corrupt political journalism and propaganda.

The foundations of political corruption are laid by electoral corruption. Ijewereme (2015) describes electoral corruption as any or all manner of electoral fraud, including manipulating voters' registers, buying votes with money, ballot stuffing, intimidation of agents of opposition parties at the polling units, and changing election results and declaring winners of elections as losers.

Economic Sector Corruption

The impact of corruption on economic growth and development in Africa is a popular subject of debate and analysis among scholars and of inquiry for researchers. Mbaku (2000, p. 54) argues that "corruption encourages inefficiency in the bureaucracy, stunts economic growth and generally impacts development negatively". Nigeria's economic sector spawns revenue from various industries, including agriculture, manufacturing, trade, communication, mining and quarrying. Nigeria's GDP amounted to 152,32 trillion Naira, over 400 billion US Dollars in 2020. The agricultural sector accounted for over 24 per cent of the country's GDP; trade accounted for over

13 per cent; the manufacturing industry generated 12 per cent; communication up to 11 per cent, and the mining sector, primarily crude oil and natural gas, contributed up to 7 per cent (Varrella, 2021). This wide-ranging economic sector provides a mecca of opportunities for pillage. Corruption in all its forms abounds and obliterates huge portions of revenue in trade, petroleum, agriculture, power, banking, infrastructural and environmental industries. There is collusion among many appendages of the economic sector, including public and private agencies. For example, the banking sector in Nigeria plays a crucial role in facilitating corruption at the highest levels of government (Page, 2018).

The impact of corruption in the agricultural sector on Nigeria's economy cannot be overemphasised, as agriculture is said to be "the backbone of Nigeria's non-oil economy, accounting for roughly 30 per cent of GDP" (Page, 2018). Also, since the agriculture sector employs more Nigerians than any other sector and is dominated by small-scale subsistence farming, the sector has a massive impact on the country's poorest and most alienated citizens (Page, 2018). There are further encumbrances on the revenue generation drive of this sector thanks to Nigeria's land tenure laws, which, among other things, make it easy for what Page (2018) dubs "corruption-prone state and local officials" to grant and revoke occupancy rights at will and simply on the whim of their benefactors or whoever fraudulently lines their pockets. These shady deals and dealings, and the susceptible laws that govern them, seriously frustrate investments in mechanised farming or farming on an industrial scale. Worse still, government officials' misappropriation of agricultural subsidies, who siphon them off to family members, friends, cronies or companies they own, leaves smallholder farmers languishing (Page, 2018).

The Economic Risk of COVID-19 Emergency Response

As governments and states take the lead in responding to the COVID-19 pandemic, they face numerous challenges and pressures on already overstretched resources, state structures and personnel. African governments' efforts at efficiently responding to the pandemic are also challenged by the added threat of corruption, as the need for rapid response handicaps existing anti-corruption procedures (Steingruber et al., 2020) and systems of accountability, thereby leaving the doors ajar for freebooters. While the COVID-19 emergency crisis did not create a new form of profiteering, it widened the already yawning gap of public service corruption and malfeasance in the management and spending of public funds (Transparency International, 2021).

Evidence suggests that even before the COVID-19 pandemic, about 20 per cent of Nigerians had to pay a bribe to access healthcare at public hospitals and clinics (Transparency International, 2021). In April 2020,

Nigeria received US$3.4 billion in emergency financial assistance from the IMF to support its COVID-19 response. The federal government of Nigeria announced a 2.3 trillion Naira (US$6 billion) stimulus package just two months after receiving the IMF grant. However, official figures show that many of Nigeria's poorest citizens have yet to see the benefit of this assistance (Transparency International, 2021). Nigeria's National Bureau of Statistics (NBS) found in 2020 that by the time of a nationwide survey in July of that year, "only 12.5 per cent of the poorest quintile of respondents had received some form of food assistance since the pandemic began", and that by August of the same year, 32 per cent of respondents nationwide were experiencing a severe food shortage, higher by 18 per cent than it was just two years prior (Transparency International, 2021).

While the federal government of Nigeria established a publicly accessible COVID-19 emergency procurement register, called the Nigeria Open Contracting Portal (NOCOPO), on COVID-19 spending and contracting, most of the measures it committed to in its request to the IMF, including the independent audit, were somewhat idealistic, still pending, or were never implemented, (Transparency International, 2021). Transparency International's report indicates that it found no beneficial ownership information or contract documentation for awarded companies when it reviewed select completed procurement processes worth US$10,000, together with Nigeria's corporate registry and an open data platform of the Bureau of Public Procurement (BPP) (Transparency International, 2021).

Moreover, containment measures being introduced by governments, such as lockdowns, border shutdowns and social distancing restrictions on public places, have had the undulating effect of increasing the economic burden on low-income households and families (i.e., most families in Nigeria), which has tripled the level of desperation of ordinary Nigerians to make ends meet, not least public service employees. A relapse into corrupt practices and illegal enrichment is inevitable. Poor coordination across government sectors, inadequate investment in digital skills and technological infrastructure, and poor disaster preparedness further complicate governments' management and oversight of state resources, not least those meant for emergency response.

In a 2020 report on corruption risks in governments' response to the COVID-19 pandemic, the World Bank Group guided addressing and mitigating corruption risks in the COVID-19 response. The report notes that "it will be essential to adjust anti-corruption efforts to support new governance arrangements and give greater attention to addressing impunity for misbehaviour, as well as to shaping norms and standards that affect public sector performance and behaviour" (World Bank Group, 2020). The report identifies the broad areas of government response prone to exploitation and where corruption risks are highest. It further provides a list of recommendations for addressing and mitigating the corruption risks associated with the pandemic response. Governments must grant access to information to ensure and enhance transparency.

Easy access to information by citizens and civil society actors, and timely and adequate response to queries from the public, as well as an increase in interface with and input from citizens, will boost public trust in government operations and make citizens and non-governmental entities allies rather than "suspects" or adversaries, as they may often be perceived by government officials who disagree with their stance on issues of public interest. Suppose the federal government of Nigeria and the IMF want to ensure that the country's most vulnerable communities and citizens receive the support and resources. In that case, they must put up with the additional adversity created by the pandemic; it is critical that the government act on the commitments to transparency and governance it had committed to in its request to the IMF for assistance and continue to prioritise integrity and transparency.

Political Party Corruption

Partisan politics – and, for that sake, multi-party elections – is arguably the most robust backbone of modern-day democratic governance. According to the political scientist E.E. Schattschneider, in his 1942 book, *Party Government*, partisan conflict is necessary for democracy, as it eliminates one-party politics, which is not democracy. "It is totalitarianism", says Schattschneider (Drutman, 2017). He also believed "modern democracy is unthinkable save in terms of parties". It is widely acknowledged that political parties mobilise and engage citizens to participate in politics, coalesce around a common purpose, and cultivate a shared sense of a collective, often indispensable for a functioning democracy (Drutman, 2017). However, partisanship presents a sad paradox for many African countries, not least for Nigeria, the most populous and one of the most ethnically diverse countries on the continent. The optimistic tale of a shared vision and collective energy that comes with party politics ends where the pulse of corruption begins. Political party structures have always played massive roles in attaining power and, by extension, access to opportunities across all government sectors to exploit public resources. Since partisanship creates a shared sense of collective energy in citizens, it is also conclusive that it strives for division. This division produces binary positions and oppositions, leading to a deliberate aggregation of citizens along party interests and transforming portions of the electorate into loyalists. The need to compensate these loyalist groups and individuals and to sustain their allegiance easily creates room for corruption. Thus, as partisanship overwhelms the political and institutional sectors, it becomes more an enabler of corruption than an impetus for unifying citizens around a common purpose.

Political parties in Nigeria are not only the main levers of political power and change; they are also – sadly – the brain and spine of the enterprise of corruption in the public service. Through electoral corruption, political parties unlatch opportunities for crime in other sectors (Page, 2018). Every time national elections usher in a new government, a new dawn of hope for more open government beams across the country. This hope is, however, quickly eclipsed by the partisanship and cronyism that ensue soon after the winning party takes the reins of power. Page (2018) notes that the transfer of political power in Nigeria in 2015 raised hopes among Nigerians "that credible elections are achievable". These hopes were, however, extinguished four years later by the shortcomings of the 2019 general elections. Nigeria's two main political parties – the ruling All Progressives Congress (APC) party and the opposition People's Democratic Party (PDP) – are, according to the assessment (Page, 2018), "constellations of fluid national, state, and local elite networks". Both parties have misappropriated public funds to finance election campaigns (Olorunmola, 2016, p. 4) and have used the reins of political authority to evade culpability for their members who are found wanton for such misappropriation. The use of public funds for party-related activities is purported to be widespread among various political factions; although it is predominantly linked with the governing parties (Olorunmola, n.d.).

Social Determinants of Corruption

The cultural basis of socio-economic and political organisations in a typical African society like Nigeria, pressures from family members, friends, and loyalists, and the lack of a distinction between personal and public property all converge into a formidable inducement for the holder of a public office to illegally enrich themselves and distribute their loot to their kith and kin (Hope & Chikulo, 2000). Social relationships are resources that can lead to the development and accumulation of human capital (Machalek & Martin, 2015). However, Nigeria's social capital has rapidly depreciated into a social deficit, as high-level and low-level corruption has permeated the social sector, especially the educational, health and social services sectors. Maira Martini of Transparency International mirrors this social norm paradigm in an article titled *Nigeria: Evidence of corruption and the influence of social norms*. Martini asserts that the "informal, personal and clientelist" networks between politicians and their buddies exist alongside and influence formal state structures (Martini, 2014, p. 2). The sad outcome of such interference is that persons and entities who have no business or expertise in making policies get to make or at least seriously influence decisions about policies and resources, which ultimately swindles the equitable distribution of public services and state resources. Thus, it is fair to say that the features of social capital, including social organisation, such as trust, norms and networks that can otherwise improve the efficiency of the country's social structures, have been hijacked and converted into an opportunity for private and pecuniary gains by persons entrusted with authority over and custody of the public good to the detriment of the public interest (Martini, 2014).

Nepotism and favouritism are other forms of societal-level corruption stemming from a solid urge to reward affinity and reaffirm allegiance to the party. Since they cannot award the whole kit and caboodle of their party base, the party fields cherry-picked personnel to receive public portfolios dished out hiring processes hijacked by the political elite in rather devious "recruitment processes". Others receive bloated government contracts, often served on a silver platter, based on spurious bidding documents scrutinised through the filters of ancestry or party affiliation and loyalty. Nepotism and favouritism do not always involve directly transferring or exchanging money. They can be the illegal and unscrupulous distribution of state resources in which a public official gifts contracts, jobs, promotions or official appointments to their family members or friends, based exclusively on bias, with flagrant disregard for merit. The effects on the social services industry are worsened by humanitarian sector corruption, which, according to Page (2018), burrows into the country's social capital and immensely impacts its most vulnerable citizens. Humanitarian sector corruption refers to all forms of corruption, including fraud, nepotism, cronyism, favouritism, extortion, political meddling, and so on, in humanitarian assistance, which encumbers the capacity of aid workers or agencies and diminishes the amount and quality of aid reaching the beneficiary populations. Sadly, this corruption is occasionally underplayed as the cost of doing business, with the "perceived trade-off between exigency and due diligence" in humanitarian contexts (Jenkins et al., 2020, p. 2). In the case of Nigeria, humanitarian sector corruption also daunts international development assistance and emergency aid, particularly in northeast Nigeria, where over 2 million people have been displaced by the Boko Haram insurgency in what is today known as one of the world's most significant humanitarian crises (Page, 2018).

Nigeria's Anti-corruption Paradox

The double standards in the fight against corruption are a giant blight on successfully implementing the federal government's anti-corruption strategy and efforts. Nigeria has three major anti-corruption agencies: the Economic and Financial Crimes Commission (EFCC), the Independent Corrupt Practices and Other Related Offences Commission, and the Code of Conduct Bureau. There is no dearth of infrastructure to fight corruption and bring offenders to book. Why does the fight against corruption in Nigeria seem to get farther away from reality? Transparency International's (TI) 2021 Corruption Perception Index, published in January 2022, ranks Nigeria 154 out of 180 countries surveyed, dropping five places from its 149th ranking in 2020 and scoring 24 out of 100 points this cycle. These statistics make Nigeria the second most corrupt country in West Africa (Transparency International, 2022). The answer lies in the unfair rules or expectations that differ between different groups of people, as it is common practice for successive presidents to use the EFCC and other anti-corruption outfits to hound political rivals while paying no heed to their cronies and allies. Allegations citing this favouritism have not spared the president of Nigeria, President Muhammadu Buhari, whose anti-corruption strategies and efforts are said to be skewed in favour of his party members, sometimes failing to investigate high-profile corruption cases (Fasan, 2022).

Moreover, there is a reasonable amount of anti-corruption legislation and strategies to curb corruption in Nigeria. So, why is crime so hard to prosecute and offenders so hard to convict? The best place to look for answers to why corruption persists in Nigeria is the preponderance of individuals in government and the expanse of power and control they have over government structures, which they can easily abuse without consequence. Anti-corruption laws and institutions are created by lawmakers, many of whom cannot uphold the very laws they promulgate when these laws have a chance to encumber their pursuit of private gain. The executive arm of government that can mete out punishment for misconduct can easily change colours from government to party and dole out pardons or look the other way in utter permissiveness towards the ruling elite (Hope & Chikulo, 2000). Corruption impedes the ability of governments to maximise the welfare of their citizens. The recent threats to Nigeria's internal security, including massive protests in 2020 over incidents of extreme police brutality (Reuter, 2020) and corruption in the ranks of the Nigerian police, are not unconnected with the government's inability to maximise the welfare of its youth population (U.S. Department of State, 2021). The United States Department of State's 2020 human rights report blamed "endemic corruption" as one of many factors impeding human rights and due process in Nigeria (U.S. Department of State 2021, p. 11). The report claims, for example, that the Nigeria Police Force remained susceptible to corruption and that the federal government of Nigeria did not consistently implement the law in convictions of "official corruption", even though the law provides criminal penalties for such convictions (U.S. Department of State 2021, p. 27). In other words, there are laws and policies, as well as institutions and structures of government, to be leveraged in the fight against corruption if only they would be used and applied indiscriminately to all Nigerians, regardless of class or partisan affiliation.

Conclusion

Successive governments of the Federal Republic of Nigeria have not successfully prosecuted corruption, and several heads of state and executive members have been at the centre of the massive pillage of state resources the country has seen over the past two decades. The legislature in Nigeria, like in many other countries, is responsible for executive accountability. Hence, a massive chunk of the blame for the collapse of Nigeria's budget process and many other fiduciary government businesses requiring shrewdness, efficacy, honest stewardship and integrity. Over the years, successive Nigerian government administrations have had many commissions and campaigns to rid Nigeria of corruption or to stem the prevalence of what has become an epidemic. However, the menace of corruption remains firmly rooted in the system. It rears its head in symptoms such as a lack of basic amenities and an absence of affordable livelihood in the country (Obutte, 2016).

There should be more than mere intentions and infinite recommendations for action. Year-in-year-out, African governments, not least the government of Nigeria, amass oodles of reports and recommendations for action as civil society organisations, international development partners, government contractors, and government ministries and departments conduct the perennial business of "feasibility studies", "monitoring and evaluations", "performance audits", "stakeholder engagements", "position papers", "White Papers", you name it. These recommendations lie about and rot on shelves and office tables. Bribery, extortion, nepotism and fake contracting go on unabated. It makes the subordination of public interests to private gains and abuse of general duty the rule rather than the exception.

Some measures that would improve and strengthen the government's response to corruption include creating a legal framework to provide greater public participation and narrow the gap between citizens, civil society organisations and the government, especially its three arms – the legislature, the executive and the judiciary. According to Stapenhurst and colleagues, Nigeria has over the years received "a low budget transparency and participation rating" (Stapenhurst et al., 2019, p. 82) by the International Budget Partnership (IBP), which recommended that Nigeria prioritises credible and effective mechanisms for public participation in and monitoring of the budget planning and implementation processes respectively, though, for example, public hearings and surveys (Stapenhurst et al., 2019). The government of Nigeria should be more proactive in enlisting public support and be more comfortable with civil society participation in implementing its anti-corruption mechanisms. In a study to examine the role of Civil Society Organizations (CSOs) in the electoral process and the impact therein on the credibility of electoral outcomes in Nigeria, Paul Ani Onuh and Chinedu Cyril Ike sampled the 2019 general election in Nigeria. The authors found that while the participation of civil society organisations in the electoral process of 2019 was substantial, their participation was emasculated by an awful lot of factors, including funding shortfalls, bureaucracy and administrative barriers, insecurity, and limited ability to independently monitor sensitive election materials (Onuh & Ike, 2021, p. 1). In Nigeria, coupled with the lack of political will, these bureaucratic encumbrances heighten citizens' apathy and limit public participation in the fight against corruption (Odusote, 2021). Thus, increasing civic participation in the government's anti-corruption drive is imperative for successfully implementing strategies to curb or control corruption in Nigeria.

Research supports the proposition that corruption can be stemmed or, to a large extent, rooted out of a country if institutional changes, bolstered by political will, block seepages, strengthen judicial independence and improve fiscal discipline. However, corruption in Nigeria will remain a focus for scholarly inquiry and national and international policy discussions for decades to come.

References

Adelaja, A. & George, J. (2019). *Terrorism and land use in agriculture: The case of Boko Haram in Nigeria*. Elsevier.

Akinwotu, E. & Olukoya, S. (2017). *'Shameful' Nigeria: A country that does not care about inequality*. The Guardian.

Alatas, S. H. (1990). *Corruption: Its nature, causes and consequences*. Aldershot, Avebury.

Ani, N. A. (2018). *Decades of corruption have held Nigeria back – it is time for change*. Apolitical.

Arimoro, A. E. (2023). Beyond economics! The (evolving) role of law in the eradication of extreme poverty. *Journal of Human Rights and Social Work*, 1–13. doi: 10.1007/s41134-023-00247-2

Banini, D. K. (2019). Security sector corruption and military effectiveness: The influence of sin on countermeasures against Boko Haram in Nigeria. *Small Wars & Insurgencies*, Vol. 31, No. 1, pp. 131–158.

Bauhr, M. (2017). Need or greed? Conditions for collective action against corruption. *Governance: An International Journal of Policy, Administration and Institutions*, Vol. 30, No. 4, pp. 561–581.

Chinweuba, G. E. (2018). Culture and corruption: A critical analysis of the basis of Nigerian depraved experience. *UJAH: Unizik Journal of Arts and Humanities*, Vol 19, No. 2, p.112.

d'Agostino, G., Dunne, J.P. & Pieroni, L. (2016). *Corruption and growth in Africa*. ResearchGate.

Drutman, L. (2017). *We need political parties. However, their rabid partisanship could destroy American democracy*. Washington, D.C., Vox Media.

Fasan, O. (2022). *Beyond Buhari's anti-corruption rhetoric: Where is the natural substance?* Business Day. https://businessday.ng/columnist/article/beyond-buharis-anti-corruption-rhetoric-wheres-the-real-substance/

George, L. (2020). *Why are Nigerians protesting against police brutality?* Reuters. www.reuters.com/article/idUSKBN2711T6/#:~:text=Because%20SARS%20was%20initially%20designed,rape%2C%20extrajudicial%20killings%20and%20torture

Ghabbir, G. & Anwar, M. (2007). Determinants of corruption in developing countries. *The Pakistan Development Review*, Vol. 46, No. 4.

Glaeser, E. L. and Goldin, C. (Eds.). (2006). *Corruption and Reform: Lessons from America's Economic History*. The University of Chicago Press.

Hope, K. R. & Chikulo, B. C. (Eds.). (2000). *Corruption and development in Africa: Lessons from country case studies*. Palgrave.

Ijewereme, O. B. (2015). *Anatomy of corruption in the Nigerian public sector: Theoretical perspectives and some empirical explanations*. SAGE.

Jenkins, M., Khaghaghordyan, A., Rahman, K. & Duri, J. (2020). The costs of corruption during humanitarian crises and mitigation strategies for development agencies. CMI: U4 Anti-Corruption Resource Center.

Johnston, M. (2005). *Syndromes of corruption: Wealth, power and democracy*, Cambridge University Press.

Koyuncu, J. Y. & Unver, M. (2017). The Association between corruption and globalisation in African countries. *Social Sciences Research Journal*, Vol. 6, pp.20–28.

Lessig, L. (2013). Foreword: "Institutional Corruption" defined. *Journal of Law, Medicine and Ethics*, Vol. 41, No. 3, pp. 553–555.

Machalek, R. & Martin, M. W. (2015). Sociobiology and sociology: A new synthesis. *International Encyclopedia of the Social & Behavioral Sciences*, (2nd ed.).

Martini, M. (2014). Nigeria: Evidence of corruption and the influence of social norms. U4 Expert Answer. www.u4.no/publications/nigeria-evidence-of-corruption-and-the-influence-of-social-norms

Mbaku, J. M. (2000). *Bureaucratic and political corruption in Africa: The public choice perspective*. Krieger Publishing Company.

Mukolu, M.O. & Ogodor, B.N. (2018). Insurgency and its implication on Nigeria's economic growth. *International Journal of Development and Sustainability*, Vol. 7, No. 2, pp. 492–501.

Obutte, P. C. (2016). *Corruption, administration of justice and the judiciary in Nigeria*. SSRN.

Odusote, O. T. (2021). *We are investigating and prosecuting corruption in Nigeria: An empirical analysis of legal and institutional frameworks* (Doctoral dissertation, University of Surrey).

Okonjo-Iweala, N. (2018). *Fighting Corruption is Dangerous: The Story behind the Headlines*. The MIT Press.

Olarinmoye, O. (2009). Godfathers, political parties and electoral corruption in Nigeria. *African Journal of Political Science and International Relations*, Vol. 2, No. 4, pp. 066–073.

Olorunmola, A. (n.d.). Cost of Politics in Nigeria. *Westminster Foundation for Democracy*.

Olorunmola, A. (2016). *The cost of politics in Nigeria*. London: Westminster Foundation for Democracy.

Onuh, P. A. & Ike, C. C. (2021). Civil society organizations and electoral credibility in Nigeria, *Africa Review*, Vol. 13, No. 2, pp. 233–250.

Page, M. T. (2018). *A new taxonomy for corruption in Nigeria*. Carnegie Endowment for International Peace.
Philp, M. (2002). *Conceptualizing Political Corruption*, 3rd Ed. Routledge.
Seay, L. (2021). Seven years ago, #BringBackOurGirls was a global campaign. What happened? A compelling book details the story of Nigeria's kidnapped Chibok girls–*The Washington Post*.
Stapenhurst, R., Draman, R., Larson, B. & Staddon, A. (Eds.). (2019). *Anti-Corruption evidence: The role of Parliaments in curbing corruption*. Springer.
Steingruber, S., Kirya, M., Jackson, D. & Mullard, S. (2020). *Corruption in the time of COVID-19: A double-threat for low-income countries*. U4 Anti-Corruption Resource Centre, Chr. Michelsen Institute.
Suleiman, M. N. & Karim, M. A. (2015). *Cycle of bad governance and corruption: The rise of Boko Haram in Nigeria*. SAGE.
Transparency International (2019). *Citizens speak out about corruption in Africa*. Berlin. Transparency International.
Transparency International (2021). *CPI 2020: Sub-Saharan Africa*. Transparency International.
Transparency International (2021). *IMF COVID-19 Emergency loans: A view from four countries*. Transparency International.
Transparency International (2022). *Corruption perceptions index 2021*. Transparency International.
United Nations Office on Drugs and Crime (2019). *Corruption in Nigeria: Patterns and trends. Second survey on corruption as experienced by the population*. UNODC Research.
U.S. Department of State (2021). *Nigeria 2020 Human Rights Report*. The United States Department of State.
Varrella, S. (2021). *Gross domestic production (GDP) distribution across activity sectors in Nigeria as of 2020*. Statista.
Wei, S. (2001). *Corruption and globalisation*. Brookings.
World Bank Group. (2020). *Ensuring Integrity in the Governance and Institutional Response to COVID-19*. World Bank eLibrary.

3
RECOUNTING HOW ELECTORAL CORRUPTION MANIFESTS IN SIERRA LEONE

Stories and Lessons from the Field

Marcella Samba-Sesay née Macauley

Recounting How Electoral Corruption Manifests in Sierra Leone: Stories and Lessons from the Field

Corruption has become a binding constraint on the agenda-setting of Sierra Leone's public policy, and the electoral space must be carefully watched as it is not exempted. Electoral corruption or fraud takes various forms, from vote buying, vote rigging, outright violence on voters, and violation of procedures. Little literature exists on this topic in Sierra Leone. However, a typology of abuse is emerging in the form of the flagrant display of money in elections and outright disruptions and electoral violence, which put electoral integrity at stake. This situation makes this topic an area of interest for further election discussions and intervention. Therefore, this study will use the 2018 Presidential, Parliamentary, Local Council elections and beyond as insights into the patterns of electoral corruption and the basis for analysis and potential actions.

Through a practitioner's perspective and case study approach, the study will explore two common manipulative strategies, i.e. vote buying and electoral violence in local politics. It will examine the extent, scope, nature, causes and subsets. It will zero in on the gender dimension of electoral corruption and how violence is a readily available tool to prevent women from assuming political office through the ballot box. It will show how money politics deter women's political representation by exposing women's struggle in party politics. In the final analysis, the chapter recounts how an organised, vibrant, and fully functional Civil Society (CS) can support electoral integrity as watchers. It shows how CS can forestall subtle forms of manipulations in the electoral process to promote electoral integrity; it further discusses the

DOI: 10.4324/9781003468608-5

limitations of CS in addressing critical aspects of electoral corruption, like campaign finance and the unregulated use of money. The study also points to the failure of state institutions, especially law enforcement agencies, to take the necessary actions to curb disruptions, violence and other forms of electoral corruption. It emphasised that such failings will only exacerbate the practice, thus undermining the quality of elections, with citizens gradually losing faith in democratic processes. By and large, this chapter seeks to discuss the issue of electoral fraud in the Sierra Leone context, bringing out its scope, nature and causes, drawing evidence from witnesses in the frontline and elections observation reports, thus adding to the body of literature on this subject.

In 2018, during the General elections, political party operatives were filmed publicly distributing cash to supporters, and political songs were sung with sentiments of vote buying (Sierra Leone News, 2018). Evidence of 'turn-out' buying also exists where influential people such as chiefs and party functionaries publicly pledge to hand over a whole tribe, chiefdom or district to a party. In circumstances where electoral laws are primarily silent on money politics, it becomes difficult to pursue further actions. Women aspirants for the 2018 elections were beaten, and the aggressors' slogan was 'pay attention'. In a 2019 bye-election in Ward 196, Tonko Limba Kambia District, National Election Watch (NEW) observers for the first time saw evidence of attempted ballot-box stuffing, leading to the arrests of some of the culprits ('NEW Raises alarm over irregularities in Tonko Limba Bye-Election', 2019). Despite these types of abuses occurring and co-existing with the electoral processes, strategies and activities of political parties and electoral stakeholders are less inclined to unearth electoral corruption and to promote an agenda to deal with it. Furthermore, this growing negative trend equally falls within the unsettling phenomenon of democratic backsliding. This is where elections are undermined, citizens' choices are stolen through disruptions, especially on polling day, and governments become less accountable to citizens (Lust &Waldner, 2015).

Electoral Fraud undermines the electoral process, citizens' trust and a flagrant display of power and control. Drawing from the International Foundation for Electoral Systems' (IFES) numerous experiences worldwide, Vickery and Shein (2012, p. 4) state that 'perpetrators of blatant fraud often make no efforts to hide them. Blatant vote buying, intimidation and violence may all be part of a strategic public display of power intended to evidence their (or their party's) control over the political process'.

Cheeseman and Klaas (2018) state that the most effective autocrats steal elections before Election Day. As such, 'counterfeit democrats use a wide range of strategies to hold on to power that have negative social and political impacts, including vote-buying and violence'. Therefore, the aim of unleashing violence during elections must not be divorced from the grand plan to influence the electoral outcome and to terrify women from mainstream democratic participation. Using the 2018 multi-tier elections and subsequent bye-elections as points of reference, it is evident that this pattern is becoming more organised and increasingly contentious. Before, manipulations were rumoured and, if they occurred, would have possibly been done tacitly, mostly in hiding and hardly spotted; hence, there is limited evidence for discussions and even prosecution. In recent times, however, manipulation has come to the fore with public cash distribution, one attempt of ballot-box stuffing recorded by election observers, and ballot box and sensitive voter materials destroyed in the full view of election officials and observers by political party supporters or burnt by marauders. Evidence abounds in a 24th of August 2019 re-run and heavily contested bye-election in constituency 110 in Western Rural District where, in one Polling Centre, sensitive voting materials, including ballots and equipment, were destroyed by thugs. The National Electoral Commission (NEC) had to cancel this election despite all voting centres being counted except for one disrupted centre ('Constituency 110 by-election conducted amid chaos', 2019) Similar disruption was evident in the bye-election for District Chairperson in Koinadugu district, where marauders disrupted voting, carted with ballots and burned voting materials. In Ward 091 in Constituency 027 in Sandor Chiefdom Kono District in Yayah Town, cast ballots were carted away by party supporters ('Koinadugu Bye-elections Marred by Widespread Political Intimidation', 2021). This situation will further be expanded on as the piece proceeds.

Sierra Leone has voted out of office two governing parties and elected the opposition into office since 1996, taking a break from the entrenching of incumbent government that is commonplace in Africa. Political theorists believe this represents democratic growth, shows that citizens can determine their fate through the ballot box and compel leaders to rule justly. More importantly, as Moehler and Lindberg (2007, p. 2) point out, electoral turnovers significantly moderate the citizens as winners and losers converge in their attitudes about the legitimacy of their state and government institutions. They further opine that this gives 'new meaning to Huntington's "two-turnover-test"'. According to them, turnovers are not just indicators that elites have accepted democracy, 'but power alterations also appear to generate shared levels of legitimacy between winners and losers in the general population, thus furthering democratic consolidation'.

Conversely, citizens' demand to use elections as a tool for political accountability can give rise to politicians resorting to visible electoral corrupt strategies and practices to clinch or remain in power. Therefore, elections in Sierra Leone have high stakes for apparent reasons; patronage politics is rife with clear evidence of mostly winner-takes-all by successive governments. The strategy is undoubtedly to evade citizens' dissatisfaction through the ballot box. Arguably, the strategies and activities of political parties and electoral stakeholders are less inclined to unearth electoral corruption in advance. Reports, findings and actions are either latent or mainly concentrated on the formal election cycle activities per the election calendar: boundary delimitation, voter registration and exhibition of the voters' roll, distribution of voters' ID cards, nominating candidates, polling and collation. Little work has been done on what transpires in the communities before Election Day.

It is essential to point out that unregulated spending in elections is rife. The law on campaign finance is relatively weak because there are no ceilings for campaign expenditure in Sierra Leone. Money spent on advertising, including posters and T-shirts, adverts and cash distribution, remains untracked. The lines between party spending and candidates' spending are equally blurred. This situation makes it difficult for the Political Party Registration Commission (PPRC) to regulate money's influence in the electioneering process; the law also makes provision for all registered political parties to disclose their party finances annually to the PPRC mandatorily. Still, compliance is often limited where state funds are not allocated to political parties. The regulatory powers of PPRC are also limited to enforcing this provision (The Political Parties Act, 2002).

The realities of the 2018 Presidential and General elections and beyond show worrying signs for upholding electoral integrity and trust in electoral outcomes. There was an injunction on the 2018 Presidential Run-off election due to fraud allegations on the one hand. Still, on the other hand, some citizens alleged that the judge who slammed the injunction was also under undue influence and directives. Although this caused wanton delays in conducting the polls and raised questions about new forms of alleged manipulations, this piece did not research the claim's authenticity and the integrity of the counterclaims. However, several questions and thoughts have come to the fore. Firstly, the occurrence reinforces how the courts have become central to the discourse on election outcomes and decisions in Africa and a must-watch space in Sierra Leone. When this is backed by a May 2019 decision by the high court removing ten opposition MPs from the Parliament of Sierra Leone and replacing nine of them with representatives from the governing party without a re-run of the constituencies, it only manifests undermining citizens' choice, and the concerns become even more compelling. (Freedom House, 2020). This issue is a point I will further dilate on as the chapter ensues. In addition, it calls for careful reflection on how the law is now perceived as a 'manipulative' tool for the political contest. It further exposes the fact that personal biases can influence legal interpretations. Mainly as a practitioner, I have observed a worrying trend of legal practitioners who once argued in favour of specific provisions that protect democracy and rights and have now flipped their line of arguments as political parties swap sides on the table.

Governance and political issues affect men and women differently. This difference is rooted in patriarchy, which manifests in traditional and cultural practices, laws, levels of literacy, and economic inequality among men and women. According to the IFES, Violence against Women in Elections (VAWE) is a threat to the integrity of the electoral process and the quality of democracy because it coercively excludes women from having a voice in the political and governance processes in their country. It is a violation, a criminal code that harms voters, candidates, elections officials, activists, security, and political professionals worldwide, occurring online and offline.

Bjarnegard (2018) believes that 'election violence should be studied as a simultaneous violation of personal and electoral integrity'. Furthermore, she defines election violence as 'occurring when the act's goal is to affect an electoral outcome or prevent someone from running in an election'. Next, how it is carried out violates the personal integrity of individuals involved in the electoral process. This point and using case studies, this piece will highlight how election fraud manifests and thrives in the 2018 elections and beyond, pointing out how VAWE violates women's 'personal integrity', thus illegitimately affecting democratic outcomes. It will discuss civil society's effort to forestall the same in growing democracies like Sierra Leone. This is especially so where formal structures are challenged, responses by law enforcement agencies are minimal or even existent in certain instances, and patriarchy is dominant.

Thus, this section identifies and discusses three major types as subsets of electoral corruption in the Sierra Leonean context. It explores how such manipulations, i.e. money/rewards, electoral violence, and VAWE manifest. It further examines the role of law enforcement agencies in securitising democracy and elections.

Electoral Fraud Strategies

Electoral manipulations vary according to context. In a post-conflict state like Sierra Leone, elections provide a non-violent alternative to gain political power and allow citizens to have excellent through the ballot box on how they are governed. As Vickery and Shein (2012) rightly put it, electoral wrongdoing violates domestic norms or internationally accepted free and fair elections standards.

Unfortunately, violence has become a significant threat to safeguarding elections, undermining the fundamentals of a process well designed for peaceful power transfer. Fabrice Lehoucq (2003) describes electoral fraud as a 'clandestine and illegal effort to shape elections results', but this definition, though straightforward and appealing at a glance, is limited in how fraud unfolds. Vickery and Shein (2012) argue that 'such issues consider fraudulent activities that a brazen incumbent candidate or party might commit in the open, such as voting or ballot stuffing'. Perhaps the most appropriate and workable definition for this piece is Andreas Schedler's (2002) definition in a paper titled '*The Menu of Manipulation*'. Electoral fraud involves the introduction of bias into the administration of elections. It can occur at any stage of the electoral process, from voter registration to the final tally of ballots. It covers such activities as forging voter ID cards, burning ballot boxes or padding the vote totals of favoured parties and candidates. Invariably, though, it violates the principle of democratic equality. Fraudulent practices distort the citizenry's preferences by denying some citizens' voting rights while amplifying others (Vickery & Shein, 2012, p. 4).

There has hardly been a holistic strategy developed by Elections Management Bodies (EMBs) to deter fraud in elections. It is difficult to see an Electoral Fraud Control Plan that will hold political pundits and leaders responsible for violent actions in Sierra Leone. An integrated plan that will consider the collective roles of all agencies and institutions having direct responsibilities to address aspects of electoral fraud, i.e. the Sierra Leone Police (SLP), the Office of National Security (ONS), the Anti-Corruption Commission (ACC), NEC, the Political Party Registration Commission (PPRC) and the Civil Society. For example, a smear campaign ensued to discredit NEC in the 2018 elections where 'political parties and state institutions provoked and potentially sabotaged NEC's reputation'. Thus 'NEC was subject to politically motivated criticism. All of the major political parties, at one point or another, alleged unspecified vote rigging in the first round; they, however, provided no genuine evidence of significant and systematic problems to support their claims' (EUEOM Preliminary Statement, 2018). It was premeditated and intentional to undermine the credibility of NEC as not fit to conduct the elections. When the first-round results were announced, the smear campaign intensified. The commission endured such high psychological stress whilst performing their national service. In the wake of allegations of electoral irregularities after the first round of the polls that had the potential of undermining the electoral process, NEC decided to allow political parties and CSOs to accompany the movement of election materials to all polling stations across the country during the Presidential Run-off elections. NEW, as a result, deployed 17 District Election Material Movement Observers (DEMMOs) and 428 Ward Elections Material Movement Observers (WEMMOs) to accompany the elections materials across the country, putting additional stress on the local elections observer's strategy and budget. Notwithstanding, this swift response by NEW exemplify how collective efforts can forestall allegations and promote electoral integrity (NEW Observation Report, 2018).

Regarding peace promotions and securitising elections, there is usually an integrated security plan mainly focusing on deploying officers for elections, peace and security. The PPRC usually mobilises persons to encourage political parties to sign Peace Pacts. It will become a treaty often flouted, as evidenced by NEW observation reports on how political parties sometimes use party supporters and thugs to disrupt polling day activities (NEW Press Statement, 2021). For the most part, electoral observation strategies focus on polling activities, mainly Voting, Counting and Collation. They can hardly unearth and combat electoral fraud in the communities where allegations of money change hands. EMBs and elections monitors should not be oblivious that violence is a strategy used by political party activists, pressure groups and individuals for their candidates to win elections at all costs, thereby influencing the course and outcomes of electoral contests.

Vote Buying and 'Turn-out Buying'

The Public Elections Act 2012 precludes the vote buying and selling of franchises. It describes a vote buyer in Section 120 (1) as such: 'A person who gives, lends, offers, promises to procure, any money or valuable consideration to or for a voter, or to do for any other person to induce a voter to vote or refrain from voting or corruptly does any such act on account of such voter having voted or refrained from voting at an election'. In the 2018, General elections, political party operatives were publicly filmed distributing money to supporters. These videos and photos circulated widely on social media with a government minister, a presidential aspirant, and political party campaign teams giving cash to voters (Sierra Leone News, 2018). Supporters chanted political songs with sentiments of vote buying. Ten thousand (10,000) Leone notes, a little over a dollar then, were distributed by lead political pundits in exchange for a T-shirt. The reason is that citizens are tricked into believing that numbers in public rallies amount to mass voting. Although the legal framework outlaws vote buying, it is becoming a growing concern and enterprise in the local democratisation. It is fueled by unregulated spending, and election observers can hardly investigate such issues. As a practitioner, I must state that civil society has not used its expertise and space enough to unearth this thoroughly. Primarily, the approach should be robust civic education, giving ordinary citizens knowledge to report as such incidents occur outside the observation/monitoring schedules. In addition, protracted human, technical and financial resources are needed to mount thorough and accurate investigations, which are mostly unavailable.

Conversely, citizens have learned to collect cash from the two dominant parties to service their desperate needs and vote for the party of their choice. This act has been termed 'Watermelon Politics', as green and red are the colours of the two dominant political parties. Voters will now be 'watermelon supporters' benefiting from cash from both sides of the divide but vote as they wish. Evidence abounds from the 2018 NEW Observation Report that the National Grand Coalition (NGC) party and the Alliance Democratic Party (ADP) called on their supporters to accept the rewards and vote for their choices (NEW Observation Report, 2018). Unfortunately, the law governing political parties is limited in provisions concerning campaign finance. In such circumstances, the PPRC can hardly track the source and threshold of spending; this situation has given rise to abuse of incumbency. The European Union Election Observer Mission (EUEOM) Report (2018) states that in 36.5% of observed first-round All Peoples Congress (APC) rallies, there was evidence of government resources being used. This was most often used in government vehicles, but other civil servants and soldiers were involved in campaigning. Money was observed being given to attendees in 3.3% of Sierra Leone's Peoples Party (SLPP) and 5% of NGC events, whereas it was observed in 18.4% of APC events (EUEOM Final Report, Sierra Leone, 2018, p. 22).

Money impacts the political scene during elections and in varying forms. Data shows that in editorial programmes for the 2018 Presidential and Parliamentary elections, the incumbent attracts more coverage and becomes the dominant party in the state broadcaster Sierra Leone Broadcasting Corporation (SLBC) than other parties (EUEOM, Final Report Sierra Leone, 2018 p. 26). The political campaign and publicity materials also outnumber the others with giant billboards and advertisements. Buying the hearts of voters using national development projects has been a recurrent tactic by politicians. The strategy is to launch community development projects to entice voters during campaigns. Ahead of a 2020 second re-run election in Constituency 110 in Western Rural District, political party supporters from the ruling SLPP party and the main opposition APC party clashed over who should complete a Community Centre ('NEW Incident Reporting Ahead of Re-Run Elections', 2020). Through analysis, the costs for these sophisticated rallies, including mobilisation of people, costs of canopies, music, and food, can part-fund the mostly unsophisticated community projects promised and launched.

There has been an implicit operation of political parties through a mass movement of communities in buses to register for the election, expecting to have their votes in return. This situation is mostly mainly observed during voters. The ferrying of voters is an expensive exercise. Politicians can hardly repeat the same because it has to be done three times, including the exhibition of the final Voters Register and on polling day. Although there is no corresponding evidence that such actions change the electoral choice of voters, many believe that this action has the potential to influence voters' behaviour.

In a 2019 re-run bye-election in Ward 196 in the Tonko Limba chiefdom Kambia District, NEW observers, for the first time, saw evidence of attempted ballot-box stuffing with allegations that voters have been paid overnight and given fake ballot papers to stuff the box. In polling centre 08056, station 3, Kagbonkoh, a voter was caught with six pre-marked and stamped ballot papers inside the polling station and was handed over to the police. Evidence of voting with ballots of a previously cancelled 2018 bye-election in the same ward exists ('NEW Raises alarm over irregularities in Tonko Limba Bye-Election', 2019). Another extreme form of vote buying is 'turn-out buying'. Nichter (2008) introduces this term when he argues that 'scholars typically understand vote buying as offering particularistic benefits in exchange for vote choices'. He posits that the term 'turn out buying' is more applicable and, in essence, as an alternative explanation that 'parties might offer rewards even if they cannot monitor voter choice'. From his argument, 'turn out buying' is rewarding 'unmobilised supporters' for 'showing up and targeting strong supporters rather than monitoring individual vote choice'. Evidence of 'turn out buying' exists where influential chiefs and party functionaries pledge to hand over the whole tribe, chiefdom, or district to a political party. Following Nichter's (2008), the critical question is, how does this arrangement sin with a secret ballot? This action compromises the voters' individualistic identity and civic and political right to choose. Further, it puts individuals in the tribe or community in a precarious situation, benefiting the leaders who make the public pledge/declaration. It becomes an opportunity for recognition and reward for themselves while their subjects and followers show unquestioning loyalty in many instances. I describe this action as a bullying strategy tending to mortgage individual voters' identity because they belong to a group. Therefore, it is not cash but using humans as collateral in exchange for political rewards, hence the politicisation of ethnic identities. NEW observed in the 2018 elections reported how some Paramount Chiefs (PCs) restricted confident party supporters to campaign in their chiefdom. In the 2018 Presidential, Parliamentary and Local Council Elections, many leaders attempted to declare their communities and tribes for political parties. The question remains on who or what accords the authority to anyone to pledge a whole tribe or chiefdom when the underlying tenets of democracy presuppose one person, one vote.

Furthermore, in a society like Sierra Leone, where digital records of births hardly exist for many, underage voters are also mobilised to register in support of primary relatives and other candidates. In addition, there exists cross-border registration and voting from people in neighbouring Guinea and Liberia. These registrants/voters argue that they are Sierra Leoneans living in the border communities, but evidence supporting or refuting the claim hardly exists. However, recent developments, pre and post-2018, point to evidence of digitised records on national civil registration or vital statistics.

Electoral Violence: Conceptual Clarifications and Manifestations

Electoral violence is a corrupt tool distinctively used for perpetuating fear and resentment in the masses and a strategy for electoral manipulation. Höglund (2019) notes that timing and motive separate electoral violence from other forms. The time aspect relates to violence carried out during the election period. The objective of electoral violence is to influence the electoral process and, by extension, its outcome. Laakso (2007) expands on the cynical and manipulative motive and notes that electoral violence is an activity motivated by an attempt to affect the results of the elections either by manipulating the electoral procedures and participation or by contesting the legitimacy of the results. From this definition, electoral violence can be perpetrated by various governments, EMBs, political parties and individual citizens (The Electoral Knowledge Network, ACE Project). It is also essential to distinguish it from other forms of political violence and to further underscore that careful analysis must be undertaken, as not all election-related violence is geared toward the desire to influence the conduct and outcome of an election. As Alston (2005) puts it, some electoral killings are not motivated by an intention to influence an election, especially killings between private citizens in an election context. In a country emerging from violent armed conflict like Sierra Leone, the consequences of violence as fear and intimidation tactics can be dire as it sends chills and outright fear in the populace (The Electoral Knowledge Network, ACE Project).

Birch et al. (2020), drawing from Seeberg et al. (2018), point out that electoral violence can take various forms and can happen in all parts of the electoral cycle, from the registration, award of symbols, campaigns, voting and the announcement of results. More importantly, it can be 'promoted by state and non-state actors'. The prevalence and dynamics of electoral violence leading to the 2018 elections and after are worrying trends for democratic consolidation.

As mentioned, every election in the history of Sierra Leone has been associated with some form of violence; the difference in recent times is that such violent actions and aggression bring about immediate recognition for political rewards and appointments. So violence is now legitimate, and political ambitions have allowed some politicians to support unbridled electoral corruption publicly. Democratic elections now go hand in hand with political rent-seeking. Cronies, therefore, are becoming more desperate from one election to the other. Those with cash contribute to party campaigns, whilst youths and the struggling masses display force as a bargaining chip for recognition. A 2013 publication by International IDEA p. 11 sums it up by stating that 'allegiance to political parties is based on promises of money, jobs and services' (Anning, 2013). Generally, political parties' conduct during their campaigns undermined multiparty democracy. Political parties' activities in the 2018 elections created and aggravated tension based on ethnicity, language, and region. NEW captured several incidents of political parties' leaders and supporters using radio, television and open meetings to propagate and spread hateful ethnic sentiments (NEW Observation Report, 2018).

This trend has led to undue mis/disinformation in Sierra Leone's politics, weaponing information. Many pose as keyboard warriors and WhatsApp audio/video journos spewing hate and uttering verbal abuse. There are also anti-rights groups targeting activists, media professionals and democracy watchers, each framing fear and intimidation on social media. Mackintosh (2020) states that WhatsApp is the most popular social media affecting politics in Sierra Leone, hosting countless political interest groups seeking truth shrouded in hate.

Young people are the readily available reservoirs used as thugs by political parties to wreak havoc on political opponents and disrupt the peace during elections. In the run-up to the 2018 elections, immediately after and subsequent bye-elections, the actions of thugs have been far-reaching. Ranging from stabbing to assault leading to bodily harm such as removing teeth and breaking limbs, posters and banners, killing and arson (NEW Observation Report Final, 2018). The consequences have led to the alleged death of a journalist and youths. Some of these thugs have come publicly on social media to threaten their paymasters. As mentioned, violence is perpetrated mainly by the two lead political parties who have controlled power since independence and criticised the police as 'regime serving' and are unlikely to act or, when they act, arrest the opposition supporters. A pattern of unprofessional policing has been taking root in the nation's democratic process for more than ten years. I have observed political parties' more organised and coordinated investments in thugs to disrupt an election. I wonder why such investments are not positively directed to capacitating party agents watching the polls. Sadly, and in my opinion, most politicians and their supporters believe that violence can win elections; therefore, it seems that mobilising, preparing and deploying thugs are part of their electoral strategy. Thuggery now appears to be a permanent feature in the electoral cycle. Unfortunately, each violent election limits the quality, integrity, and trust in the polls and undermines national stability.

Some of the bye-elections post-2018 have been marred with systematic patterns of violence. On 29 September 2018, a bye-election held in Ward 196, Tonko Limba Chiefdom, Kambia District, was cancelled by NEC as 'violence erupted in Polling Centre Code 8057 St Mary's Junior Secondary School Mile 14 and Polling Centre 8060 (Wesleyan Church of Sierra Leone Primary School, Masunthu)' ('Bye-Election in Ward 196 Constituency 58', 2018) There were also violent clashes between supporters of the APC and SLPP. NEW reported gross intimidation and suppression of election officials by party operatives. Aggressive Party supporters were ferried in open vehicles to polling places, used invectives and threw stones at each other. This violent act extended to polling staff, observers, and voters near polling centres. Though state police officials were present, the violence could not be forestalled, leading to the death of a 14-year-old boy ('Cancellation of Local

Council Bye Election', 2018; 'Bye-Election in Ward 196 Constituency 58', 2018). This was one of the first sets of bye-elections after the 2018 polls that brought the SLPP to power, and party supporters from both sides were desperate to win as a show of political hegemony.

Perhaps the most worrying trend of election violence and its manipulative effects on election outcomes was the tacit role displayed by state security agencies on the 24 August 2019 re-run election in Constituency 110 in the Western Rural District in Sierra Leone. In a statement after the polls, NEW writes, 'Despite the heavy security presence and the invocation of Military Aide to Civil Power (MACP), polling stations were invaded and election materials destroyed and perpetrators not arrested'. Democracy watchers and citizens alike were stunned as thugs and party functionaries destroyed sensitive voting materials. The NEC cancelled the election, and state resources were wasted. Even with the circulation of videos on social media, criticisms and condemnations by civil society, sections of the media and some political parties, no arrests of some of the main culprits have been made to date.

Similarly, in a bye-election for Local Council Chairperson in Koinadugu district, 'unidentified youths' entered the polling precinct of Centre code 6115, RC Primary School Saint Balia, causing panic and burnt down voting materials. These exceptional incidents undoubtedly cast a sombre light on electoral integrity ('Koinadugu Bye-elections Marred', 2021)

Party Primaries are not absolved from violence and manipulations. Internal democracy is equally challenged as the legislation about sanity is non-existent. In some instances, candidates have attempted to acquire party symbols through violence or alliance with political godfathers.

Violence against Women in Elections (VAWE)

Although Sierra Leone is a signatory to several international, regional and sub-regional instruments that promote an enabling environment for women's participation in elections, the realities on the ground can be hostile and far from encouraging.

The March 2018 Presidential, Parliamentary and Local Council Elections in Sierra Leone impacted women's participation and representation. For the 2018 elections, there was a ban on dual citizens. However, it is essential to point out that though this law is a statutory requirement for nomination, it has never been enforced. This ban negatively affected women's chances of a level playing field and thwarted opportunities to gain more political representation for women. As the EUEOM Report (2018) rightly puts it, 'the banning of dual citizens . . . had a disproportionate effect on female candidates because it was often those women with international backgrounds who were most likely to put themselves forward as MP candidate standing, the government's temporary ban on secret societies became an implicit support system for women in the 2018 elections'. Women had complained that secret societies, for the most part, restrict their political activities and limit campaigns, especially at night.

Thus, women's experiences were diverse depending on their platform. Women were optimistic about a more level playing field based on the amount of training, advocacy, lobbying and the widespread public debates around including more women in political leadership. Next, various political parties promised to promote women's representation. A Knowledge, Attitude and Practice (KAP) survey done in April of 2016 by the civil society Standing Together for Democracy Consortium was promising. The findings revealed that 70% of the respondents said they were for women. Unfortunately, evidence in the elections was contrary. The elections were indeed not free from fear and violence. In retrospect, it became clear that the intent and the reality were directly opposite, especially in a context where citizens' voting decisions largely depended on political party affiliation instead of policies and individual competence.

The ordeals of women in the pursuit of contesting elections were revealing. This situation was thoroughly documented by the Campaign for Good Governance CGG) (a civil society organisation promoting inclusive citizens' participation in governance) in post-2018-election dialogue sessions held with various categories of women who had interfaced with elections nationwide. The nature of horrible experiences ranges from physical and psychological abuse, intimidation, and destruction of property to their person, family members, and loyal supporters. Sometimes, close friends were terrified to associate with female aspirants or candidates for fear of being targeted. Therefore, the politics of violence was a key strategy used in the 2018 elections to shut women from the political contest. Electoral violence against women was thus a calculated ploy to forestall women's win with techniques that instilled outright fear, stalking and intimidation (Campaign for Good Governance Report, 2018).

In a study by Trocaire partners entitled 'On the Campaign Trail: documenting women's experiences on the 2018 Elections', candidates admitted having to pay for votes, whether this is in the form of 'respect' or 'borra' or through the provision of 'transport', rice, or food. One candidate mentioned giving money to community people as she went door-to-door as a sign of respect and to pay for their time. Thus, women had to endure varying forms of electoral corruption as they struggled to claim their right to vote and be voted for within and outside their political parties. What was even more worrying was the struggles within political parties.

Some case studies will be narrated in this section to present compelling stories and experiences of election violence towards other women in 2018. A lady who contested as councillor in one of the new parties recounts her experience of being humiliated, assaulted, and property vandalised. Her first direct encounter with violence was when two men allegedly disguised as police officers attacked her whilst visiting a neighbour. Not long after that incident, a group of thugs stormed her residence, vandalised her shop and went away with Le 15,000,000 (fifteen million Leones), a business she runs from a bank loan. Her husband was also assaulted; she identified the thugs and their associated party, but the attacks continued unabated. She believes the constant attacks showed that the thugs were assigned to her. As the physical, verbal and psychological abuse persisted, she left her home to seek solace with her friends. When the thugs realised she had moved, they resorted to cheap and cruel acts such as emptying human excrete in her home. She reported the issue on several occasions to the police. Unfortunately, the thugs were never apprehended. She alleged that the instigator behind the violence in the district was a very influential politician and government official at the time. She faked carrying acid to protect herself and threatened to retaliate if any of the thugs confronted her again. The situation was her everyday experience until a Run-off of the 2018 Presidential Polls was declared. This female candidate was, however, unsuccessful (Campaign for Good Governance Report, 2018).

One would imagine that with the eagerness with which the thugs perpetrate these offences, state authorities would have initiated some redress measures to hold the perpetrators accountable in her case. It became evident that the assailants had political backing, and the police were limited in addressing the complaints. Several women equally recount how they were attacked by thugs and asked to step down. A female councillor wanting to run for a second term was denied the party symbol as she could not afford the requested bribe, as alleged. The party symbol was withdrawn from a female candidate 16 days after being awarded. According to her, the incumbent parliamentarian, her opponent and his thugs orchestrated the violence. The MP was vying for the same symbol. After such physical and psychological abuse, some women were later invited to the party headquarters in Freetown to negotiate a peaceful settlement with promises of other favourable offices or opportunities when the party won. When analysed, the acts of violence point to inter and intra-partisan struggles and factors of entrenched patriarchy and systemic gender discrimination in elections.

Despite these challenges, women supported women aspirants and candidates through diverse financial, moral and other forms of support (such as hosting in their homes when women are under threat). Women created solidarity spaces where law enforcement failed (Campaign for Good Governance Report, 2018).

It will make sense to reflect on these case studies and note how unresponsive security and law enforcement inactions can embolden perpetrators, exacerbate crime and delineate repressive pathways for democratic practice and political culture. Most of these matters did not move from the police stations to be heard in court. It is important to note that there were also offences relating to double voter registration, which remain inconclusive.

According to judicial officials, some of the matters lack the essential ingredients, resulting in the manner of acquittals.

Efforts to Address Elections-Related Violence

In the absence of appropriate rights-based strategies, the SLP, on polling day for the 2018 elections, enforced transport restrictions as a direct response to demobilise violent groups and thugs across the country, but this met heavy criticisms from right-based organisations and individuals. Only accredited vehicles by the NEC were allowed to ply. Security agencies enforced the ban in all urban towns; the restriction did not cover the rural communities and areas outside the district headquarters towns. The statement released by the SLP encouraged stakeholders that 'the restriction is not in any way inhibiting the free movement of voters and other persons going about their normal lawful business as long as they do not loiter within 300 meters of a polling centre' (Shaban, 2018).

The law enforcement agencies' independence has seriously been questioned, and citizens' trust in the police and judiciary has waxed and waned. This is because impunity is rising, and elections are becoming more contentious from one cycle to the other. Citizens rely on law enforcement authorities to act. The continuous failure of law enforcement agencies, especially the judiciary, to uphold democratic tenets will bolster despotic tendencies and open elections to even more violent, manipulative strategies. For us democracy watchers, we believe the unseating of ten MPs without the court calling for fresh elections in most constituencies is a usurpation of the citizens' mandate to elect their leaders.

However, it is essential to recognise some efforts to address thuggery and electoral and political-related violence. The Office of National Security (ONS), after a consultative meeting with stakeholders and political parties on 3 March 2021, released a statement banning political party bodyguards used as marshals. The Inspector General of police, during the consultative meeting, stated, 'How can we have the police as a national law enforcement body and have another seemingly to serve the same purpose?' The practice has been a growing syndicate where political parties train party loyalists as marshals. It is important to note that despite this proactive action, compliance with the ban is minimal. It is interesting to observe how actions of informal violent groups, if left unaddressed, can metamorphose into formal space, distorting the principles of good governance and democratic oversight of security.

The Role of Organize Civil Society in Tackling Aspects of Electoral Manipulations

NEW has been observing elections in a structured manner since 2002 and has reported the processes in many elections with precision. This 'long-running tradition' of the coalition has helped prevent subtle forms of rigging through a comprehensive strategy of national coverage of polling stations and the display of consistency in respecting democratic principles and the knowledge of the local context (EUEOM Report, 2018). For the 2018 elections, NEW publicly advocated for the announcement of the election date through its diverse networks across the country. As part of a grand plan to derail the electoral process, anti-rights groups and individuals had emerged with an organised 'more time' campaign calling for a third for the presidency ('NEW calls on NEC', 2016). This 'more time' campaign was a flagrant violation of the 1991 constitution. It was an affront to democracy as all representatives must emerge through the ballot box after four or five years, depending on whether the elections are local, presidential or parliamentary. NEW will either validate or condemn events and stages in the electoral process through its press statements and advocate for actions where delays could stall the process.

An example was getting parliament to approve the Boundary Delimitation Exercise twice by NEC after a controversial law, the Provinces Act 2017, was passed, redistricting the country and forming new regions and districts less than a year before the elections. This complicated situation was enough to distort the remaining electoral activities and timelines. Today, citizens still grapple with understanding the new formations, mergers and boundaries. For the first time, NEW deployed observers to follow sensitive and non-sensitive voter materials for the March 2018 Presidential Run-off elections. After the first round of the 7 March Presidential, Parliamentary and Local Council elections, political parties alleged widespread irregularities discredited the NEC leadership as incompetent and arrested some NEC officials. Although these allegations, for the most part, were far from the reality, NEW, to add value to the Run-off elections and muster citizens' confidence in the process for the first time, deployed new categories of observers in the regions, districts and wards to follow the delivery and retrieval of sensitive voter materials. Politicians alleged that manipulations were done to and from the Polling stations where observers were absent. NEW had observers on motorbikes at the community level trailing sensitive materials to the last mile (NEW Observation Final Report, 2018).

NEW set up a Citizens Situation Room to monitor and report incidents from the field on Election Day, calling on stakeholders for real-time responses and actions. Perhaps the most impressive is NEW's use of Parallel Vote Tabulation (PVT) in 2018; NEW has used this methodology since 2007 but in 2018, made public the findings of the PVT, using a representative random sample of 506 polling stations to detect possible procedural shortcomings throughout polling day quickly. This strategy forestalled potential violence. In appraising the NEW PVT, the EUEOM 2018 concludes in its final report that 'the PVT exercise, based on this random sampling of Polling stations, confirmed with a high degree of precision the integrity of the official presidential elections in both rounds'.

Unfortunately, like most local elections observer outfits, I want to state that civil society working on elections does not have the requisite skills and time to follow through on organised electoral corruption like monitoring campaign finance, money politics, and vote buying. This is even more complex with the limited opportunities the legal framework presents. Money is necessary for political participation and representation in our local context; the political culture presupposes that candidates must mount massive campaigns with electorates eating, drumming, drinking and dancing. I will argue that unregulated money stifles democratic choice and pressures candidates, especially women, who cannot muster the requisite financial muscles to mount such sophisticated campaigns. So, whilst women's groups and women-serving agencies would have trained female candidates on strategies for a democratic contest, the reality on the ground and the challenges prove otherwise.

NEW has engaged in various strategies to support electoral integrity and credibility, and these have evolved. It is essential to fully support domestic election observers to cover every aspect of the electoral process. Support to civil society should consider the capacity to monitor aspects of campaign finance and money politics and carefully follow litigation processes to ensure electoral justice. If political actors and supporters could think of such strategies to manipulate electoral outcomes in these forms, the control of corruption when they assume state governance is equally challenged.

Why Policy Actions and Reforms Matter

If elections must be meaningful and democracy not jeopardised, violence and other manipulative strategies such as vote buying, turn-out buying, smear campaigns and VAWE must be called out and addressed through the right policy actions. The 2018 elections in Sierra Leone and the subsequent bye-elections present extraordinary lessons for advocacy groups and policy actors to consider necessary steps towards safeguarding electoral integrity.
Some key actions could be:

- The continued presence of election monitors and observers to keep the processes in check, report the outcomes and for government and independent state institutions and EMBs to integrate recommendations by Observer missions into the electoral process and legal reforms.
- Efforts towards changing political behaviour are essential to building a culture of electoral integrity. This could be done through robust civic education with non-violent messages targeting youth and political leaders.

Intra-group social contract through intra-party dialogue and political party liaison committees.
- Regular multiparty liaison committee meetings provide a forum for communication. It can also serve as a platform for dispute resolution and political party peer review mechanisms and accountability.

Additionally, political will is needed at the policy level to combat patronage politics and political rewards. Appointments to manage independent state institutions must be based on merit.

In growing democracies, effort must be made to protect the people's will because this translates into a government that cares rather than oppresses. Enforcement of laws relating to elections and criminalising electoral corruption is of the essence. This will combat blatant impunity. Conversely, corrupt actors must be brought to justice and rights groups should be well positioned to sustain the advocacy as safe havens for perpetrators must be denied.

Conclusion

Electoral violence, thuggery, vote buying or 'turn-out buying', smear campaigns, and VAWE are well organised and part of the grand corruption scheme to influence electoral outcomes. It is a gradually growing strategy that must be carefully watched, with laws and policy actions initiated to address the situation. Violence and fraudulent strategies now co-exist with formal electoral processes and gradually become patterns in our democratisation processes, and they must not remain unchecked. VAWE was increasingly visible in the 2018 Elections. These abuses range from assault, and intimidation to escalated forms of harassment. This piece notes limited spaces for redress, especially from traditional state security agencies. Law enforcement agencies' tacit role and lack of action allow such crime to flourish, distorting sound governance principles and democratic practices.

It is uncontested that organised civil society plays a significant role in safeguarding democracy and promoting electoral integrity. The political context has evolved, and civil society entities like NEW working on elections must be supported with the required resources and technical capacity to venture into electoral fraud, campaign finance and vote buying, which take place outside the formal electoral calendar. This support and capacity building must be a permanent and continuous engagement.

After twenty-five years of democratic renewal since 1996, these issues are becoming deep-seated in our political culture and socialisation and require genuine dialogue and collaborative strategies for redress by stakeholders. The smear campaign used to discredit NEC and soiled its reputation in 2018 was forestalled by collective initiatives stakeholders. Elections related to violence against women and polling disruptions post-2018 require an integrated approach to promote electoral integrity. As the country advances, it will be helpful for election stakeholders to have a collaborative fraud control plan to help address this situation in the Sierra Leonean context.

References

ACE Project. (n.d.). Preventing Election Related Violence. ACE Electoral Knowledge Network. Retrieved from https://aceproject.org/ace-en/topics/ve/overview

Alston, P. (2010). Report of the Special Rapporteur on extrajudicial, summary or arbitrary executions, Addendum : Study on targeted killings. UNCHR. www.refworld.org/reference/themreport/unhrc/2010/en/73516

Anning, K. (2013). *Legal and Policy Frameworks Regulating the Behaviour of Politicians and Political Parties-Sierra Leone*. International IDEA.

Birch, S., Daxecker, U., & Höglund, K. (2020). Electoral violence: An introduction. *Journal of Peace Research*, 57(1), 3–14.

Bjarnegård, E. (2018). Making gender visible in election violence: Strategies for data collection. *Politics & Gender*, 14(4), 690–695.

Bye-Election in Ward 196 Constituency 58 Tonko Limba Chiefdom Kambia District marred by Gross intimidation, Thuggery, and Excessive Violence Cancelled (2018, September 30), National Election Watch, Press Statement.

Campaign for Good Governance (2018). *Reflecting on Women's Experiences with Violence during the 2018 Multi-Party Democratic Elections*. https://slcgg/reflecting-on-women's-experiences-with-violence-during-the-2018multi-party-democratic-elections/

Cancellation of Local Council Bye Election in Ward 196. Kambia District held on Saturday 29th September 2018 (2018, September 29), NEC, Press Release.

Cheeseman, N., & Klaas, B. (2018). *How to Rig an Election*. Yale University Press.

Constituency 110 by-election conducted amid chaos, (2019, August 27), Concord Times Communications. http://slconcordtimes.com/constituency-110-by-election-conducted-amid-chaos

EUEOM Final Report (2018). *European Union Election Observation Mission Final Report Republic of Sierra Leone Presidential, Parliamentary and Local Council Elections* http://eeas.europa.eu/sites/default/files/eu_eom_sl2018_final_report_4pdf

EUEOM Preliminary Statement (2018, April 3). http://eeas.europa.eu/election-observation-missions/eom-sierra-leone2018_en/42402/Preliminary%20Statement%20of%20the20EU%20EOM%20for%20the%20presidential%20run-off%20election

Freedom House (2020). *Freedom in the World 2020 Sierra Leone*. https://freedomhouse.org/country/sierra-leone/freedom-world/2021

Höglund, K. (2019). Electoral violence in conflict-ridden societies: Concepts, causes, and consequences. *Terrorism and Political Violence*, 21(3), 412–427.

Laakso, L. (2007). Insights into electoral violence in Africa. In M. Basedau, G. Erdmann, & A. Mehler (Eds.), *Votes, Money and Violence: Political Parties and Elections in Sub-Saharan Africa*, 224–252, Nordic African Institute.

Lehoucq, F. (2003). Electoral fraud: Causes, types, and consequences. *Annual Review of Political Science*, 6(1), 233–256.

Lust, E., & Waldner, D. (2015). Theories of Democratic Change. *Retrieved from* https://pdf.USAIDd. gov/pdf_docs/PBAAD635. Pdf

Mackintosh, R. B. (2020). *Sierra Leone: Social Media –New Power of Political Influence*, Concord Times, Freetown.

Moehler, D. C., & Lindberg, S. I. (2007). Narrowing the legitimacy gap: Turnovers as a cause of democratic consolidation. *The Journal of Politics*, 71(4), 1448–1466.

National Election Watch (2018). *National Election Watch (NEW) Observation Report of the 2018 Electoral Cycle in Sierra Leone*. July 2018, http://nationalelectionwatchsl.org

Nichter, S. (2008). Vote buying or turnout buying? Machine politics and the secret ballot. *American Political Science Review*, 102(1), 19–31.

NEC Conducts Bye-elections in Ward 069 and Ward 091 (2021, November 15), National Election Watch, Press Statement https://nationalelectionwatchsl.org/press/

NEW calls on NEC to release the specific date for Elections in 2018 (2016, November 28), NEW Press Release, Freetown. http://nationalelectionwatchsl.org

NEW Incident Reporting Ahead of Re-Run Elections- Politicians Scramble over completion of Goderich Community Centre (2020, November 11), National Election Watch, Press Statement. https://nationalelectionwatchsl.org/press/

NEW Press Statement. (2021). Koinadugu Bye-elections Marred by Widespread Political Intimidation, Incidents of Thuggery and Suspension of Tallying (2021, October 4).

NEW Raises alarm over irregularities in Tonko Limba Bye-Election (2019, March 13), National Election Watch. http://thecalabashnewspapr.com/new-raises-alarm-over-irregularities-in-tonko-limba-bye-election/

Schedler, A. (2002). Elections without democracy: The menu of manipulation. *Journal of Democracy*, 13(2), 46.

Shaban, A. (2018). Sierra Leone Police to enforce transport restrictions on election day. www.africanews.com/2018/03/01/sierra-leone-police-to-enforce-transport-restriction-on-election-daywww.africannews.com/2018/03/01/sierraleone-police-to-enforce-transport-restriction-on-election-day//

Sierra Leone News: Vote buying prevalent during 2018 elections –IGR (2018, August 3), Awoko Publications. https://awokonewspaper.sl/sierra-leone-news-vote-buying-prevalent-during-2018-elections-igr/

The Electoral Knowledge Network, ACE Project. 1998-2002. http://aceproject.org/

The Political Parties Act (2002). Supplement to the Sierra Leone Gazette Vol. CXXXIII. No8.

The Public Elections Act (2012). www.sierra-leone.org/Laws/2012-04.pdf

Trocaire (2019). *On the Campaign Trail: Documenting Women's Experiences on the 2018 Elections in Sierra Leone*. www.trocaire.org/documents/on-the-campaign-trail-2/

Vickery, C., & Shein, E. (2012). Assessing electoral fraud in new democracies: refining the vocabulary. *Washington, DC, White Paper Series*, Retrieved from International Foundation for Electoral Systems.

Violence against Women in Elections, www.ifes.org/VAWE

4
UNDERSTANDING POLITICAL CORRUPTION IN UGANDA THROUGH THE LENS OF COMPLEXITY THINKING AND HISTORICAL INSTITUTIONALISM

Clare Cheromoi, Asiimwe Godfrey,
Charlotte Karungi Mafumbo and Richard Sebaggala

Introduction

While corruption predates the colonial era in Uganda and was also used as an instrument of colonisation, its post-colonial legacies deserve specific scholarly attention. Post-independent African states have experienced a manifold of problems (Chime & Enor, 2016; Onongha, 2014), but corruption is a significant problem constraining economic progress and political development (Mlambo et al., 2019). Corruption has become endemic in most African countries, so much so that pathological metaphors have become common to describe it – terms such as cancer, virus, cankerworm, parasite, epidemic, and so on (Apata, 2018). Apata (2018) has argued that these metaphors applied to African corruption are not merely embodiments of long-term stereotypes but also colour and distort contemporary thinking about corruption in Africa. Pillay (2014) shows that economic, social, or political corruption can be ruinous. Economically, it misdirects resources and discourages investment by the private sector. Socially, it creates a culture of poverty and crime and deprives the neediest elements of a society of the benefits of government resources. Politically, it destroys people's confidence in their government and undermines the legitimacy of political institutions. Indeed, in some circumstances, corruption can be a source of political instability.

Uganda is no exception to that analysis. The country's history has been marked by endemic corruption. Transitions between governments over the last five decades have been preceded and followed by allegations of corruption, encouraging perceptions that every post-independence government has been corrupt. According to Transparency International Corruption Perception Index (CPI) reports (2015, 2016, 2017, 2018, 2019, 2020 and 2021), Uganda consistently ranks among the most corrupt nations in the CPI annual reports. For instance, Uganda was ranked 131st out of 167 countries in 2015 ranked 151st of 176 countries in 2016, and 149th out of 180 countries in 2018, 2019, 2020, and 2021, it ranked 137th, 142nd, and 144th, respectively. Afrobarometer (2006) revealed that more than two-thirds (68%) of Ugandans said corruption in the country had increased in the preceding twelve months. Estimates from ActionAid Uganda show that between 2000 and 2014, Uganda lost more than Ugx 24 trillion (around US$6.6 billion as of 2023), an amount that would have financed the nation's entire 2015/2016 budget (Afrobarometer, 2006). It is easy to point to contemporary corruption as a cause or symptom of many current dilemmas. However, until we understand Uganda's history of crime in its full complexity, we will be hard-pressed to respond to the issue today or in the future. This chapter aims to contribute to a better understanding of the evolution of political corruption in Uganda and how it has entrenched itself in independence.

Gyekye (1997) argues that post-colonial Africa is undeniably among the worst victims of political corruption. However, while corruption may be traced to ancient Greece and Rome (Hill, 2013), the subject has recently gained research momentum. This is mainly because contemporary political corruption leads to the misallocation of resources and affects decision-making at both micro and macro levels of governance. Unlike bureaucratic corruption, which ruling figures can control – for better or worse – if they so desire, the problem with political corruption is that it helps those actors maintain control of the state, which can outweigh their determination to fight crime (Amundsen, 2019). Consequently, political corruption negatively affects political institutions' functioning, leading to maladministration and institutional decay (Amundsen, 1999; Balachandrudu, 2006).

For many years, the systematic study of corruption generally, and of political corruption in particular, needed to be improved by the need for adequate definitions (Peters & Welch, 1978; Banerjee & Sengupta, 2008). Unlike the earliest reports of political corruption that were classified according to three criteria – *legality*, public *interest*, or public *opinion* (Peters & Welch, 1978) – we adopt a recent definition advanced by Amundsen, who proposed two essential and often interrelated forms: "extractive" and "power-preserving": "Extractive political corruption is when a politician uses corrupt means to extract wealth to the benefit of themselves, their families and friends, for example embezzlement, bribery and fraud", while "Power-preserving political corruption takes place when the resources mentioned above (gained via corruptive means) are utilised to strengthen the position of the politician and party in question" (Amundsen, 2019, p. 1).

Amundsen argues that both forms of corruption are purposely driven by wealth, status, and power gains, but extractive political corruption is mainly for wealth and status. For example, "it is extractive when political power-holders enrich themselves, their family and relatives, their political friends and allies, and their ruling parties and governments". Therefore, it includes practices such as embezzlement, economic crime, "privatisations" and crony capitalism (favouring their businesses), and, most importantly, bribe-taking in public procurement (Amundsen, 2019). Power-preserving political corruption is mainly for maintaining and strengthening its practitioners' hold on power. Examples include practices such as buying friends (favouritism, co-optations, clientelism and nepotism), buying support from businesses (by favouring the companies of political supporters), buying institutions of oversight and control (through appointments and inducements), the use of state resources to win elections, and buying judicial impunity.

The Amundsen definition of political corruption has been used to analyse mining and extracting corruption scandals from historical archives. It aligns with Vannucci and Della Porta's (1999) argument that political corruption is more than a simple exchange of money and favours. It also circumvents legitimate procedures by exchanging resources, including political influence, access to restricted information, political protection, and money. Amundsen's definition is also operationally consistent with Mbaku's (2010) definition of political corruption as the use of laws and institutions to build political parties and help certain politicians become leaders of the state (pp. 11–13).

Even with the above, most attempts to understand political corruption in post-independence Uganda have focused on the effectiveness of anti-corruption reforms. Few have studied corruption as a complex historical political problem; most of those that have emerged have been descriptive and have emphasised colonial history as causal influences (see examples, Asiimwe, 2013; Tangri & Mwenda, 2001, 2003, 2006, 2008, 2013; Mwenda, 2007; Mbabazi & Pyeong Yu, 2015; Tangri & Mwenda, 2019). For example, Mbabazi and Yu (2015) argue that Uganda's patronage and corruption emanated from the British colonial administrative system, which relied on a section of local people to rule over the rest and consequently rewarded them for supporting colonial policies and interests. Without democratic rule, institutions that could condemn corruption, exert public control, and demand accountability from public officials never developed. While Mbabazi and Yu show how Uganda's post-independence political history has contributed to today's corruption, they do not explore transhistorical linkages. The transhistorical lens considers corruption as a phenomenon that transcends individual events and circumstances and exhibits consistent characteristics or patterns throughout history. This approach seeks to identify recurring themes, commonalities, and systemic issues that persist across periods.

No subsequent analysis traces the origin and continuities of political corruption in Uganda. Other scholars have attributed all African ills, including breakdown, to neopatrimonialism (Mkandawire, 2015). However, The neopatrimonialism perspective needs to be more blunt and formulaic to understand political corruption in any detail. (Pitcher, Moran, & Johnston, 2009) argue that the term "Neopatrimonialism" has been wrongly applied to attribute all of Africa's issues, including corruption, to this term. The authors challenge that patrimonialism accurately characterises African political situations, whether historical or current (Pitcher et al., 2009). Important questions remain regarding the persistence of political corruption despite the regulatory frameworks, anti-corruption institutions, and public awareness campaigns crafted over the years. We must use a historical lens informed by complex thinking to understand the persistence of political corruption in Uganda. This study utilised periodisation to establish a chronological framework for analysing historical data and narratives related to political corruption. The aim was to trace connections and patterns across different political regimes in post-independence Uganda, encompassing various manifestations, underlying causes, key actors, and responses to corruption. By employing periodisation, the study highlighted the interwoven links between past occurrences and their relevance to the present context.

Theoretical Background

Several schools of thought have been advanced to explain the phenomenon of corruption. They include public choice and bad-apple theories, others emphasising clashing moral values, institutions and organisational cultures, and collective-action approaches. The principal-agent idea is the most dominant (Klitgaard, 1988; Rose-Ackerman, 1998). According to Walton and Jones (2017), the principal-agent theory has two tenets: the principal (variously depicted as government ministers/agencies, or voters) who is charged with performing an organisational function, and the agent – groups or individuals whom the principal monitors, and who are responsible for actually carrying out the function. In such a situation, corruption might occur when information and preference asymmetry between the principals and agents incentivises agents to engage in corruption. In that situation, corruption occurs when the principals fail to monitor agents' actions adequately. Alternatively, a principal might engage in preferential hiring and pressure agents to divert revenues, or even a portion of their salaries, to the principal's benefit.

The critics of the principal-agent theory argue that it is well suited to analysing bureaucratic corruption but less fit for broadly based forms such as political corruption (Johnston, 1996; Groenendijk, 1997). Others contend that principal-agent theory is too simplistic to unravel the complexities of corruption and, therefore, ambiguous, weak and contradictory in empirical applications given the complexities of corruption as an endemic problem (Calderón Cuadrado & Álvarez-Arce, 2005; Walton & Jones, 2017). This may explain the shortcomings of anti-corruption reforms originating from principal-agent theory (Persson et al., 2013). The lack of understanding that corruption is a complex problem undermined early studies that assumed a fundamental linear dichotomy between cause and effect (Cantú & Center, 2017). Recent perspectives draw analogies between corrupt agents and viruses that mutate and adapt to new environments (Habtemichael, 2009). Deeply embedded in social, political, and economic dynamics, corruption causes and effects influence each other non-linearly; thus, a change to any one piece within such a system will reverberate in or affect other parts, often in ways that can be difficult to predict. Finally, corruption is robust and adaptive, and thus highly resilient and evolutionary. New forms of corruption emerge in response to anti-corruption efforts as people's norms and practices adapt to the new environment (Graaf et al., 2010; Scharbatke-Church, 2016). Warburton (2013) described corruption as an ant-artefact of social and political organisation and, as such, is a phenomenon of infinite complexity. The term "ant-artefact" conveys that corruption is not a deliberate creation or intended outcome of social and political organisation. Instead, it emerges due to these systems' complex interactions and dynamics. This emphasises that corruption is a highly intricate and multifaceted phenomenon, reflecting the complex interplay of various factors within social and political contexts.

However, while numerous studies have alluded to the fact that corruption generally, and political corruption, in particular, are complex system problems with infinite complexity to its causes and consequences (Sardan & Olivier, 1999; Amundsen, 1999; Calderón Cuadrado & Álvarez-Arce, 2005; De Graaf, 2007; Habtemichael, 2009; Graaf et al., 2010; Warburton, 2013; Dimant & Tosato, 2018), applications of complexity theory in the analysis of corruption are few (Yaser, 2005; Calderón Cuadrado & Álvarez-Arce, 2011; Cantú & Center, 2017). A literature review on Uganda found no study employing a complexity perspective in understanding political corruption.

The failure to study corruption as a complex phenomenon has limited our understanding of the factors responsible for its emergence, how it evolves over different historical junctures, and its adaptability to changing political circumstances, and hence, narrows the range and effectiveness of anti-corruption reforms. Studying corruption through the lens of complex thinking informed by historical institutionalism provides a better conceptualisation, enables process-tracing of its evolution, and thus explains the failures of anti-corruption efforts in countries like Uganda.

While not dismissing rational-choice perspectives, principal-agent theory, and collective-action explanations, we regard political corruption as a complex problem. Its origins are deeply embedded in social, political and economic historical structures and cannot be isolated because of its interconnected causes and effects. It evolves through complex processes and thus tends to remain resilient against institutional. Our analysis is rooted in the cybernetic theory of Norbert Wiener (1948). The reasoning behind cybernetics is this: *functional relations* among system parts, rather than the parts themselves, are critical. This theory offers a novel way to conceptualise the complexity of political corruption; it does not create a step-by-step methodological research process but allows researchers to view corruption from a non-linear perspective. It involves integrating different viewpoints to construct a theoretical framework for historically tracing corruption over time. To understand the behaviour of a complex system, we must understand not only the behaviour of the parts but *how they act together to form the behaviour of the whole* (Bar-Yam, 1997; see also Van Mil et al., 2014).

Further complicating our analysis is that complex system and their evolution are very sensitive to initial conditions or small perturbations. According to historical institutionalists, initial conditions have enduring and self-reinforcing patterns (Farrell, 2018). Understanding the initial requirements and the disruptions that have influenced political corruption over time provides avenues for understanding transhistorical patterns, evolution, factors, and interrelationships related to political corruption in Uganda. Historical institutionalism is a sociological perspective that views institutions differently from a rationalist perspective (Hall, 2010) – in these cases, as arenas for power-distributional conflicts. It focuses on temporal processes that explain how institutions emerge and change (Suárez & Bromley, 2016). The approach thus emphasises understanding contextual conditions and sees institutions as enduring legacies of political struggles (Thelen, 1999). For example, Leiren and Reimer (2018) focus on how institutions develop over time and can affect actors in ways that may have been unintended or undesired by their creators. Path dependence is another concept often applied by historical institutionalists and refers specifically to the dynamics of self-reinforcing systems or positive feedback loops whereby initial effects trigger responses that reinforce the recurrence of a pattern. The core idea behind "path dependence" is that some institutions become increasingly difficult to change once established. So, small choices early on can close off various possibilities later and thus have significant long-term impacts.

Finally, a complex-systems approach enables us to construct historical nodes that link contemporary corruption to some empirically verifiable process in the country's past, such as configurations of complex networks of actors whose behaviours and conduct sowed seeds of corruption that have been nurtured over the years. A historical institutionalist approach provided the process-tracing resources necessary for applying complexity theory. The primary objective was to show how institutions and their settings mediate, influencing how processes evolve. This approach emphasises examining the state's role, government institutions, and social norms in this context (Farrell 2018). According to Sanders (2006), historical institutionalists are primarily concerned with understanding how institutions are constructed, maintained, and adapted across temporal dimensions.

Methodology

The study employed a historical research design. During the study, complexity thinking provided insights into issues that need investigation about political corruption problems. In contrast, historical institutionalism provided insights into the long-term historical processes underpinning Uganda's political corruption. Suárez and Bromley (2016) noted that historical institutionalism helps explain how institutions emerge and change. Based on this perspective, the researchers examined how institutional formations were borne in the post-independent period, focusing on temporal historical circumstances. Through document review or analysis of historical information and documentary literature on political corruption, the researchers searched and identified the relationship between past happenings and their links with the present. However, the fact that historical narrative cannot violate the sequence of the actual flow of time (Groat & Wang, 2013), periodisation was explicitly introduced to cater for a time sequence. "periodisation" refers to the deliberate division of historical time into distinct periods or segments. It involves identifying specific timeframes or epochs with common characteristics, events, or trends. This study utilised periodisation to establish a chronological framework for analysing historical data and narratives related to political corruption. The purpose of periodisation was to trace the transhistorical links in the manifestations of political corruption across the different political regimes in post-independent Uganda. The central assumption driving the periodisation of political corruption across different rules is embedded in the fact that political context is essential in understanding how public administrators or political actors behave.

Results and Discussion

Uganda's political history has been characterised by numerous government changes, with eight changes within sixty-one years (1962–2023). Therefore, to understand the evolution and manifestation of political corruption in Uganda, an inquiry into the corruption occurrences within each central political regime helped us to know whether the patterns and evolution of political corruption in Uganda are transhistorical and not just confined to particular rules. The document review and analysis of corruption cases experienced in each post-independent political regime may not reveal the whole story of how corrupt the governments were. However, it at least gives us an idea of how corrupt the regimes have been and helps us trace the historical patterns and evolution processes. In this section, findings of investigated or published and reported corruption cases in post-independent political regimes are presented and explained in detail to understand the forces behind political corruption and its evolution in Uganda.

Political Corruption in the Milton Obote Regime (1962–1971)

A reasonably strong economy characterised Uganda at independence with a domestic savings rate averaging about 15 per cent of GDP (Sejjaaka, 2004); well-established legislative and parliamentary institutions, sound electoral procedures, a high level of accountability; a lively and free press; efficient civil service; and promising future outlook (Langseth, 1995; Flanary & Watt, 1999). However, a few years into the post-independent period, things started falling apart politically. The dual leadership of President Sir Fredrick Mutesa and Prime Minister Milton Obote (who later became president) collapsed primarily due to ethnic tensions. In a quote attributed to Machiavelli, Balachandrudu (2006, p.812) stated, "Even the best individuals are capable of being bribed by a little ambition and avarice". In the early years of independence, the visionary and nationalistic Milton Obote started to subordinate himself to the pursuit of private interests at the expense of the common good. Ethnicity, state power, and regime survival became the critical variables of Obote's regime. Indeed, these variables are central to understanding the evolution of political corruption during the Obote 1 regime (1966–1971) (Okuku, 2002). Corruption was done by those holding high political offices in Obote's government. For instance, in 1965, Obote, Idi Amin, Minister of Defence Felix Onama, and Minister of Planning Adoko Nekyon were put on the spot over corruption and smuggling of gold, ivory and coffee in the Democratic Republic of Congo, formally the Republic of Zaire (Okuku, 2002). The scandal was sparked when Amin walked into a commercial bank in Uganda with a bar of gold and demanded cash in exchange. On 4 February 1966, Daudi Ochieng, the secretary general of the Kabaka Yekka (KY) political movement, tabled a motion before Parliament implicating ministers Felix Onama, Adoko Nekyon and Prime Minister Milton Obote as accomplices in the looting of gold, ivory, and coffee from Congo.

Ochieng, in the parliament, submitted proof of a deposit from Idi Amin's bank account as evidence that Amin was smuggling gold, ivory and coffee from Congo and claimed that the loot was being shared among four people, including Obote (Umeya, 2019). Although the accusations against Obote and Amin collapsed and they were exonerated, the scandal sparked a political crisis. In the aftermath, the Constitution was abrogated, kingdoms were abolished, ministers were arrested, and Uganda's first president, though ceremonial, was forced into exile. From there on, dictatorship and rule by the gun defined Uganda's politics. While Tangri and Mwenda (2008) have argued that the Obote I regime 1962–71 was relatively clean apart from the evidence of ministerial involvement in the gold smuggling scandal, the political crisis and dictatorship tendencies that defined the Obote government in the years after 1966 created conditions for political corruption including nepotism–particularly towards the ethnic groups most loyal to him: the Langi and Acholi.

Political Corruption and the Idi Amin Regime (1971–1979)

Idi Amin came to power through a coup, and like many post-independent African states, the legacy of military dictatorship befell Uganda (Tindigarukayo, 1988; Kiyimba, 1998). Amin was in power for only eight years, but those are regarded as some of the worst years in Ugandan history. Amin is widely regarded as Uganda's most notorious dictator and, like authoritarian regimes elsewhere (Yadav & Mukherjee, 2016), was marked by pervasive corruption. Tangri and Mwenda (2008), citing Kasfir, (1993) and Prunier (1983), note that the black market became pervasive and private entrepreneurs amassed fortunes, mainly through coffee smuggling.

Amin's regime is remembered as a period famous for political and economic mismanagement, leading to severe economic hardships, political chaos, and civil strife. Severine Rugumamu and Osman Gbla (2003) depict Amin's weak and inefficient government as characterised by excessive controls over the economy and society that propagated pervasive caprice, arbitrariness, rent-seeking and corruption. The militarisation of politics contributed to the collapse of the Ugandan state, society, and economy. While Amin used force to exact compliance, the regime lost its organisational clarity and functional role as a social manager. The collapse of the state and institutionalisation of violence undermined civilian leadership and institutions, and the resulting destruction of legitimacy culminated in political anarchy. In that environment, political players had strong incentives to pursue extortionary activities at the expense of the wider society. For example, Amin expropriated Uganda's Indian merchants in 1972, handing formerly Asian shops to his loyalists while contributing to the economy's collapse.

The culture of taking what did not belong to you, provided you are politically connected, has become the norm. That impunity was the worst form of political corruption Ugandans witnessed during Amin's regime. The looting, fear and anxiety, and loss of life were worse than the stealing of state resources we see today.

Political Corruption, Obote II (1980–1985) and Tito Okello (1985–1986)

During the second Obote presidency, petty corruption continued to pervade the public sector, but only the occasional high-profile scandal involving state elites came to light (Tangri & Mwenda, 2008). However, Obote's administration had all the conditions for corruption to thrive. Mapolu (1985) argues that the Obote II leadership was in disarray. The uneven distribution was evident within the army and had permeated virtually all workforce segments. Civil servants frequently went unpaid for months, and it was officially acknowledged that even senior civil servants could never survive on their stated salaries. They, therefore, had to fend for themselves by engaging in all sorts of legal and illegal activities to survive. Like Idi Amin, Obote II disregarded the interests of the country as a whole and pooled all resources for the arms for personal enrichment. The army was so corrupt that they exploited the civilian population for survival. They placed roadblocks in the guise of security checks but were stealing from people. The overthrow of Obote II through a coup and the rise of Tito Okello to the presidency of Uganda, backed by his angry, undisciplined, and influential colleagues in the army, did not change the political situation. During Okello's regime, power belonged to people who did not know what to do with it (Mapolu, 1985). For instance, this can be seen in the failure to re-establish civilian supremacy that led to widespread economic challenges and terror during that period. As a result, the first two post-Amin leaders (Yusuf et al.) lasted hardly a year before being removed by the military. Yusuf Lule briefly served as President from April to June 1979, followed by Godfrey Binaisa, who held office from June 1979 to May 1980.

The Yoweri Museveni Regime (1986–2017)

The National Resistance Movement (NRM) under Yoweri Museveni, which came to power in 1986, had the best opportunity to resolve the political confusion and fight corruption. They enjoyed widespread goodwill, particularly among the international policymakers, and Museveni was clearly in charge. However, as with his predecessors, political corruption defined Museveni's thirty-plus years in power (Wamara, 2017). Table 4.1 presents a sample of significant scandals that surfaced in the Museveni regime despite many anti-corruption reforms.

Museveni proclaimed "fundamental change" based on a "Ten-Point Programme", but his promises to eliminate corruption and misuse of power failed. Scholars have argued that Museveni's strategy of routinely co-opting people from past regimes through patronage and bribery (Flanary & Watt, 1999; Makara, 2010; Tangri & Mwenda, 2013) made further corruption likely.

For example, Makara (2010) argues that the NRM bought the support of leading members of the old regimes by placing them in government positions or dishing out business favours. Golooba-Mutebi (2018) has noted that whereas there may be many causes of entrenched corruption, informality in public governance is a critical facilitator. The rise, development, and spread of informal power networks rooted in the NRM's original approach to building alliances is responsible for deep-rooted political corruption:

> When the party came to power, it invited potential rivals and competitors into the government coalition, but no formal agreements or memoranda of understanding concluded. Consequently, those informal alliances

TABLE 4.1 Major corruption scandals during Museveni regime (1986–2017)

Year	Scandal	Sector/Ministry	Amount Involved (Ugx/US dollars
1989	Botched procurement of IFA, Jifeng and Santana vehicles	Ministry of Defence	US$ 100,000,000
1988	Telex services scandal	Ministry of Information and Broadcasting	US $400,000
1998	Junk helicopters scandal	Ministry of Defence	US $800,000
1998	MIG-21 jet fighters, anti-aircraft guns and T-55 tanks	Ministry of Defence	US $100 million
2000	Police payment	Uganda police	Ugx 1 billion
2003	GAVI funds scandal	Ministry of Health	Ugx 1.6 billion
2003	Training ghost soldiers	Ministry of Defence	Ugx 20 billion
2003	M1-24-helicopter gunships	Ministry of Defence	US $ 12.2 million
2006	Vivia's making	Ministry Trade and Fishers	Ugx 20 billion
2006	UPE scandal	Ministry of Education	Ugx 82 billion
2007	CHOGM	Ministry of Finance Planning and Economic Development	Ugx 247 billion
2009	NAADS scandal	Ministry of Agriculture	Ugx 2.7 billion
2010	Lost Via Posta Kenya	Telecommunication	Ugx 2.5 billion
2011	Microfinance scandal	Vice President	Ugx 60 billion
2011	Identity cards	Internal affairs	Ugx 205 billion
2012	Education monies	Ministry of Education	Ugx 375 billion
2012	Ghost firms	Ministry of Finance	Ugx 400 billion
2012	Pension scandal	Ministry of Public Service	Ugx 262 billion
2013	Internet deal	Telecommunications	Ugx 107.8 billion
2017	Uganda's ghost refuge scandal	Office of Prime Minister	US $350 million

Sources: Uganda Debt Network, 2013; Black Monday Newsletter, 2014.

collapsed, and the former network allies became active party adversaries. To counter their power, the NRM made new alliances, some of whom were members of the same opposition parties that had exited the previous coalition or even members that defected to the NRM in return for opportunities for self-advancement.

(Golooba-Mutebi, 2018, p. 5)

Indeed, it is accurate to state that specific informal power networks, as elucidated by Makara (2010) and Golooba-Mutebi (2018), exerted more substantial influence compared to the intended governance role of official institutions and mechanisms within the country. Therefore, although Museveni's regime publicly advocated democratic ideals, economic prosperity, and sanity in public administration, corruption remained a way to keep the government in power (Tangri & Mwenda, 2013).

Political commentators, particularly Andrew Mwenda, who has written so much about corruption in Uganda, have argued that in the post-independent history of Uganda, no one has been as openly nepotistic as Museveni. Without remorse, he has recruited his wife, brother, son, daughter, sister, and in-laws into government positions. Mwenda equates Museveni to African chiefs of old, such as Nyungu Ya Maawe of the 19th-century Nyamwezi empire.

Patterns of Political Corruption in Uganda

Corruption has persisted as an important political and economic exchange mechanism between Uganda's state elites and businesses. Within this context, corrupt interactions between state elites and well-connected individuals flourish. This pattern is characterised by a skewed power structure that facilitates institutional and social manipulation, as Asiimwe (2013) outlined. Tangri and Mwenda (2008) have argued that high-level corruption in Uganda has enabled the government to cement the loyalty of individual state leaders as well as to mobilise political support for maintaining the regime in power. The twin objectives of political corruption to generate wealth and preserve the government have undermined the anti-corruption reforms and efforts to fight it. For example, the dual focus of corruption to amass wealth and maintain regime stability has had the adverse effect of weakening measures and reforms aimed at combating corruption. These intertwined objectives have resulted in the lack of strong incentives to fight corruption.

In the course of the history of Uganda's post-independence political regimes, two facts have been evident. From the start, and in all the post-independent administrations, political corruption served the twin purposes of wealth extraction and power preservation. Second, although corruption has changed in magnitude and pervasiveness, it has continued to administer those goals. As Figure 4.1 shows, as corruption evolved in Uganda from occasional/everyday corruption to endemic and finally to systemic or institutionalised corruption, and as it has become more pervasive, it has been shaped by long-standing social patterns of values and behaviour. Whereas any form of corruption is harmful, endemic and systemic, political corruption is profoundly detrimental because predatory elites are many, and particularism is dominant. Rotondi and Stanca (2015) argue that where particularism is the cultural norm, relationships come ahead of abstract social codes, and models and appropriate behaviour are context-dependent. As a result, social relations are shaped by strong, cohesive group ties informed by principles of tradition, conformity, and benevolence.

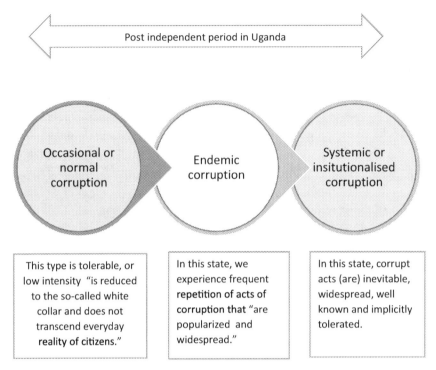

FIGURE 4.1   The evolution pattern of political corruption in Uganda.

Conclusion and Implications

This study uses the lens of complexity and historical institutionalism to analyse the evolution and manifestations of political corruption in the post-independence period. Our central argument in this paper is the evolution of political corruption and its manifestations in post-independent Uganda. However, varying in magnitude and extent, reflect underlying causes across Uganda's several political regimes. The common threads among them are the corrupt tendencies covertly or overtly exercised by those in power. They are deeply rooted in a historical political structure that has enabled and encouraged state actors to accumulate wealth and preserve power. The study's findings show that the drivers of extractive and power-persevering corrupt practices are embedded in and act through enduring informal processes and social connections. In this paper, looking at political corruption through the lens of complexity enabled us to discover that post-independence has witnessed leaders whose behaviours are primarily driven by power preservation and wealth accumulation. Even political leaders such as Yoweri Museveni, who had looked like the beacon of hope for Uganda, have fallen into traits like political leaders that have come before. This resembles the findings of

Thomas Dye (2015), who, in his classic book "Who is Running America?", demonstrates how power in America is concentrated in large institutions no matter who inhabits the White House. Post-independence Uganda has seen many political regimes, leaders, and public officials at various levels; they look similar when considering their corrupt behaviour.

Uganda has suffered from a leadership crisis ever since attaining independence in 1962. Political corruption for extractive or power-preserving purposes has been the common feature of seemingly diverse political regimes since independence. A lack of nationalistic, patriotic, and clean leadership has continued. Uganda's past and present leaders have chosen to fight and destroy each other to grab resources and consolidate state power instead of building viable institutions and putting the interests of ordinary people first. The consistent acts of post-independent leaders focusing on building strong personal capacity based on their political parties, families, relatives, tribes, friends, and puppets have influenced the behaviours, incentives and sanctions of the formal institution's conduits of political corruption.

Mbandlwa's (2020) paper, Challenges of African Leadership after the Independence, warns that development in Africa will only happen if corruption is addressed correctly, and corrosion can only be controlled if the leadership crisis persists. Therefore, fighting political corruption in Uganda, and in many African countries that have taken Uganda's political trajectory, will require addressing the historical political issues that have created and sustained the leadership crisis. The main takeaway from this paper is that a comprehensive understanding of African societies goes beyond merely addressing their immediate economic or administrative challenges. We should avoid blaming colonialism and focus on ongoing political and leadership dynamics within African societies. This involves examining the factors that incentivise, enable, or hinder certain behaviours and patterns among different regimes. In essence, the narrative encourages a more nuanced view of African politics, moving beyond the perception of it as just a display of corruption. Instead, it underscores the significance of historical patterns in shaping the complexities of African politics.

References

Action Aid International, Uganda (2014) *Black Monday*, Issue 22. Citizen action against theft of our money without shame, https://uganda.actionaid.org/publications/2014/black-monday-newsletter-

Afrobarometer Network. (2006). *Citizens and the African state: New results from Afrobarometer round 3–Afro barometer Working Papers.*

Amundsen, I. (1999). *Political corruption: An introduction to the issues.* Chr. Michelsen Institute.

Amundsen, I. (2019). Extractive and power-preserving political corruption. In *Inge Amundsen* (Ed.), Political *Corruption in Africa*, 1–28. Edward Elgar Publishing.

Apata, G. O. (2018). Corruption and the postcolonial state: How the West invented African corruption. *Journal of Contemporary African Studies*, 1–14.

Asiimwe, G. B. (2013). Of extensive and elusive corruption in Uganda: Neo-patronage, power, and narrow interests. *African Studies Review*, 56(2), 129–144.

Balachandrudu, K. (2006). Understanding political corruption. *The Indian Journal of Political Science*, 67(4), 809–816.

Banerjee, S., and Sengupta, P. K. (2008). Conceptualizing political corruption: Issues and problems. *The Indian Journal of Political Science*, 69(3), 473–482.

Bar-Yam, Y. (1997). *Dynamics of complexxa systems* (Vol. 213). Addison-Wesley Reading, MA.

Cantú, A. B. S., and Center, J. F. R. (2017). *Complexity and corruption: The need for a synthetic understanding of corruption in Mexico*.

Chime, J., and Enor, F. N. (2016). Foreign direct investment and the development of Neo-Colonial economies: A survey approach. *International Journal of World Policy and Development Studies*, 2(3), 15–19.

Calderón Cuadrado, R., and Álvarez-Arce, J. L. (2005). *The complexity of corruption: Nature and ethical suggestions*. Pamplona, Facultad de Ciencias Económicas y Empresariales Universidad de Navarra, Working Paper, (05/06).

De Graaf, G. (2007). Causes of corruption: Towards a contextual theory of corruption. *Public Administration Quarterly*, 31, 39–86.

Dimant, E., and Tosato, G. (2018). Causes and effects of corruption: What has the past decade's empirical research taught us? A survey. *Journal of Economic Surveys*, 32(2), 335–356.

Dye, T. R. (2015). *Who is Running America?: The Obama Reign*. Routledge.

Farrell, H. (2018). The shared challenges of institutional theories: Rational choice, historical institutionalism, and sociological institutionalism. In Johannes Glückler, Roy Suddaby, Regina Lenz (Eds.), *Knowledge and institutions* (pp. 23–44). Cham, Springer.

Flanary, R., and Watt, D. (1999). The state of corruption: A case study of Uganda. *Third World Quarterly*, 20(3), 515–536.

Golooba-Mutebi, F. (2018). *Informal governance and corruption – Transcending the principal agent and collective action paradigms Uganda country report*. Basel Institute on Governance.

Graaf, G. de, Maravic, P. von, and Wagenaar, P. (2010). *Introduction: Causes of corruption-the right question or the proper perspective?* B. Budrich.

Groat, L. N., and Wang, D. (2013). *Architectural research methods*. John Wiley and Sons.

Groenendijk, N. (1997). A principal-agent model of corruption. *Crime, Law and Social Change*, 27(3–4), 207–229.

Gyekye, K. (1997). *Tradition and modernity: Philosophical reflections on the African experience*. Oxford University Press.

Habtemichael, F. S. (2009). *Anti-corruption strategies in the South African public sector: Perspectives on the contributions of complexity thinking and ICTs (PhD Thesis)*. Stellenbosch, University of Stellenbosch.

Hall, P. A. (2010). Historical institutionalism in rationalist and sociological perspective. In James Mahoney and Kathleen Thelen (Eds.), *Explaining institutional change: Ambiguity, agency, and power*, 204–223. Cambridge University Press.

Hill, L. (2013). Conceptions of political corruption in ancient Athens and Rome. *History of Political thought*, 34(4), 565–587.

Johnston, M. (1996). The search for definitions: The vitality of politics and the issue of corruption. *International Social Science Journal*, 48(149), 321–335.

Kasfir, S. L. (1993). On "Africa Explores". *African Arts*, 26(3), 16–18.

Kiyimba, A. (1998). The ghost of Idi Amin in Ugandan literature. *Research in African Literatures*, 29(1), 124–138.

Klitgaard, R. (1988). *Controlling corruption*. University of California Press.

Langseth, P. (1995). Civil service reform in Uganda: Lessons learned. *Public Administration and Development*, 15(4), 365–390.

Leiren, M. D., and Reimer, I. (2018). Historical institutionalist perspective on the shift from feed-in tariffs towards auctioning in German renewable energy policy. *Energy Research and Social Science*, 43, 33–40.

Makara, S. (2010). Deepening democracy through multipartyism: The bumpy road to Uganda's 2011 elections. *Africa Spectrum*, 45(2), 81–94.

Mapolu, H. (1985). Second Coup d'Etat. *Economic and Political Weekly*, 1473–1475.

Mbabazi, G., and Yu, P. (2015). Patronage-driven corruption undermining the fight against Poverty in Uganda. *African Social Science Review*, 7(1), 54–70.

Mbaku, J. M. (2010). *Corruption in Africa: Causes, consequences, and cleanups*. Lexington Books.

Mbandlwa, Z. (2020). Challenges of African leadership after tIndependence. *Solid State Technology*, 63(6), 13241–13254.

Mkandawire, T. (2015). Neopatrimonialism and the political economy of economic performance in Africa: Critical reflections. *World Politics*, 67(3), 563–612.

Mlambo, D. N., Mubecua, M. A., Mpanza, S. E., and Mlambo, V. H. (2019). Corruption and its implications for development and good governance: A perspective from post-colonial Africa. *Journal of Economics and Behavioral Studies*, 11(1(J)), 39–47.

Mwenda, A. M. (2007). Personalising power in Uganda. *Journal of Democracy*, 18(3), 23–37.

Okuku, J. (2002). *Ethnicity, state power and the democratisation process in Uganda* (Vol. 17). Nordic Africa Institute.

Onongha, K. (2014). Corruption, culture, and conversion: The role of the church in correcting a global concern. *Journal of Applied Christian Leadership*, 8(2), 67–82.

Persson, A., Rothstein, B., and Teorell, J. (2013). Why anticorruption reforms fail–systemic corruption as a collective action problem. *Governance*, 26(3), 449–471.

Peters, J. G., and Welch, S. (1978). Politics, corruption, and political culture: A view from the state legislature. *American Politics Quarterly*, 6(3), 345–356.

Pillay, S. (2014). *Development corruption in South Africa: Governance matters*. Springer.

Pitcher, A., Moran, M. H., and Johnston, M. (2009). Rethinking patrimonialism and neopatrimonialism in Africa. *African Studies Review*, 52(1), 125–156.

Prunier, G. (1983). Le magendo. *Politique africaine*, 9, 53–62.

Rose-Ackerman, S. (1998). Corruption and development. *Annual world bank conference on development economics 1997*, 35–57. World Bank Washington DC.

Rotondi, V., and Stanca, L. (2015). The effect of particularism on corruption: Theory and empirical evidence. *Journal of Economic Psychology*, 51, 219–235.

Rugumamu, S., and Gbla, O. (2003). *Studies in Reconstruction and Capacity Building in Post-Conflict Countries in Africa: Some Lessons of Experience from Uganda*. African Capacity Building Foundation.

Sanders, E. (2006). Historical institutionalism. In Sarah A. Binder, R. A. W. Rhodes, Bert A. Rockman (Eds.), *The Oxford handbook of political institutions*, 39–55. Oxford University Press.

Sardan, D., and Olivier, J.-P. (1999). A moral economy of corruption in Africa? *The Journal of Modern African Studies*, 37(1), 25–52.

Scharbatke-Church, C. (2016). *Corruption, Justice and Legitimacy*. Institute for Human Security, The Fletcher School of Law and Diplomacy, Tufts University, 617, 627–7940.

Sejjaaka, S. (2004). A political and economic history of Uganda, 1962–2002. In *International Businesses and the Challenges of Poverty in the Developing World* (pp. 98–110). London, Palgrave Macmillan.

Suárez, D., and Bromley, P. (2016). Institutional theories and levels of analysis: History, diffusion, and translation. In Jürgen Schriewe (Ed.), *World culture re-contextualised: Meaning constellations and dependencies in comparative and international education research*, 139–159. Routledge.

Tangri, R., and Mwenda, A. M. (2003). Military corruption & Ugandan politics since the late 1990s. *Review of African Political Economy*, 30(98), 539–552.

Tangri, R., and Mwenda, A. (2013). *The politics of elite corruption in Africa: Uganda in comparative African perspective*. Routledge.

Tangri, R., and Mwenda, A. (2001). Corruption and cronyism in Uganda's privatisation in the 1990s. *African Affairs*, 100(398), 117–133.

Tangri, R., and Mwenda, A. M. (2008). Elite corruption and politics in Uganda. *Commonwealth and comparative politics*, 46(2), 177–194.

Tangri, R., and Mwenda, A. M. (2006). Politics, donors and the ineffectiveness of anti-corruption institutions in Uganda. *The Journal of Modern African Studies*, 44(1), 101–124.

Tangri, R., and Mwenda, A. M. (2019). Change and continuity in the politics of Government-business relations in Museveni's Uganda. *Journal of Eastern African Studies*, 13(4), 678–697.

Thelen, K. (1999). Historical institutionalism in comparative politics. *Annual Review of Political Science*, 2(1), 369–404.

Tindigarukayo, J. K. (1988). Uganda, (1979).-85: Leadership in transition. *The Journal of Modern African Studies*, 26(4), 607–622.

Uganda Debt Network (2013). *Dossier. Corruption in Uganda*. Kampala, Uganda Debt Network.

Umeya, K. (2019). *Reflexive accounts on Uganda general election 2016: The agency of the dead and its effect among Western Nilotes*. Citizenship in Motion: South African and Japanese scholars in conversation, 149.

Van Mil, H. G., Foegeding, E. A., Windhab, E. J., Perrot, N., and Van Der Linden, E. (2014). A complex system approach to address world challenges in food and agriculture. *Trends in Food Science and Technology*, 40(1), 20–32.

Vannucci, A., and Della Porta (1999). *Corrupt Exchanges. Actors, Resources and Mechanisms of Political Corruption*. Aldine de Gruyter.

Walton, G., and Jones, A. (2017). *The geographies of collective action, principal-agent theory and potential corruption in Papua New Guinea. Development Policy Centre Discussion*, Paper No. 58.

Wamara, C. K. (2017). Corruption in Uganda: Does this have anything to do with social work? *Journal of Human Rights and Social Work*, 2(1), 52–61.
Warburton, J. (2013). *Corruption as a social process*. Corruption and anti-corruption.
Wiener, N. (1948). *Cybernetics or control and communication in the animal and the machine*. Technology Press.
Yadav, V., & Mukherjee, B. (2016). *The politics of corruption in dictatorships*. Cambridge University.
Yaser, M. M. (2005). A complex system model for understanding the causes of corruption: Case Study – Turkey. University North Texas.

5

UNRAVELLING THE COMPLEXITIES

Identifying Persistent Factors Hindering Anti-corruption Efforts in Cameroon

Kwei Haliday Nyingchia

Introduction

It is no news that corruption is a severe scourge that has infected Cameroon's public and private spheres. This has created a negative image of the country and has grossly affected public service delivery due to the systematic looting of public resources. Consequently, the economic development of one of sub-Saharan Africa's most diversified production and resource bases, involved in exporting a broad range of raw materials, has been delayed and distorted (Ntangsi, 2008). Corruption has spread across all facets of life, severely threatening the state's survival. It is manifested through the misappropriation of public property, payment of kickbacks to obtain public contracts and services, and exemption from obligations imposed by law (Vondou, 2015).

No sector is immune from corruption in Cameroon. Indeed, measures aimed at fighting corruption are used simultaneously to protect corrupters and conceal corruption, thus making the fight against corruption extremely difficult. Those advocating or writing against corruption with robust condemnation are not clean from this scourge. For example, it is common to see law enforcement agencies turn a blind eye to illicit payments or concoct offences to extort money from drivers, university lecturers exchange marks for money, judges demand bribes for favourable judgments, and police, customs, and gendarmerie agents at traffic checkpoints extort money from truck drivers (Pigeaud, 2021). The country's corruption level came to the limelight in 1998 and 1999 when Cameroon was the absolute cellar-dweller in Transparency International's Corruption Perception Index. Since then, the country has continued to be classified as one of the most corrupt in the world

(National Programme on Governance, 2016). Since then, a cornucopia of legal and institutional mechanisms has been implemented since early 2000.

The primary step took place in 2004 when the government, via Decree no. 2004/124 of 18 May 2004, ratified the United Nations Convention Against Corruption, adopted in New York on 31 October 2003; and by ratifying this Convention, State Parties committed themselves to adopt legislative and other measures that may reduce corruption (Anoukaha, 2017). In Cameroon, numerous national instruments were enacted to tighten administrative cracks, reform the public service, introduce new accountability standards, and hold perpetrators of corruption accountable (Avitus, 2019). These measures were enforced through CONAC, the French acronym for the National Anti-Corruption Commission (considered the central organ in fighting corruption), created by Decree no. 2006/088 of 11 March 2006. There followed an anti-graft campaign, dubbed by the press as 'operation Sparrow hawk'; a government anti-corruption campaign (Charly, 2011) which has ensnared many top governments and State officials; a former Prime Minister, three former Secretaries General of the Presidency, over a dozen former ministers, two former Vice Chancellors of State Universities (the Special Criminal Court has acquitted both), General Managers and Directors of Public Establishments and Corporations, and a host of top-ranking State functionaries, who were imprisoned for the misappropriation of public property and other offences related to corruption. Despite all these measures, economic opportunism, predatory administrative habits, embezzlement of State funds, theft of public resources, bribery, and the corruption of state organs, the executive, judiciary and legislature have neither reduced nor slowed down (Avitus, 2019).

Incentives for systemic corruption have remained rife with devastating consequences. Corruption has eaten away the power of the State, its resources, and its credibility, with unknown effects on young people who once hailed the 'future of the nation' (Onga, 2012). The incentives for corruption are usually attributed to the inordinate pursuit of wealth, a weak institutional security system, bad leadership and a weak socio-economic system (Adeyemi et al., 2012). This is further amplified by limited adherence to the rule of law resulting from the absence of accountability, just laws, open government, and accessible and impartial justice (World Justice Project 2021). As per the Ibrahim Index of African Governance (IIAG) for 2020, issues of transparency, anti-corruption and accountability are some areas where Cameroon is delivering its worst performances, although a slight improvement has been witnessed over the last decade (Mo Ibrahim Africa Governance Report, 2022).

Corruption differs from country to country in its causes, though it is possible to identify some of the critical joint driving forces that generate it (Sumah, 2018). Among the most important are culture and the credibility of public institutions. Understanding such causes of corruption is complex because, at times, we may be referring to the grounds of a particular type of corruption and, at others, to what caused a specific corrupt act. Similarly, there are many varieties of unethical behaviours, as there are multitudinous factors contributing to corruption. So many explanations are offered that it is difficult to classify them systematically. De Graaf et al. (2010) argue that the phenomenon's complexity makes it impossible to account for its causes comprehensively. The main question to be answered here is why the opportunities for corruption in Cameroon remain rife despite all the anti-corruption mechanisms put in place for the last two decades.

Theoretical Conception

Luo's institutional model of corruption argues that corruption is encouraged when uncertainty and power concentration occur with regulation and institutional pressures, such as opaqueness, injustice, and complexity. His model focuses on influences in the organisational environment that enable corporate corruption to develop (Soma, 2014). Institutional models hold that deterioration at the organisational level is caused by a lack of support from the task environment, poor comprehension of regulations and flawed execution of these regulations. Other causal factors are weak commitment to eradicate corruption, lack of institutional environment transparency, and the administrative system's complexity (Yudha & Jianfu, 2015). Corruption is generalisable and, as a result, is found in government and many other institutions, creating a need to study institutional corruption in private institutions. Accordingly, organisational studies have sought to understand the organisational settings in which corruption takes place – whether by one or several members within an organisation, by individuals on behalf of organisations, or by entire organisations in cases where corruption operates as an institutionalised practice (Pinto et al., 2008).

The institutional arrangements of power, the rule of law, anti-corruption norms and anti-corruption agencies found in Cameroon indicate limited political will in the fight against corruption. Many in political and economic power benefit from corruption, making it less likely that they will try to eradicate it. While over thirty-six anti-corruption activities were launched and executed by over a dozen NGOs or Civil Society Organizations beginning in 2009, the level of corruption in the country is either stagnant or on the increase (Michel, 2010).

For the past fifty years, the political establishment in Cameroon has blindfolded the citizens with empty slogans such as 'planned liberal economy', 'national unity', 'rigour and moralisation', 'new deal', 'liberation and democratisation', 'greater ambition' and 'greater accomplishments' without the architects ascribing much actual importance to these ideas. Instead, these and other political slogans thwart the development process and entrench enormous personal benefits while impoverishing the population (Forje, 2008). This state of affairs is amplified by institutions designed so that power is highly centralised on the executive, facilitating rent-seeking and state capture. Given the formal powers provided to the presidency and the Cameroon People's Democratic Movement's (CPDM) decades-long domination of the country's institutions, neither the legislature nor judiciary can hold the executive accountable (Bertelsmann, 2020). Cameroon is a strongly personalised electoral autocracy with little commitment to democratic institutions. The President's centralisation of power enables him to manipulate institutions to reward supporters and punish detractors (Bertelsmann, 2020). The catastrophic effects of corruption on the Cameroonian economy seem to have been completely ignored or miscalculated by the authorities. Officially, corruption has been dismissed as nothing more than occasional acts of indiscretion or dishonesty by some civil servants (Fombad, 2000).

In Cameroon, as in most parts of Africa, corruption has been normalised, becoming a usual practice at all levels of government and the private sector, perpetrated in different forms (Avitus, 2019). In other words, corruption has officially been dismissed as nothing more than occasional acts of indiscretion or dishonesty by some civil servants (Fombad, 2000). Even the 'Operation Sparrow Hawk' that has ensnared several top government officials has not deterred their successors from looting public property (Avitus, 2017). The looting of public resources is the only form of corruption that the courts have constantly punished, while other forms, which also have tremendous consequences, are ignored (Avitus, 2017).

Materials and Methods

We argue that corruption in Cameroon and its underlying causes have remained rife due to a culture of impunity and irresponsibility that has found solace in the Cameroonian society and an inadequate political will to fight against it effectively. We focus on the qualitative analysis of primary and secondary data sources, enabling an in-depth analysis of statutes, textbooks and other sources on the causes of corruption in Cameroon. Content analysis, a formalised method of studying documents using a qualitative approach, enabled us to scrutinise documents and articles on the grounds of indecency.

For example, the historical method was used to study the devaluation of the Franc CFA and salaries in the public service. Along with salary cuts, devaluation reduced general agents' pay by more than sixty per cent. Depreciation increased the cost of living, while salary cuts aggravated poverty, thus pushing most public agents to resort to corruption.

The descriptive method was similarly used to analyse anti-corruption strategies adopted by the government. An in-depth analysis of these strategies reveals that they have proved ineffective, thus accounting for the prevalence of systemic corruption in Cameroon.

Results and Discussion

It is glaring that just as there are wide varieties of corrupt behaviours, so there are multitudinous factors contributing to corruption (Graaf et al., 2010). In 2019 and 2020, Cameroon was ranked 153 and 149 in the TI Corruption Perception Index out of 180 counties and 37 out of 54 countries in the 2020 Ibrahim Index of African Governance, scoring 43.5 out of 100 (Mo Ibrahim Foundation, 2020). Acts of corruption in Cameroon had become so common and widespread that the US Ambassador Niels Marquardt in 2006 wondered if the word corruption had a different connotation in Cameroon (Pigeaud, 2021). According to information published on the website of the Ministry of Posts and Telecommunication, about 1,845 billion Francs CFA (approximately US$3.8 billion) was stolen from the public coffers between 1998–2004 (Republic of Cameroon, Ministry of Posts and Telecommunication, 2017), while other sources indicate that in the last decade over US$16 billion which almost twice the budget of Cameroon has been lost to corruption. This buttresses the fact that the causes of corruption are multifarious in Cameroon.

Historical Causes of Corruption in Cameroon

Cameroon's socio-political history is integral to any explanation of corruption in Cameroon. Before the colonial period, African regimes were shaped by patron-client relationships that generated royalty systems (Pigeaud, 2021). Subsequently, the slave trade spurred the expansion of tributary systems, promoting other corrupt practices. There was the systematic use of material inducements to compel African chiefs/administrators to collaborate with colonial masters, aiding their project of dominating and exploiting their people (Munyae & Lesetedi, 1998). Colonialism contributed to the advent of the predatory state wherein key figures circumvented authority through the corruption of individuals at the centre of the repressive apparatus (Pigeaud, 2021). This state of affairs did not change at independence despite a strong culture of responsibility. For example, when Paul Biya took over as President of the Republic from Amadou Adhidjo in 1982, he ignored the fight against corruption. He focused more on his power and security (Pigeaud, 2021) despite his promised slogans of rigour and moralisation. It has been argued that the practices of post-colonial Africa's political and bureaucratic elites are merely an extension of such colonial policies and procedures that have entrenched corruption (Munyae & Lesetedi, 1998).

Once a prosperous nation, Cameroon slipped into an economic crisis in 1986 due to the changing international economic and domestic policy environment (Bernard, 1996). This caused a tremendous financial crisis, hindering the government from providing specific social amenities. As a result, the government agreed on stabilisation and structural adjustment programmes with the Bretton Woods Institutions in 1989 to counteract the deleterious impact of the crisis. This led to successive salary cuts in 1993, which saw public agents forgoing over sixty per cent of their monthly salaries. As noted earlier, those cuts and the devaluation of the Franc CFA significantly amplified poverty, thereby encouraging corruption (Tangham, 2005); even today, salaries for civil servants are still meagre. For example, magistrates in the country, upon graduation from school, earn approximately US$460 monthly, while their counterparts in countries like Ivory Coast, Gabon, Senegal, and Rwanda, with the same level of development, earn about US$1050 monthly (Séverin, 2015). The judiciary, often classified among the three most corrupt institutions in the country, also suffers from poor compensation, mainly as magistrates are typically under social pressure to construct good houses and be respected as people who have money (Séverin, 2015).

Civil servants' salaries in Cameroon are miserable and remain among the lowest in Africa, ranging from 44,000 Francs CFA (US$70.43) to 340000 Francs CFA (US$571.92) per month (Pigeaud, 2021). As noted above, poorly compensated public servants have powerful financial incentives to search for additional sources of income through bribes, extortion (Martinez et al., 2007), or outright theft. However, it can be argued that corruption cuts remuneration barriers (Iyanda, 2012). Wage inequality in the public sector is an essential determinant of the effectiveness of anti-corruption policies, and increasing the salaries of public officials could help reduce corruption in countries with low public sector wage inequality (Asli et al., 2021). Low salaries or poverty are not the sole causes of corruption because some people become corrupt in environments that allow such abuses. Comparative studies have shown that corruption relates positively to lack of control and political will to redress it (Michel, 2010). The Cabinet Ministers and General Managers of Public Corporations and Public Establishments arrested and prosecuted for embezzling public funds notwithstanding the tremendous advantages they already enjoy as top officials are suggesting that low salaries or poverty by themselves do not entirely account for corruption in Cameroon when it comes top-ranking officials, who are entitled to very juicy advantages and still resort to corruption. Some rich people or well-paid public agents are greedy and have an insatiable appetite to accumulate further wealth (Michel, 2010). Business people evade taxes by paying kickbacks to customs and taxation officials, while national and expatriate companies resort to corruption to maintain their position in national and world markets (Michel, 2010). Low salaries and poverty in Cameroon make room for the amplification of corruption in the country, but corruption in Cameroon also results from other factors (Kwei, 2020).

Inadequate Political Will to Fight Corruption

Authors are divided on the nature and significance of political will in corruption control, especially as there is little systematic analysis of the concept. Political will is commonly cited in the policy literature, the media and civil society as a critical factor necessary for change. In this perspective, civil society experts point to a lack of political will as one of the main challenges to realising anti-corruption reform (Grimes et al., 2021). Political will involves the genuine aspiration of political leaders and significant stakeholders to check perceived causes or effects of corruption (Ugoani, 2016). It is commonly defined as the 'demonstrated credible intent' of political actors. Kukutschka (2015) holds that a lack of political will is often invoked as a reason for the failure of anti-corruption reforms and a significant obstacle to economic performance and achievement of development goals. He further posits that political leadership and a commitment to fight corruption at the highest level are prerequisites for initiating and sustaining reforms until results are achieved. Unfortunately, the concept of political will has received relatively little study and remains poorly defined and understood, referred to by some authors as 'the slipperiest concept in the policy lexicon' (Kukutschka, 2015). Considering that there is political will, we can see actions visible in combating corruption. This should be expected in a country like Cameroon, where the President wields absolute power to create public services, appoints all top military and civil ranking positions, and equally defines their power. A leader in this context who has the will should take zealous actions to combat corruption without discrimination and favour. Furthermore, such acts can be measured since most actors have observed that political will can be demonstrated through actual policy outcomes. However, this approach conflates political will with the work it is expected to generate as policies may fail for reasons other than lack of political will, especially in the area of anti-corruption and especially where corruption is prevalent (Grimes et al., 2021). Notwithstanding, I join issues with those who hold that lack of political will significantly undermines anti-corruption efforts. Kpundeh (1998) posits that political will is a critical starting point for sustainable and effective anti-corruption strategies and programs and that lack of political will to fight corruption systematically allowed abusive practices to continue and eventually became a way of life for Sierra Leoneans under the former presidents Stevens, Momoh and Strasser. One could be tempted to describe Cameroon in a manner where corruption has equally become a way of life. Also, Ugoani (2016) holds that corruption has persisted in many countries, especially Nigeria, due to weak political will or the lack of it to curb the menace. Thus, a remedy to corruption should demonstrate credible intent by political leaders and stakeholders to attack perceived causes of corruption or its effects at a systemic level.

There has been much political discourse among Cameroon's political elite, especially the Head of State, to fight corruption. On 15 September 2011, at the ordinary congress of the CPDM, the President of the Republic reiterated his determination to fight corruption by stating that the fight shall be intensified without complaisance, discrimination and independently from the social status or political inclination of those suspected (*Jeune Afrique Economie*, 2012). Most of such discourse has been considered as window dressing because corruption is an integral element in political power relations in Cameroon. In practice, state resources and opportunities such as jobs are allocated to individuals based on their tribal, ethnic or political connections. Corruption has catalysed class formation and capital accumulation (Avitus, 2019).

Considerable political effort was involved in ratifying the UN Convention Against Corruption and the African Union Convention on Preventing and Combating Corruption. That was followed by the creation of the National Anti-Corruption Commission (CONAC) in 2006 and the Special Criminal Court by Law no. 2011/028 of 14 December 2011, steps portrayed as repressing the looting of public property. On 2 September 2021, the National Daily *Cameroon Tribune* disclosed that judgments rendered by this Court and the Specialized Section of the Supreme Court since 2013 amounted to 400 billion Francs CFA, approximately US$672,844,917. This could nurture the belief that there is political will to fight corruption in Cameroon, but the political elite is aware that the system survives on corruption. State capture remains challenging as political or state agents manipulate government institutions and alter the political and legal system to maintain their hold on power to enrich themselves (Avitus, 2019).

Article 66 of the 1996 Constitution enjoins the President, Prime Ministers, Members of Government, other top functionaries of the State, those holding elective office, and anyone in charge of handling public funds and managing public property to declare their assets at the beginning and the end of their tenure. Law no. 2006/003 of 26 April 2006, to lay down procedures for declarations, creates a Commission responsible for receiving them. All these have remained on paper, and it is widespread to see a public agent in Cameroon who earns less than 220.000 Francs CFA (approximately US$369) monthly brandishing estates worth hundreds of millions (CONAC, 2016) without anyone raising an alarm.

The government has failed to criminalise illicit enrichment, which is one of the predicate corruption offences, typically resulting from looting public property and receiving kickbacks. The offence has become part of the criminal law of several countries. It can be found in the three multilateral conventions that make up the global anti-corruption regime (Ndiva, 2012) and would thus be defined as illegal in any country legitimately fighting corruption. Non-criminalisation is an unequivocal justification that political will is absent in eliminating corruption in Cameroon.

The government still needs to send a draft anti-corruption law prepared in 2008 to the Parliament for adoption into law. The bill, agreed between the government and donor bodies, was part of the CHOC Project, which stands for '*Change Habits, Oppose Corruption*', a three-year multi-donor initiative to develop strategies to combat and reduce the incidence of corruption in Cameroon from 2006 to 2009. The program coordinator began work in Cameroon on 28 March 2008 but resigned on 20 December the same year. According to him:

> The fight against corruption was not over; it had hardly begun. Although the Government of Cameroon was prompted to fight corruption by the Western ambassadors and some international agencies like the World Bank, European Union and UNDP (who invited me), their support for my work failed.
>
> *(Michel, 2010)*

According to him, the Minister of Justice had declared in a meeting that corruption was not a serious offence (indicating that it was not a problem) in Cameroon. In contrast, in the same session, his counterpart in the Ministry of Finance considered a lack of jobs and investments a more significant problem than corruption (Michel, 2010). Kingsley (2015) indicates that in Cameroon, the sectors of customs, police, judiciary, public procurement, environment, natural resources and extractive industry are all particularly prone to corruption. This could result from the government's insincerity and lack of political will to fight fraud and corruption in the system.

This is further compounded by lousy leadership in a country that has since 1982 known only one leader. Cameroon is seen as an autocracy wherein impunity and corruption have become a way of life (Jacques, 2011). As such, the absence of exemplary leadership is a strong incentive for corruption. In fighting corruption, the enactment of laws and the establishment of institutions are insufficient by themselves. Laws do not enforce themselves; neither do institutional mechanisms set themselves into motion. Both must be actively implemented at all times, at all levels, without fearing recrimination or victimisation (Avitus, 2019). In Cameroon, by contrast, impunity seems to be the order of the day.

Impunity and the Absence of a Culture of Responsibility

Impunity survives where there is no respect for the rule of law and where the laws of a country and decisions of the courts are not enforced. Corruption is tolerated in countries with high impunity levels because everyone is not equal before the law (www.news24.com/News24/impunity-fuels-corruption-20180 817, accessed 10/06/2022). Where management encourages godfatherism in the workplace or does not respond to offences promptly, corruption will find comfort in the organisation (Iyanda, 2012). Some corrupt practices like purchasing influence for job seekers within public institutions are standard in Cameroon: bribes are paid, or nepotism is the rule, all to the detriment of meritorious candidates (*Repères* newspaper no. 495 of 5 October 2016). This leads to recruiting incompetent civil servants who become loyal to patrons or clans rather than the state (Pigeaud, 2021). Law enforcement authorities collect kickbacks on the highway in plain view of citizens. The situation is much the same in public hospitals, financial administration and other services of the State (Kwei, 2020). The 2016 report on the state of corruption, presented by CONAC in December 2017, indicated that between the period 2010–2016, customs officials had swindled over 1300 billion Francs CFA (approximately US$2.2 billion), with some having liquid cash worth hundreds of millions of Francs CFA, in their bank accounts, land titles, and mansions (*Cameroon Tribune*, no. 11504/7703 of 28 December 2017). None of these public agents have faced any form of sanction. Similarly, between 2012 and 2017, over 6000 billion Francs CFA (approximately US$10 billion) disappeared from the public treasury (Pigeaud, 2021). The most apparent deterrent cost of corruption is the risk of getting caught and punished, and the probability of getting caught depends on the effectiveness of the country's legal system (Treisman, 2000). When people indulge in corruption and are not sanctioned, even when it is glaring, they are motivated to engage in more corruption. In Cameroon corruption has become automatic and regular to many such that economic actors stand out by reflexes pushing them to seek corruption even when they have the right to legal gains (Pigeaud, 2021).

In Cameroon, the discretionary powers of many public agents are extensive. Moral principles in public affairs are less developed, and law officers who ensure their implementation must be prepared for the task (Gbetnkom, 2012). A supervisor engaged in corruption is unlikely to reprimand others who are similarly involved. Lack of adherence to the rule of law is as common as corruption in Cameroon, instilling systemic impunity. This is further compounded by fear of recriminations or other negative consequences from reporting corruption. As a result, neither public nor private sector employees are willing to be whistle-blowers (Kingsley, 2015).

As per the 8 December 2017 ranking of the Global Index on Impunity (GII) by the Center for Studies on Impunity and Justice (CESIJ), Cameroon was the titleholder with the highest impunity index in Africa and the third-highest at the world level (Center for Studies on Impunity and Justice, CESIJ, 2017). Impunity is encouraged by a culture of irresponsibility that has plagued all the segments of the State (Kwei, 2020). A study conducted within the framework of the National Governance Program reported that Cameroonian society experiences a culture of tolerance and solidarity that does not favour the sorts of sanctions considered an essential element of accountability and good governance (ARMP, 2006). Those expectations trigger the non-systematic application of sanctions in the fight against corruption (Kwei, 2020). That is a capture of State institutions that only helps fuel corruption since there is no systematic application of sanctions. In Cameroon, most administrations do not have a code of ethics. This contributes to the spread of corruption as most public agents are not held to professional standards. To combat impunity, we must promote a culture of respect for laws, accountability and transparency; foster a democratic system that ensures checks and balances; and put an effective and independent judiciary and anti-corruption bodies in place. Breaking the culture of corruption and impunity requires a comprehensive governance approach that ensures access to justice and information and the development of effective, accountable and transparent institutions at all levels (Keuleers, 2015).

The Quality and Independence of Institutions

It is no longer news that the quality of institutions and their independence are robust elements that greatly limit opportunities for corruption. Institutional quality can reduce corruption and limit the scope of the shadow economy (Dominik & Heldman, 2017). In Cameroon, public policy and feeble institutions are subject to the whims of the executive, which constantly reflects authoritarian or populist tendencies. While the Constitution provides for the separation of powers, the dominance of the executive affects the functioning of other powers, undermining governance and encouraging systematic corruption. The National Assembly and Senate are dominated by CPDM, the ruling party, which makes checks against the executive ineffective. Party discipline often prevails over the responsibility of Parliamentarians who should quite freely vote for or against issues of national significance, depending on their convictions and the interests of electors (AfDB, 2004), but prefer not to be barred by the party when it comes to time for renewal of their mandates. Control mechanisms like the motion of censure and parliamentary inquiries have never been used, even when the press denounces serious corruption scandals, and the judiciary and executive are inactive. Like other French African countries, Cameroon inherited the rationalisation of Parliament under the 5th Republic (Evina, 2005). This system does not guarantee effective control of government action in Cameroon and is further compounded by the dominance of the CPDM in Parliament. In an ideal system, institutions should be open to influences and feedback from different sources, yet at the same time sufficiently independent to effectively carry out their work. Where the openness and independence of the institutions are in balance, officials are accessible but not excessively exposed to private influences; if they can make authoritative decisions while not using their power in arbitrary ways, corruption will be relatively low. However, where the officials' independence is reflected in excessive exploitation of their power, they are likely to do as they please, increasing the possibility of extreme corruption. In Cameroon, anti-corruption institutions are easily influenced by those with political and economic power because of the absence of independence.

The Constitution, in Article 37, stipulates that the Judicial Power shall be independent of the Executive and Legislative Powers and that the President of the Republic shall guarantee its independence. This gives the impression that the judiciary is a weaker power. The Constitution further stipulates that the President shall be assisted by the Higher Judicial Council, which provides him with its opinion on all nominations for the bench and disciplinary action against Judicial and Legal Officers. However, the President presides over the Higher Judicial Council, assisted by the Minister of Justice as Vice President, as encapsulated in Section 1 of Law no. 82/14 of 26 November 1982 as amended in 1989. Accordingly, there is no functional independence of the judiciary in Cameroon. The National Governance Program observes that inefficiency, corruption, bribery, lack of autonomy, and pressures of all kinds make the Cameroonian Judicial system less credible (National Programme on Governance, 2016). Courts operate as external services of the Ministry of Justice, and the prosecution service is directly subordinated to the Minister of Justice. As a result, prosecutorial discretion in some issues is determined by the Minister of Justice, who may receive instructions or files from the President before transmitting them to the competent prosecuting authority. Thus, the prosecution is usually powerless when corrupt acts are committed but has yet to be instructed to initiate proceedings. In Cameroon, the press has denounced the looting of public funds in constructing stadiums to host the African Cup of Nations. More recently, what has been called Covid-Gate featured the embezzlement of billions of Francs CFA intended to fight the COVID-19 pandemic by cabinet ministers and other top functionaries. The Audit Bench of the Supreme Court (equivalence of Supreme Audit Institutions in Anglo-Saxon countries) published a report in 2021 indicating suspicious cases of embezzlement of funds destined for the COVID-19 pandemic, but prosecution has not been initiated. The silence of the judiciary shows that it is waiting for instructions, which significantly undermines its independence in controlling corruption. The absence of the independence of the judiciary in Cameroon creates serious incentives for such cases of serious corruption (Kwei & Doris, 2021).

All anti-corruption agencies in the country are faced with a similar problem. CONAC, the central authority in charge of corruption control, is directly under the authority of the President of the Republic, lacks the power to probe specific top public agents, and does not have prosecuting powers. Article 24 of Decree no. 2006/088 of 11 March 2006, creating this body, provides that the Commission will submit a report to the President of the Republic. Those arrangements make the impartiality of the Commission questionable (Kingsley, 2015). The Commission has often remained toothless when government ministries refuse to provide information.

The Supreme State Audit , responsible for protecting public property by controlling managers and imposing administrative sanctions for mismanagement, suffers a similar fate. It, too, is attached to the Presidency; the President is the sole addressee of its reports, and its activities are done under his control and instructions, as mandated in Decree no. 2013/287 of 4 September 2013. Almost all its functions have been transferred to the Audit Courts under Law no. 2018/011 of 11 July 2018, organising the financial regime of the state and other public entities. The Audit Bench of the Supreme Court is still to assume such functions, and it is hoped that it might significantly improve the management of public property.

The National Agency for Financial Investigation (a financial intelligence unit), known by its French acronym ANIF, is attached to the Ministry of Finance and is responsible for fighting money laundering. It reports directly to the State Prosecutor but does have powers similar to those conferred on the Economic and Financial Crimes Commission of Nigeria (EFCC). Its inefficiency, however, can be seen as public agents displaying wealth from doubtful sources with impunity in Cameroon. Indeed, many public agents in Cameroon are richer than business people. Therefore, corruption thrives and flourishes in weak and dysfunctional structures (Ato et al., 2014). Other anti-corruption committees exist in ministries and some public establishments and corporations but lack independence, and nothing is heard about their role in limiting corruption, especially as the authorities in these units abuse public office for private gains with impunity.

Thus, excessive executive authority must be reduced drastically in Cameroon to ensure checks and balances. In the World Justice Project Rule of Law Index indicators, factor 1, which deals with constraints on government powers, indicates that the legislature, judiciary, independent auditing and review bodies must effectively limit executive powers. Government officials must be sanctioned for misconduct, powers must be subject to non-governmental checks, and transitions of power should be subject to the law. Those sorts of changes must be instituted in Cameroon if anti-corruption bodies are to handle cases effectively and without respect to prominent persons. An impartial and independent judiciary capable of holding all public officials accountable should become a top priority.

Conclusion

Corruption is a persistent feature in Cameroon, with some of its causes remaining endemic despite significant control of it. This study was based on the hypothesis that there needs to be more political will to fight corruption in Cameroon. Ultimately, we are convinced that this lack of political will is the main reason for the country's emergence and spread of corruption. This is because if the powers that be were committed to tackle corruption, incentives promoting it would have been tremendously reduced. The consequences of corruption in a country where a considerable part of its resources are lost can no longer be overemphasised.

As a result, a real struggle against corruption has not begun in Cameroon because the legal and institutional mechanisms marshalled to limit its spread need to be stronger. The government must reinvent its anti-corruption strategies by considering endemic causes, including low salaries and a lack of solid and independent institutions. Building such institutions in Cameroon can create an atmosphere of trust in the State. This must be followed by the criminalisation of conduct like illicit enrichment, the institution of declaration of assets, and severe sanctions for non-declaration. The independence of the judiciary and anti-corruption agencies must be firmly established. The anti-corruption efforts in the country can only make sense if the draft anti-corruption law, which has been in the cupboard since 2011, is sent to Parliament for adoption. This draft law provides an exciting framework for the fight against corruption, with the National Anti-Corruption Commission given absolute independence with a mandate to investigate money laundering. Creating specialised courts for sanctioning corruption is highly compelling to complement these efforts.

References

Adeyemi, O., S. Akindele, O. Abubakar, and K. Olugbemi. (2012). The manifestation of corruption in Nigeria: A critical x-ray of some selective development. *International Journal of Physical and Social Sciences (IJPSS)*, vol. 2, no. 4: 1–31.

AfDB. (2004). *Cameroon: Country Governance Report 2004*. African Development Bank.

Anoukaha, F. (2017). *The Penal Code of 12 July 2016 and the Anti-Corruption Drive in Cameroon*. Yaounde, Les Grandes Editions.

Anti-Corruption Unit, MINPOSTEL. (2017). www.minpostel.gov.cm/index.php/en/vie-associative296-types-and-impact-of-corruption (accessed 14/06/2023)

ARMP. (2006). *ARMP Bulletin, Etude sur les Sanctions Dans le Domaine des Marches Public*. Public Contracts Regulatory Agency, Yaounde Cameroon.

Asli, Demirguc-kunt, L. Michael, and K. Vladimir. (2021). *Effects of public sector wages on corruption: Wage inequality matters*. World Bank Group, Europe and Central Asia Region, Office of the Chief Economist. https://elibrary.worldbank.org/doi/abs/10.1596/1813-9450-9643

Avitus, A. (2017). Prosecuting the offence of misappropriation of public funds: An insight into Cameroon's Special Criminal Court, PER/PELJ2017(20). www.researchgate.net/publication/317111052_Prosecuting_the_Offense_of_Misappropriation_of_Public_Funds_An_Insight_into_Cameroon%27s_Special_Criminal_Court (accessed 14/06/2024)

Avitus, A. (2019). Cameroon and the corruption conundrum: Highlighting the need for political will in combatting corruption in Cameroon. *African Journal of International and Comparative Law*, no. 27.1: 50–75.

Bernard, G. (1996). La dynamique du secteur manufacturier Africain en periode d'ajustement structurel. *Revue Region et Developpement*, no. 3: 1–26.

Bertelsmann, S. (2020). *BTI 2020 Country Report – Cameroon*. Gütersloh, Bertelsmann Stiftung.

Cameroon Tribune, no. 11504/7703 of 28 December 2017.

Charly, G. M. (2011). *L'opération épervier au Cameroun, un devoir d'injustice?* KiyiKaat Editions.

CONAC. (2016). *Report on the State of Corruption in Cameroon for 2016*. Yaounde, Cameroon.

Daniel, T. (2000). The causes of corruption: A cross-national study. *Journal of Public Economics*, vol. 17, no. 3: 399–457.
Dominik, H. E., and C. Heldman. 2017. Causes and consequences of corruption overview. IW-Report 2/2017. Cologne Institute for Economic Research.
Fombad, C. M. (2000). Endemic corruption in Cameroon: Insights on consequences and control. In: Hope, K. R., and Chikulo, B. C. (eds), *Corruption and development in Africa*. Palgrave Macmillan, London.
Forje, J. W. (2008). A country in peril: X-raying Cameroon's democratisation and socio-economic transformation: From state failure to state building. *Revue Africaine d'Etudes Politiques et Stratégiques*, no. 5: 69–99.
Gbetnkom, D. (2012). *Corruption and small-sized enterprise growth in Cameroon*. African Economic Conference, Kigali, Rwanda.
Graaf, G. D., P. V. Maravic, and P. Wagenaar (Eds.). (2010). *The good cause: Theoretical perspectives on corruption*. Opladen, B. Budrich. https://doi.org/10.3224/866492639
Grimes, M., O. Huss, and K. Ivanyshin. (2021) Building political will to combat corruption. Policy Brief No. 16. ICLD.
Iyanda, D. O. (2012). Corruption: Definitions and concepts. *Arabian Journal of Business and Management Review*, vol. 2, no. 4: 37–45.
Jacques, P. Nguemegne. (2011). Fighting corruption in Africa: The anti-corruption system in Cameroon, *International Journal of Organizational Theory and Behaviour*, vol. 14, no. 1: 83–121.
Jeune Afrique Economie, 2012, no. 388.
Jorge, M.-V., A. del G. Javier, and J. Boex. (2007). *Fighting corruption in the public sector: Contributions to economic analysis, International Studies Program*. Andrew Young School of Policy Studies, Georgia State University, 1st edition, Atlanta, USA, The Netherlands, Elsevier.
Keuleers, Patrick. (2015). End impunity for corruption to boost resources for development. UNDP Anti-Corruption for Development (September 23). https://anti-corruption.org/end-impunity-for-corruption-to-boost-resources-for-development/ (accessed 26/6/2024).
Kingsley, Mua. (2015). Fraud and corruption practices in public sector: The Cameroon experience, *Research Journal of Finance and Accounting*, vol. 6, no.4: 203–209.
Kpundeh, S. J. (1998). Political will in fighting corruption. In: *Corruption and Integrity improvement initiatives in developing countries*. United Nations Development Programme, Bureau for Policy Development, New York. www.undp-acia.org/publications/other/undp/fc/corruption97e.pdf (accessed 20/02/2023)
Kukutschka, R. M. B. (2015). Building political will. Transparency International. https://knowledgehub.transparency.org/assets/uploads/kproducts/Topic_Guide-_Political_Will.pdf
Kwei, H. N. (2020). A critical appraisal of the legal mechanisms for preventing and combating corruption in Cameroon: A legal treatise. PhD Thesis, Faculty of Law and Political Science, Cameroon, University of Dschang.
Kwei, H., and N. Doris. (2021). Appraising the independence of the judiciary in Cameroon in fighting corruption. *NAUJILJ*, vol. 12, no. 1: 182–196.
Michel, Van Hulten. (2010). Power and corruption in Cameroon in 2008, seminar paper presented at the Surrey University 6-7 July 2010 on the theme: Corruption in a globalising world: challenge and change. www.academia.edu/37442606/Power_and_Corruption_in_Cmeroon_doc (accessed 12/06/2014)

Mo Ibrahim Foundation. (2020). *2020 Ibrahim Index of African Governance, Index Report.*
Mo Ibrahim Foundation. (2022). *2022 Ibrahim Index of African Governance, Index Report.*
Mulinge, M. M., and G. N. Lesetedi. (1998). Interrogating our past: Colonialism and corruption in Sub-Saharan Africa. *African Journal of Political Science*, vol. 3 no. 2: 15–28.
National Programme on Governance. (2016). *Report on the State of Governance in Cameroon in 2016.* Yaounde, Prime Minister's Office.
Ndiva, K.-K. (2012). *Combating Economic Crimes, Balancing Competing Rights and Interests in Prosecuting the Crime of Illicit Enrichment.* London and New York, Routledge.
Ntangsi, M. M. (2008). *A Balance Sheet of Economic Development Experience since Independence, Civil Society and Search for Development Alternatives in Cameroon: Chapter 1.* Council for the Development of Social Science Research in Africa (CODESRIA).
Onga, T. (2012). The fight against impunity is a normative analysis. *Antrocom Online Journal of Anthropology*, vol. 8, no. 1: 103–122. ISSN 1973-2880
Pigeaud, F. (2021). *The Mechanisms of Corruption in Cameroon.* Media part of 03/8/2021.
Pinto, J., C. R. Leana, and F. K. Pil. (2008). Corrupt organisations or organisations of unscrupulous individuals? Two types of organization-level corruption. *Academy of Management Review*, vol. 33, no. 3: 685–709.
Republic of Cameroon, Ministry of Posts and Telecommunication. (2017). Cellule Anti-Corruption. Online at https://www.minpostel.gov.cm/index.php/fr/cellule-anti-corruption/296-types-and-impact-of-corruption (accessed 26/6/2024).
Richard, E. O. (2005). *L'intégration du pilotage des performance en finances publiques Camerounaise*, Masters Dissertation, ENA de Paris.
Repères newspaper no. 495 of 5th October 2016.
Séverin, Djiazet Mbou Mbogning. (2015). *L'accès à la justice au Cameroun, étude de sociologie juridique*, Paris, L'Harmattan.
Soma, P. (2014). *Development Corruption in South Africa: Governance Matters.* Palgrave Macmillan.
Sumah, S. (2018). Corruption, causes and consequences. http://dx.doi.org/10.5772/intechopen.72953
Tangham, D. T. (2005). Economic crime in Cameroon and its impact on the sound development of the State. 126th International senior seminar, participants' paper. www.unafei.or.jp/publications/pdf/RS_No66/No66_17PA_Dohgansin.pdf (accessed 14/ 06/2024).
Ugoani, John N. N. (2016). Political will and anticorruption crusade management in Nigeria. *Independent Journal of Management & Production (IJM&P)*, vol. 7, no. 1: 72–97.
Vondou, A. (2015). *Virtue Ethics for the Prevention and Fight against Corruption in Cameroon a Thesis Submitted in Partial Fulfillment of the Requirements for the S.T.L.* Degree from the Boston College, School of Theology and Ministry.
World Justice Project. (2021). *Rule of Law Index 2021.* World Justice Project report, Washington, DC.
Yudha, A. S., and S. Jianfu. (2015). Institutional theory for explaining corruption: An empirical study on public sector organisations in China and Indonesia. *Corporate Ownership and Control*, vol. 13, no. 1: 817–823.

6
LOBBYING IN TUNISIA
Developing a Transparency Regime to Tackle Perceptions of Corruption

Barry Solaiman

Introduction

While there is much literature on corruption in Tunisia, there is a dearth of research specifically on political lobbying in that country. Analyses focus specifically on the corruption of the Ben Ali regime and on corruption in the public and private sectors since the revolution, such as bribery, petty corruption and other forms of systemic corruption.[1] The legal framework that has developed for transitional justice emphasises financial corruption, electoral fraud and the embezzlement of public money.[2]

There are shortcomings in that specific focus on corruption that may also apply to lobbying in Tunisia. For example, some bodies fail to cooperate with the special courts that adjudicate transitional justice cases.[3] Despite some minor crossover, lobbying is a distinct study. In most cases, lobbying is good for democracy because it involves citizens exercising their democratic right to influence politicians. However, left unchecked, it may have deleterious outcomes for the political process, particularly if insidious forms of conduct are involved, such as institutional corruption, which are not encapsulated in predominant examinations on corruption. This conduct is an important aspect that is often overlooked, but it is crucial to implement mechanisms sooner rather than later. Indeed, former Prime Minister of Tunisia, Youssef Chahed, noted in a speech to Parliament that corruption is a threat to fledgling democracies.[4] While his government's anti-corruption efforts involved arresting high profile figures who enriched themselves following the revolution, the threats posed by lobbying also require significant attention at this early stage in the country's democratic development.[5]

This chapter argues that an 'institutional corruption' analytical framework should be used to capture the concerns regarding political lobbying in Tunisia. That framework assists in pinpointing concerns specific to lobbying that are not accounted for in other literature and, in so doing, provides justification for a particular form of regulation to combat the related concerns. International best practices are examined to determine the most effective form of those mechanisms currently used in practice that Tunisia could follow. For reformers, the institutional corruption framework can pinpoint areas for reform and justify those reforms with coherent and logical reasoning supported by the framework. At present, transparency registers and codes of conduct are implemented by countries without a cohesive strategy or justification for their use. In some cases, lawmakers create regulations with incoherent reasoning, leading to ineffective registers.[6] This chapter does not purport to answer all the challenges faced by Tunisia. Instead, the aim is to flag the relevant concerns about lobbying and highlight how reform might be pursued.

Lobbying can be defined as the act of individuals or groups attempting to influence decisions taken at a political or administrative level.[7] Meetings, phone calls, hosting social events, protests and petitions undertaken to influence officeholders are all examples of lobbying. In most cases, those acts are inherently desirable to a democracy. They are how citizens exercise their right to speak freely and be heard by their representatives. These rights have been hard fought and won by Tunisians, and they must be protected from abuse. Thus, the argument here is not that lobbying is inherently wrong, but when manifested through institutional corruption, it can harm those democratic rights. Political science, law, sociology and economics tend to be the primary fields from which lobbying research arises. Lobbying has been regulated at the federal level in the United States since 1946 and at the state level since the early 1900s.[8] The main concern is that wealthy individuals and groups do not have disproportionate influence over decision-making.[9] While there is much literature on the topic in the US, the field is relatively underdeveloped elsewhere.

It should be emphasised that while lobbying and corruption are separate, the focus here is on corrupt activity that may arise from lobbying. In Tunisia, corruption linked to lobbying is not measured. Yet, corruption has led to a decline in trust in the government, with people also concerned about favouritism and nepotism.[10] There has also been confusion about the so-called 'war on corruption', with many in civil society not understanding who the actual enemy is nor what the appropriate tools are for tackling corruption.[11] There has been frustration that efforts have focussed on some sectors and not others (for example, a focus on smugglers instead of business, security and customs sectors).[12] This confusion is reflected in the divergent approaches to tackling corruption in the country. On the one hand, government officials have tended to focus on tackling corruption that has arisen since the revolution. On the other hand, civil society has sought to address past crimes and to institutionalise anti-corruption measures.[13]

There are a multitude of concerns that are appropriate for individual study. All the concerns cannot be rectified with one measure, and a multifaceted approach is required which likely contributes to the confused approach to tackling corruption in Tunisia. As such, the 'institutional corruption' framework is needed to provide a more accurate appraisal of problematic lobbying in Tunisia than current approaches.

The chapter proceeds as follows. First, the conceptual framework for institutional corruption that underlies many lobbying concerns is detailed. Second, the specific risks of lobbying and corruption in Tunisia are outlined. It is argued that the lack of transparency in Tunisia creates difficulties in determining whether institutional corruption from lobbying exists and to what extent. Third is an analysis of the current legal mechanisms used to tackle quid pro quo forms of corruption such as bribery. This analysis highlights the lack of a suitable mechanism for identifying institutional corruption and the need for one. Fourth, it is argued that Tunisia should introduce a lobbying transparency regulator and code of conduct. While a transparency register may not solve the corruption problems, it is a crucial first step in understanding the extent of lobbying and the associated concerns in the country.

It must be emphasised what this contribution is not. There has been a burgeoning interest in Tunisia among academicians in recent years. Some have been criticised for providing analyses of 'post-revolution dynamics' using external models rather than examining Tunisia's own history.[14] In this context, Tunisia has often been used as a case study to test or verify theories arising from Western academies.[15] This dynamic has been exacerbated by information power imbalances between academics who have access to costly journals and citizens of Tunisia who experienced the revolution but do not have access to such resources to provide their narrative.[16] At the same time, it has been noted that those concerns do not justify academic nationalism, narcissistic introspection whereby the study of Tunisian politics is replaced with one's position or binary views that 'Western academies and politicians keep exploiting the South'.[17]

With that background in mind, the following is essential to note. The approaches to lobbying regulation are broadly similar worldwide (a code of conduct and transparency register). However, the specific rules and final form of those mechanisms should be adapted by those on the ground with relevant experience. Thus, while the theory of 'institutional corruption' presented in this chapter derives from Western academies, it is at the forefront of the current understanding of lobbying in any democracy. In this manner, this chapter is intended as a starting point to encourage conversations about the need to regulate lobbying in the country.

Institutional Corruption Theory and Lobbying

Lobbying activities are best understood through 'institutional corruption' theory rather than traditional analyses of corruption premised on bribery, fraud and embezzlement. For this reason, it will be seen below how the current regulatory framework in Tunisia is geared towards the latter concerns, which does not assist in dealing with the former.

Most politicians in democratic systems do not engage in outright bribery, and most attempts to influence policy and implementation are not corrupt. Where clear-cut abuses occur, there are specific legal mechanisms to deal with them. Here, we are concerned with more insidious conduct that is more subtle, nuanced and harder to detect, such as meetings at social events, sponsoring tables at political fundraisers as a means to donate to the political party, and policies written by private think-tanks. That conduct is often perfectly legal but can be problematic. The premise of institutional corruption is thus based on *political* benefits. Individuals are not seeking a *personal benefit* for themselves (such as a bribe) but attain an advantage for their party or their corporation. An example is a donation to a political party. Assuming the donation meets the permissible donations criteria under the law, then a politician soliciting a donation for their party is acting within the law. Traditional corruption laws or financial misconduct rules are unhelpful for analysing the concerns arising from such donations. Donors can (and usually do) state that the donation was given in accordance with the law and no further investigations are needed. This is problematic because the damage caused by such lobbying can lead to a betrayal of public trust in political institutions, lead to unfavourable laws and regulations, and undermine equality, which is harmful to democracy.[18] This is explained by Thompson, who argues that:

> When the pursuit of political gain undermines the very process the money is supposed to support, politicians not only fail to do their job, they disgrace it. They betray the public trust in a more insidious way than when they use their office for personal gain, which is after all incidental to their role. When they pursue political gain improperly, they betray their duty while doing it.[19]

'Institutional corruption' can be used to analyse such lobbying. It is:

> A systemic and strategic influence which is legal, or even currently ethical, that undermines the institution's effectiveness by diverting it from its

purpose or weakening its ability to achieve its purpose, including, to the extent relevant to its purpose, weakening either the public's trust in that institution or the institution's inherent trustworthiness.[20]

This definition is provided by Lessig, who advances Thompson's theory developed in the 1990s concerning the US Congress. Lessig explains the definition in more detail. First, a 'systemic and strategic influence' means a regular and predictable systematic influence used by others to achieve a deviation. This can be money, ideology or anything that brings about that effect.[21] Second, the influence must be 'legal or ethical' because the aim is to distinguish between legal influences and illegal ones such as bribery.[22] For this reason, institutional corruption captures conduct beyond quid pro quo bribery, which current laws are predominantly designed to do. Therefore, institutional corruption can capture broader, more insidious conduct. Third, the corruption must 'undermine the institution's effectiveness'. Here, there is a focus on the effect of institutionally corrupt behaviours. Fourth, the institution must be diverted from its purpose, or there is a weakening of its ability to achieve its purpose. According to Lessig, an institution may or may not have a defined purpose. If it does not have a purpose, it cannot be corrupted in the sense of institutional corruption, but 'if it does, then corruption is manifested relative to that purpose'.[23] It may be that the institution fluctuates between deviating and not deviating from its purpose (which may suggest a weaker deviation). In general, the purpose of the executive and legislature will be to act in the general public interest rather than in the interest of a few powerful groups or individuals (something that problematic lobbying threatens to do).[24] Fifth, the deviation weakens public trust in the institution or the institution's inherent trustworthiness.[25] Citizens should trust political institutions. Institutional corruption makes it more difficult to trust the recommendations of those institutions or trust that they are operating in the public interest.

This methodology can apply to both public and private-sector institutions.[26] It can be used to capture concerns about lobbyists' using vast wealth and power to displace the public voice in policy development, to convince legislators to define policy problems in ways that advance their interests,[27] to shape the rules of the game to lower standards,[28] and to displace some public policy goals and compromise the attainment of others.[29]

At present, the legal and institutional framework in Tunisia has not been developed to identify the extent of institutional corruption that underlies many lobbying concerns in democratic countries. The following section highlights some research elucidating those concerns, but that research is ultimately limited. The institutional corruption framework may provide a more helpful method for identifying the challenges in Tunisia and its approach to reform.

Lobbying in Tunisia?

The political process in Tunisia was historically closed with influence wielded by a small circle of trusted officials, donors and special interests.[30] This limited the ability of citizens to have any meaningful influence.[31] Since 2011, Tunisia has been constructing a new citizenship based on transparency, liberty, equality and participation in the country's political life.[32] In this vein, Tunisia is in the process of a significant transition towards democracy that involves a proactive approach towards the management of public affairs.[33] There has been greater access to information, more public consultation and greater civil society engagement in the early stages of the policymaking process.[34] However, while Ben Ali has left the scene, there is now concern that corruption has simply become decentralised in the public sector more broadly.[35] This has been called the 'democratisation of corruption', with the public sector becoming susceptible to crime bosses who have paid to gain influence in political parties, the judiciary and more.[36] Ultimately, many groups are now competing for power.[37] Thus, while tightly controlled corruption is problematic, it could be argued that uncontrolled corruption is more unwieldy, disruptive, costly and harmful to democracy.

Competition for political influence is legitimate in a democracy so long as it takes place within limits of openness and fairness, and the argument here is not what type of democratic system should be pursued in Tunisia.[38] In general, lobbying can exist in systems that consider democracy a deliberative endeavour involving public discussion or systems that consider democracy to be a battle of ideas whereby a struggle to be heard ensues among different interests.[39] In any democratic system, power can become concentrated in the hands of the 'privileged elite' to the detriment of other citizens.[40] The focus here is on the mechanisms needed to protect the Tunisian political system from the subversion of democracy by wealthy and powerful interests. Tunisia has an opportunity to implement mechanisms at a relatively early stage before networks become too embedded and resistant to attempts to provide more transparency.

Unfortunately, there is a lack of literature on political lobbying in Tunisia that can provide a proper assessment of where and when such interests are exerting influence. This is another reason why a lobbying transparency register is needed. Nevertheless, there is enough research to piece together some of the facets of lobbying that presently exist. One obvious aspect is so-called grassroots lobbying, which includes citizen protests and petitions, which are a big part of the political landscape. Tunisia has among the highest levels of demonstrations in Africa.[41] During the COVID-19 pandemic, protests revolved around socioeconomic issues and the failure of successive governments to address inequalities since the Revolution.[42] But those sorts of activities are not our primary concern. Instead, it is hidden influences, networks and finances used to influence political decision-making that require transparency.[43] These examples may present systemic influences that are legal or ethical that may divert political institutions from their purpose or weaken their ability to do so, as defined under institutional corruption theory noted above.

One group that raises concerns about the concentration of power and influence is the media. For example, Nabil Karoui, a prominent businessman, politician and key figure in Tunisian media, not only supported the successful election of Beji Caid in 2014 but also his own election campaign for President in 2019,[44] which resulted in him reaching the second round of the election. For his own campaign, Karoui's television channel started a daily program covering his charitable activities and daily footage of him distributing meals to the poor for Ramadan in 2019.[45] Such influence may raise questions about the level of access that those in the media can gain to political leaders or the political process. Again, there is a lack of empirical research in Tunisia, but Karoui has previously worked with Beji Caid, and his firm provided visual services for Beji Caid's 2014 campaign. While there is no evidence in this case, such a relationship can create unequal influences in lobbying because a wealthy individual or group has supported a politician to influence them (lobbying) and may later expect a benefit in return. Ordinary people in society cannot hope to wield such influence. The media's tactics can be broader, with strategies being employed to play elites against one another or to position themselves as the voice of the ordinary person in an attempt to gain the respect of a large portion of the population.[46] These tactics create an inequality of influence that others may be unable to wield.

Lobbying may also occur indirectly through policy research undertaken in universities, public administration and independent research institutes.[47] There has been greater freedom to research and influence the policy dialogue since 2011.[48] Independent policy research institutes influencing policy dialogues have seen a particular 'boom'.[49] They undertake policy evaluation and analysis, providing decision makers with important data.[50] Kherigi and Amiri find that such institutes:

> Are developing a stake in the policymaking process in Tunisia, using new spaces for policy research and critical engagement to scrutinise and question government policies, challenge policy frameworks and government models and raise new policy problems.[51]

This influence has arisen because public officials require high quality information to make policy decisions. Such information is lacking in the Arab region, with data often being unavailable or outdated owing to the general lack of transparency at the political level.[52] In this manner, institutes that can provide such information can assist in governance. This lack of data undermines the policy evaluation process, which is beset by structural problems of poor access to information, low capacity and commitment for garnering data, and little exchange of information between researchers and policy makers.[53]

Despite this boom, interviews with institutes highlight a continued dissatisfaction from some that, in practice, institutes continue to be marginalised from the policymaking process.[54] Although, such grievances should be understood in the context of the varying ambitions of the different institutes. Some institutes are happy to undertake purely technical analyses of policy, whereas others are seeking to build political networks to funnel more comprehensive policy recommendations.[55] Some factors are important to note in this paradigm of institute influence.

A broad range of entities provide data to officeholders in democratic systems, playing a crucial role in a healthy democratic process. However, some institutes can become powerful entrenched networks themselves, negating some positive aspects. One can identify think-tanks in the United Kingdom (UK) as an example. Think-tanks have become so entrenched in recent decades with the political party apparatus that they play a significant role in creating, disseminating and legitimising policy proposals.[56] Essentially, think-tanks influence politics at the highest level but are controlled by a small number of powerful people who are unknown.

Such institutions are inaccessible to the general public and threaten to wield too much influence in the long-term once embedded. At present, the risk of policy research institutes wielding too much influence in Tunisia appears to be limited owing to a lack of public trust in their work. The public has seen lobbying and special interest influence in the media and research organisations, which has naturally led to scepticism about the intellectual integrity and credibility of policy research institutes.[57] Nevertheless, there is a legitimate place for policy institutes in the political discourse, and they can fulfil an important role. Proper transparency could not only alleviate concerns about what institutes are doing but also provide legitimacy to their good work while keeping their influence in check. For example, a transparency register that openly highlights what institutes are publishing and who they are seeking to influence.

Finally, political parties have been accused of indulging and promoting clientelism, tailoring legislation for their own interests and engaging in nepotism.[58] President Kais Saied has accused the Ennahda party of paying 'nearly three million dinars ($1.1 million) to foreign lobbying groups to harm their country'.[59] However, Saied has been criticised for attempting to garner power under the guise of tackling corruption.[60] Political parties have also been found not to have properly reported campaign finances. Former President Karoui was accused of receiving money from foreign donors and commissioning a lobbying firm paid for from an undeclared account abroad.[61]

These examples may present systemic influences that are legal or ethical that may divert political institutions from their purpose or weaken their ability to do so, as defined under institutional corruption theory noted above. There is a need for greater transparency surrounding lobbying in the country. It is challenging to determine the extent to which the executive and legislature in Tunisia may be undermined in carrying out their democratic mandate effectively owing to the influence of lobbyists. There is little data on what political benefits (if any) are derived by these and the many other unidentified groups. Without sufficient information, one cannot understand whether the lobbying that is occurring is a healthy driving force in the democratic arena or powered by institutional corruption. The lack of information is not helped by the current laws.

The Developing Legal and Institutional Framework

Following the Jasmine Revolution of 2010–2011, Tunisia managed to free public speech and created a pluralist political arena.[62] Public deliberation has been a central part of the constitutional reform process, leading to a 'significant impact on the content of the constitution.'[63] Indeed, the Constitution can be seen as a response to that history. Alongside these efforts at democratisation has been a series of anti-corruption initiatives to tackle specific concerns.[64] These include a freedom of information law, joining the Open Government Partnership, a law to protect whistleblowers, and laws on asset declarations and conflicts of interest.[65] Some efforts have been aimed at pre-revolution corruption, while others have focussed on post-revolution corruption. Both are outlined here, but the predominant focus is on post-revolution infrastructure.

Before examining the legal attempts to tackle corruption below, it should be emphasised that citizen concerns have only increased, owing to the underfunding of institutions and inadequate implementation of laws.[66] Citizens in Tunisia still feel that the government should do more to tackle corruption.[67] The public has consistently considered that the government is doing 'badly' at tackling corruption by 62%.[68] That anger is that citizens perceive government officials and members of Parliament to be the most corrupt in society.[69] These concerns are not helped by serious ongoing challenges, such as the election commission being seized by President Saied in 2022, which was seen as a blow to democracy.[70] Highlighting the changes made becomes a more critical exercise considering the ongoing challenges.

For the legal changes, the Constitution of Tunisia has several articles dedicated to combating corruption.[71] Article 10 notes that public funds shall be spent in a manner that prevents corruption. Article 15 states that the public administration should operate in accordance with the principles of impartiality, equality, transparency, integrity, and accountability. Under

Article 32, access to information is guaranteed as a right. Article 130 sets out the rules for the Good Governance and Anti-Corruption Commission (discussed below). The Constitution also requires the President, Head of Government, members of the Council of Ministers, members of the Assembly of the Representatives of the People and other public figures to declare their assets once they have assumed their role.[72] These constitutional provisions are supported by legislation implementing them.

Thus, regarding access to information, there is Organic Law No. 22 of 2016 on the Right of Access to Information which implements the right to information guaranteed under Article 32 of the Constitution. The law created the Access to Information Authority (INAI) to oversee compliance. However, executive bodies do not always comply with requests for information, which limits the impact of the INAI.[73] Further, even if compliance was high, access to information laws are unhelpful for dealing with lobbying transparency. Hundreds of incidences of lobbying may occur on a given day in politics. It would be unreasonable and unworkable if the only available avenue to securing information about those meetings were through the submission of hundreds of individual requests that may take a significant amount of time to release. The public ought to have accessible information about meetings that is frequently updated. This would give citizens transparency about any conversations that may affect them and provide an opportunity to lobby officials in response.

The constitutional requirement to declare assets is important in order to highlight potential conflicts of interest. For example, if a lawmaker holds shares in a pharmaceutical company lobbying the government for legislative changes, that would be highly pertinent for citizens to know because of potential political benefits.[74] Despite this stipulation in the Constitution, many public officials have not declared their assets.[75] There must be not only transparency about who is lobbying officials but also a comprehensive register of interests held by politicians that is publicly accessible.

Organic Law No. 10 of 2017 on Corruption Reporting and Whistleblower Protection offers protections for public servants and others who reveal information in the pursuit of combating corruption. This has been particularly needed in the region because of threats to income, life and physical safety.[76] This law is a welcome tool for tackling corruption that can work alongside a lobbying transparency regime. While most officials would declare interests honestly, mechanisms for whistleblowers to raise concerns about declarations that they know to be untrue are needed. Also welcome are civil service rules prohibiting public servants from having personal interests that may unduly influence their independence, restrictions on employment upon leaving office for work related to their public function, and a prohibition on participating in undertakings that might compromise the dignity of the public service.[77]

Together, these laws constitute a range of disparate tools (varying in effectiveness) that may apply in specific lobbying contexts. While it has been argued that 'Tunisia's legal measures provide a strong framework to combat corruption, many are not fully implemented or enforced.'[78] There are also questions about how effective the legal measures will be at deterring corruption once implemented.[79] Most importantly, the tools are not designed specifically to tackle concerns with institutional corruption that may underlie lobbying. The closest mechanism appears to be the Code of Conduct and Ethics of Public Officials, created by decree in 2014.[80] The Code applies to all public officials working at the central, regional or local levels of government.[81] The Code's existence is a significant development for a young democracy. It would have been unthinkable for all public officials to be subject to a code of conduct and ethics under the Ben Ali regime. The purpose of the Code is to support public officials in upholding an 'upright public service, beyond the doubt of corruption in order to restore confidence in the State apparatus'.[82] This includes enabling the public official to 'overcome the situations of interest conflict that he can be faced with during his professional life'.[83]

Several principles are espoused, including transparency, integrity, accountability, nepotism, favouritism and clientelism.[84] Integrity denotes the values of 'sincerity, integrity, loyalty and devotion' to public service 'in order to preserve the image of the institution to which he belongs'.[85] Favouritism alludes to preferences given illegally to one political party to the detriment of another during the provision of a service.[86] Clientelism concerns the appointment of a person owing to an existing relationship.[87] Further, beyond the principles, there are several 'values' stated in the Code. One is 'probity' – the notion that a public official is 'bound to practice his duties with devotion and honesty without aiming at reaching personal interest'.[88] 'Neutrality' means that public officials should not 'give preferential treatment, or be partial towards the provision of services'.[89] These provisions can apply to lobbying, but they are vague. Terms such as 'sincerity', 'devotion' and 'honesty' are open to wide interpretation, and 'personal' interests sidestep the need to account for 'political' benefits explained under an institutional corruption framework.

The Code does contain specific provisions on conflict of interest, declaration of assets, privileges and parallel activities.[90] On 'conflict of interests', a public official who considers that they may have a conflict 'shall inform immediately his hierarchical superior, who shall take appropriate measures to resolve the situation'.[91] However, this procedure is not robust because it relies on an official taking the initiative to declare a conflict and, even then, only to their supervisor. Instead, there should be mandatory reporting periods by those in public office registered with an independent regulator. On 'official declaration of assets', a public official must declare any private interests belonging to them, their spouse or children upon taking their post.⁹² Yet, one is not left with much faith that officials will comply with the Code considering the lack of compliance with the Constitution on the declaration of assets.

On 'gifts, advantages and other privileges', the public official must 'abstain from requesting or requiring or accepting gifts, donations or any other advantage presented to him or to other persons and that could affect, directly or indirectly, the objectivity in performing his duties'.⁹³ This provision could be central to a specific Code on lobbying because it rightly focuses on 'objectivity' in decision-making and the potential for that to be undermined by the receipt of 'political' benefits as captured within institutional corruption theory, which stipulates that an individual attains a benefit for the political system, their party or their corporation. On 'parallel activity', the code states that 'the status of the public official is incompatible with every activity which is contrary to the honour and dignity of the profession or affecting the performance of his duties'.⁹⁴ Again, vague terms such as 'honour' and 'dignity' are not helpful from a regulatory perspective owing to the broad possible interpretations.

Overall, the Code provides a clearer articulation of principles that ought to be followed but is presented as a 'grab bag' of incoherent and vague rules that do little to protect against the risks of lobbying. A detailed rulebook is needed alongside an empowered regulator. That is not to say that institutions have not been created. However, the experience thus far with creating institutions highlights that much work is needed to establish a robust body. For example, the Authority for Good Governance and the Fight Against Corruption (INLUCC) was created to monitor and investigate cases of corruption in the public and private sectors.⁹⁵ While the INLUCC has examined thousands of cases, referring some to the ministries and others to the courts, the authority is underfunded and understaffed, and few cases have been ultimately prosecuted.⁹⁶ Other institutions have also been difficult to establish.⁹⁷ It has been a challenge, for example, to establish institutions dedicated to protecting human rights.⁹⁸ The inability to appoint members of the Constitutional Court is a glaring concern.⁹⁹ The work of the Truth and Dignity Commission was ended, having been deemed a failed experiment by some.¹⁰⁰ Its work was also a secondary concern for a government focussed on more pressing economic and security challenges.¹⁰¹ There have been numerous challenges, not least the need for money to fund constitutional commissions.¹⁰² The common theme that arises is a lack of human and financial resources, which is a 'serious impediment to investigating and prosecuting a large volume of corruption-related cases.¹⁰³ Underpinning these shortcomings are concerns about President Saeid recentralising power, closing the anti-corruption commission, placing the former head of the agency under house arrest, and offering amnesty to businessmen who invest in state projects.[104] This has had a chilling effect on whistleblowers, and ministries are also more reluctant to respond to requests for access to information.[105]

The intention here is not to be overly critical. There has been incredibly hard work involved in creating institutions and operating them day-to-day. A significant constitutional and institutional overhaul has been accomplished in Tunisia in a very short period, one that any country in the world would struggle to match. The point here is to emphasise that lobbying regulation is critical to safeguarding the democratic arena from institutional corruption and that the experience so far highlights the risks and hurdles faced by any regulator in order to be successful. The precarity of the new laws and institutions is further underscored by the potential of a lurch back towards the centralisation of power and the loss of freedom of speech.

If that is to be avoided, overcoming the institutional hurdles will be necessary. Tunisia must fulfil its aspirations within the Open Government Partnership (OGP). Tunisia's associated Action Plan for the OGP for 2018-2020 highlights important ambitions that are relevant to lobbying.[106] Tunisia aims, for example, to enhance the right of access to information and public data.[107] To achieve this aim, the Action Plan proposes establishing a legal and regulatory framework that would anchor a new culture based on principles of openness, transparency and cooperation.[108] Transparency is premised on making more data publicly available and improving the process of accessing information.[109] In doing so, authorities hope to enhance public participation in the political process.[110] Tunisia has also committed to establishing regulatory and organisational mechanisms premised on enhancing integrity in the public sector and combating corruption.[111] The Action Plan cites the law on whistleblower protection and declaration of asset laws in support, as well as establishing the Authority of Good Governance and Anti-Corruption.[112] The problems with those endeavours have already been highlighted. Creating a lobbying law and regulator would help to address the aims of the Action Plan.[113] It is that issue to which this chapter finally turns.

Regulating Lobbying through the Institutional Corruption Framework

A comprehensive regulatory framework requires a detailed empirical study in Tunisia. For now, the purpose is to outline current best practices that Tunisia should consider in developing a regulatory regime through the institutional corruption framework.

As noted above, Tunisia implements disparate approaches to tackling corruption. Some of that corruption may arise from or be linked to lobbying activities. As is common in many jurisdictions, anti-corruption initiatives are created to deal with specific problems and do not deal with the underlying causes holistically. Returning to Lessig's definition of institutional corruption, the problem is:

> A systemic and strategic influence which is legal, or even currently ethical, that undermines the institution's effectiveness by diverting it from its purpose or weakening its ability to achieve its purpose, including, to the extent relevant to its purpose, weakening either the public's trust in that institution or the institution's inherent trustworthiness.[114]

The analysis in this chapter raises a consistent problem: a lack of data about lobbying. Institutional corruption refers to legal or ethical systemic and strategic influence that is regular and predictable. That influence reduces the institution's effectiveness, diverting it from its purpose or weakening its ability to achieve its purpose (such as acting in the public interest rather than in the interest of a few powerful groups or individuals) and undermines public trust in the institution or the institution's inherent untrustworthiness. Identifying these individual facets can lead towards specific reforms, but the current 'grab bag' approach to regulation is a symptom of the lack of a systemic diagnosis of the underlying problems in Tunisia. A significant increase in transparency is required to obtain the necessary data for the diagnosis and treatment.

With more data, the institutional corruption framework can provide a more robust dissection of the matters in question. When Nabil Karoui supported the election of Beji Caid as President in 2014, that support may have been legal, but it still gave Karoui more access and influence than the average person. If the duty of elected leaders is to act in the public interest, then Karoui's support may have caused a diversion from that purpose by influencing Caid to heed Karoui's narrow interests more readily. Policy research institutes have developed a stake in the policymaking process in Tunisia, yet there are no means of identifying whether those (or other) institutes may engage in institutional corruption. An institute can become entrenched in the party's political and governance mechanisms, influencing the entire decision-making environment. This could be entirely legal yet result in decision makers being diverted towards the aims and interests of an influential institute with a particular political leaning.

Of course, it may be that there is no institutional corruption in any of those cases, but greater transparency is necessary for a clearer examination and identification of any problematic lobbying that might be occurring. Institutional corruption analysis provides for the identification of these issues. The lobbying involved in each case is different, yet an analysis can be undertaken using the same framework. This holistic analysis can support a coherent regulatory strategy to disrupt problematic cycles of influence. But Tunisian institutions do not have the required data to undertake this analysis nor the remit to tackle lobbying-related institutional corruption concerns.

Rather than submitting hundreds of requests for information to the INAI, there should be a central public register of lobbying that is updated frequently. Politicians are not declaring their assets, creating critical information gaps for identifying potential institutional corruption. The declaration of assets should be enforced, and those declarations should be highlighted on a central lobbying register for any relevant entry.

The vague principles established in the Code of Conduct and Ethics of Public Officials should be overhauled, with greater clarity surrounding the responsibilities of politicians. That Code should be tied directly to a lobbying register so that the obligations of transparency are read and applied alongside the ethical obligations of public officials. Bodies like the INLUCC are bound to fail if they are underfunded, operate without a coherent ethos for what they are precisely tackling, and are demoralised in a system where politicians do not fulfil their constitutional obligations. The Action Plan for the OGP is a good aim in principle, but what will opening up government data accomplish if there is no clear strategy over what that is meant to achieve? The institutional corruption framework could provide a clearer focus for such objectives. In the first instance, the framework could be applied to a specific sector that has courted particular controversy in Tunisia to test its usefulness, such as the media. Which sector ought to be tested by the framework will depend on the challenges arising at a particular moment in time and should be determined by society.

If that were to be achieved, what would be the legal structure underpinning such a move? Canada is relevant here owing to its relative success in maintaining a long-established lobbying transparency register and accompanying code of conduct. While no system is perfect, Canada's approach can help link the concepts of institutional corruption to the law. This chapter does not claim that the Canadian and Tunisian political systems are easily transposable to each other. Instead, it merely presents a tool (a lobbying register), which is considered to be an international best practice for lobbying transparency applied in numerous countries globally. Canada's register is a well-known and comprehensive register from which a more bespoke and tailored lobbying register could be created in Tunisia.

Lobbying legislation would be necessary to create a register for tackling institutional corruption. In Canadian law, there are four cornerstones: first, the principles underlying the law; second, the range of communications covered; third the range of officeholders that will be covered, by the law; and fourth, the types of lobbyists covered.

First, for the principles, the governing legislation in Canada is the Lobbying Act 2008.[115] This is the most recent iteration of a law first enacted in 1989. It lists four underlying principles:

1. free and open access to government is an important matter of public interest;

2. lobbying public office holders is a legitimate activity;
3. it is desirable that public office holders and the public be able to know who is engaged in lobbying activities;
4. a system for the registration of paid lobbyists should not impede free and open access to government.[116]

A statement of principles is essential to emphasise that lobbying regulation is not about stifling free speech but rather safeguards the democratic arena. These principles could be modified for Tunisia's case to take account of its history as determined by Tunisian society. The emphasis on freedom of speech should be retained, but it should also be emphasised that the law exists to help identify influences that may raise concerns about corruption. The agreed principles will provide justification for the range of communications that are registerable activities.

Second, for the range of communications, the Canadian law requires those to register who make communications with regard to:

1. the making, developing or amending of federal legislative proposals, bills or resolutions, regulations or policies or programmes;
2. the awarding of federal grants, contributions or other financial benefits; and
3. in the case of consultant lobbyists, the awarding of a federal government contract or arranging a meeting between their client and a public office holder.[117]

In general, how the communication is made should not matter (phone call, email, meeting). The one distinction in the provisions above is under (3) regarding arranging a meeting. This involves considerations about the type of lobbyist, which is discussed below. These provisions are necessary for identifying whether legal and ethical influences may cause the institution to be diverted from acting in the general public interest, thereby causing institutional corruption.

Third, the law normally outlines to whom the communications must be directed to be registerable. In Canada covered targets under the Act are defined as 'public office holders'.[118] These are explained by the former registrar of lobbyists to be 'virtually all persons occupying an elected or appointed position in the Government of Canada, including members of the House of Commons and the Senate and their staff, as well as officers and employees of federal departments and agencies'.[119] The law is, therefore, broad-reaching. However, any law should not be too broad. It would not be advisable for Tunisia to implement a transparency register involving all public officials because it would be impossible to implement and administer effectively. As a practical matter, the larger the regulator, the more unwieldy and challenging it becomes to regulate effectively. Instead, an effective regime would focus on high-level officeholders such as those in the executive and legislature (and their staff). Again, these provisions will be necessary for identifying the public official involved and whether they have acted in the public interest or have been involved in institutional corruption.

Fourth, the law should stipulate the type of lobbyist covered. In Canada, three types of lobbyists are positively defined by the Federal Lobbying Act 2008: consultant lobbyists, in-house lobbyists for corporations and in-house lobbyists for organisations. Section 5(1) covers consultant lobbyists who are individuals who receive 'payment, on behalf of any person or organization'. Section 7(1)(a) defines in-house lobbyists to include corporations and organisations which employ one or more individuals 'any part of whose duties it is to communicate with public office holders on behalf of the employer . . . or subsidiary'. In other words, in-house lobbyists employed by *corporations* are persons who work for 'compensation in an entity that operates for profit'.[120] In-house lobbyists for *organisations* are persons who work 'for compensation in a non-profit entity'.[121] In-house lobbyists are required to register where the total lobbying activity of all employees equals 20% or more of their overall duties.[122] Consultant lobbyists are persons who are 'hired to communicate on behalf of a client'. This is explained as those who are deemed to be professional lobbyists but also includes any individual who 'in the course of his or her work for a client, communicated with or arranged meetings with a public office holder'.[123]

In-house lobbyists make up the vast majority of lobbyists, yet some countries, such as the UK, omit them. To garner public trust, any law in Tunisia must include in-house lobbyists. Further, with respect to 'consultant lobbyists', such individuals would be required to register where they make direct representations on behalf of their clients but may not be required to register where they simply draw attention to correspondence from their client to a public official. There is significant scope for nuance and for loopholes to develop, which is why a rigorous process is required for creating any law. These provisions are critical for identifying institutional corruption because it is necessary to uncover who is lobbying the politician (information that is generally lacking in Tunisia). The law in Canada has resulted in a transparency register, an example of which is seen in Figure 6.1.

Figure 6.1 highlights the essential facets of a robust lobbying register with specific details of who is lobbying, what is being lobbied, who is being lobbied, and who is the lobbyist involved. Such a register would significantly enhance the transparency of governance in Tunisia and help to highlight any instances of institutional corruption. For example, by revealing meetings between entities and government figures, what was discussed, and what issues the entities sought to influence. By revealing such meetings, civil society could investigate any existing links between an entity and the government using other tools (such as campaign donation reports). Not shown in Figure 6.1 are

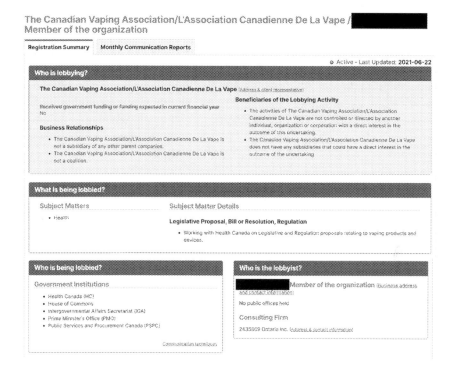

FIGURE 6.1   Example of an entry on the Canadian Registry of Lobbyists (29 April 2021).

Source: Office of the Commissioner of Lobbying of Canada, 'Registry of Lobbyists: The Canadian Vaping Association' (Lobby Canada, 29 April 2021) https://lobbycanada.gc.ca/app/secure/ocl/lrs/do/clntSmmry?clientOrgCorpNumber=364337&sMdKy=1624280986850; Note: this contains information licensed under the Open Data Licence Agreement—Office of the Commissioner of Lobbying and is in compliance with the conditions enumerated in the Open Data Licence Agreement, see Office of the Commissioner of Lobbying of Canada, 'Open data licence agreement' (Lobby Canada) https://lobbycanada.gc.ca/en/open-data/open-data-licence-agreement/

the detailed monthly communication reports, which provide a comprehensive picture of the lobbying involved.

A final element of a robust lobbying transparency regime is to create a code of conduct to accompany the register. Not all countries have implemented codes of conduct, but they are needed if the law is to require not only that lobbying be registered but also that those activities be conducted ethically – a matter that will be of importance to Tunisians who have little trust in public officials. Canada's Lobbyists' Code of Conduct emphasises key principles that are enforced by the Lobbying Commissioner (although the Commissioner's powers are limited to reporting violations to Parliament rather than levying criminal sanctions).[124] The Code includes principles of transparency, integrity and honesty, openness, professionalism, conflicts of interest, preferential access, political activities, and gifts.[125] Such principles are already articulated in Tunisia, but it would be more effective to enhance those principles and channel their application through an enforced lobbying register.

By developing legislation that follows a similar rubric, one could envisage a register that highlights what lobbying is occurring and whether there may be institutional corruption. None of the current approaches ensure the type of transparency needed to undertake such an analysis.

Conclusion

Tunisia stands apart from other countries in North Africa. Transitions to democracy do not come easy, and newfound freedoms can be fragile. Institutionalising that transition will be a critical challenge that Tunisia must navigate in the years and decades to come. At the same time, the country has an opportunity to design robust checks and balances for its democratic system, such as lobbying regulations. It is more challenging to design and implement such regulations in countries with long-established democratic systems that have entrenched mechanisms of political influence. Once powerful interests become embedded, they are often resistant to changing the status quo in an attempt to retain power.

There have been many attempts at dealing with corruption concerns in Tunisia but those have faced challenges such as a lack of compliance, lack of funding and understaffing. Further, the measures are not designed to address institutional corruption concerns typically associated with political lobbying. While much has happened since 2011 in Tunisia, a decade or so remains very early in any country's democratic development. Democracy can take decades to embed and develop. Now would be a good opportunity for Tunisia to pre-empt a future where networks become so embedded and entrenched that calls for meaningful transparency may be rejected. Developing robust lobbying regulations and an associated code of conduct would be a crucial step in shining a light on the lobbying that is taking place and would enable proper analyses of institutional corruption indicators. This approach would be pivotal to enhancing public trust, which has been languishing for too long.

Notes

1 Sarah Yerkes and Marwan Muasher, 'Tunisia's Corruption Contagion: A Transition at Risk' (October 2017) Carnegie Endowment for International Peace 1, 4.
2 Law No 53 of 2013 on the Establishment and Regulation of Transitional Justice; For an analysis of this legal framework, see, Adnen Nouioua, 'Fighting Corruption within the Framework of Transitional Justice: The Impact on Democratic Transition in Tunisia' (2020) 3(1) AlMuntaqa 9, 10.

3 Nouioua (n 2) 13.
4 Yerkes (n 1) 14.
5 Ibid.
6 See, Barry Solaiman, 'Lobbying in the UK: Towards Robust Regulation' (2021) 76(2) Parliamentary Affairs 270–297. https://doi.org/10.1093/pa/gsab051 accessed 11 May 2024.
7 See, Raj Chari, John Hogan and Gary Murphy, *Regulating Lobbying: a global comparison* (Manchester University Press 2010) 4.
8 Federal Regulation of Lobbying Act 1946 (US); Clive S Thomas, 'Interest Group Regulation Across the United States: Rationale, Development and Consequences' (1998) 51(4) Parliamentary Affairs 500, 505.
9 Cass R Sunstein, 'Political Equality and Unintended Consequences' (1994) 94 Colum L Rev 1390, 1392; see also, Julian Bernauer, Nathalie Giger and Jan Rosset, 'Mind the Gap: Do Proportional Electoral Systems Foster a More Equal Representation of Women and Men, Poor and Rich?' (2015) 36(1) International Political Science Review 78, 78.
10 Yerkes (n 1) 11–12.
11 Ibid. 15.
12 Ibid.
13 Ibid. 13.
14 Nadia Marzouki and Hamza Meddeb, 'The Struggle for Meanings and Power in Tunisia after the Revolution' (2016) 8 (2–3) Middle East Law and Governance 119, 120.
15 Ibid.
16 Ibid. 121.
17 Ibid.
18 Dennis F Thompson, 'Two Concepts of Corruption' (2013) Edmond J. Safra Working Papers, No. 16, 10.
19 Ibid.
20 Lawrence Lessig, 'Foreword: "Institutional Corruption" Defined' (2013) 41(3) JLME 553, 553.
21 Ibid.
22 Ibid.
23 Ibid. 554.
24 This 'best interest' argument is made by Solaiman. See, Barry Solaiman, 'Evaluating Lobbying in the United Kingdom: Moving From a Corruption Framework to 'Institutional Diversion' (PhD Thesis, University of Cambridge, 2017) https://doi.org/10.17863/CAM.15615 accessed 11 May 2024; see also, Barry Solaiman, Lobbying, Democracy and Public Trust: An Institutional Diversion Framework (Hart, Forthcoming 2025).
25 Lessig (n 20) 554.
26 Gregg Fields, 'Parallel Problems: Applying Institutional Corruption Analysis of Congress to Big Pharma' (2013) 41(3) JLME 556, 556.
27 Paul D Jorgensen, 'Pharmaceuticals, Political Money, and Public Policy: A Theoretical and Empirical Agenda' (2013) 41(3) JLME 561, 561.
28 Marc-André Gagnon, 'Corruption of Pharmaceutical Markets: Addressing the Misalignment of Financial Incentives and Public Health' (2013) 41(3) JLME 571, 572–573.

29 Marc A Rodwin, 'Five Un-Easy Pieces of Pharmaceutical Policy Reform' (2013) 41(3) JLME 581, 581; Abigail Brown, 'Understanding Pharmaceutical Research Manipulation in the Context of Accounting Manipulation' (2013) 41(3) JLME 611.
30 Intissar Kherigi and Khalil Amiri, 'Public Policy Making in Tunisia: The Contribution of Policy Research Institutes' (2015) 7(1) Middle East Law and Governance 76, 80; Bob Rijkers, Caroline Freund and Antonio Nucifora, 'All in the Family: State Capture in Tunisia' (March 2014) World Bank Policy Research Working Paper 6810.
31 Kherigi (n 30) 82.
32 Mohamed Nachi, 'Transition to Democracy in Tunisia: Learning about Citizenship in a National and Transnational Context' (2016) 55(4) Social Sciences Information 429, 431; Kherigi (n 29) 83.
33 Nachi (n 32) 432.
34 Kherigi (n 30) 83.
35 Jennifer Schoeberlein and Matthew Jenkins, 'Corruption in the Middle East and North Africa: Regional Trends from the 2019 Global Corruption Barometer and Country Spotlights', *Transparency International* (10 Dec 2019) 18–19.
36 Krista Lee-Jones and Kinda Hattar, 'Tunisia: Overview of Corruption and Anti-Corruption', *Transparency International* (31 August 2018) U4 Helpdesk Answer 2018:15, 4; Carlotta Gall, 'Corruption Crackdown Intensifies in Tunisia, and the People Cheer' *New York Times* (2017) www.nytimes.com/2017/06/25/world/africa/corruption-crackdown-intensifies-in-tunisia-and-the-people-cheer.html accessed 11 May 2024.
37 Lee-Jones (n 36) 4.
38 For a discussion on this, see Nachi (n 32) 435.
39 ibid. 436; Jürgen Habermas, *Droit et démocratie. Entre faits et normes* (Paris, Gallimard 1997).
40 Nachi (n 32) 436.
41 Armed Conflict Location & Event Data Project, 'Demonstrations Spike in Tunisia Despite COVID-19 Pandemic' (29 June 2020) 1 www.jstor.org/stable/resrep25631 accessed 11 May 2024.
42 Ibid. 2.
43 It is also a concern when some groups use violence to squelch the democratic right of others to lobby. For example, accusations have long existed of the harassment and physical violence directed towards the media by the police and army. Although, such harassment is beyond the scope of this chapter. See, Roxanne Farmanfarmaian, 'Media and Politics of the Sacral: Freedom of Expression in Tunisia after the Arab Uprisings' (2017) 39(7) Media, Culture and Society 1043, 1053.
44 Katrin Voltmer, Kjetil Selvik and Jacob Hoigilt, 'Hybrid Media and Hybrid Politics: Contesting Informational Uncertainty in Lebanon and Tunisia' (2021) 0(0) The International Journal of Press/Politics 1, 8.
45 Ibid.
46 Ibid. 15.
47 Kherigi (n 30) 76 & 86.
48 Ibid. 87.
49 Ibid. 88.
50 Ibid. 76.

51 Ibid.
52 Ibid. 79.
53 Ibid.
54 Ibid. 90.
55 Ibid. 93.
56 Peter Dorey, *Policy Making in Britain* (2nd edn, Sage 2014) 68.
57 Kherigi (n 30) 93.
58 Francesco Tamburini, "How I learned to Stop Worrying and Love Autocracy": Kais Saied's "Constitutional Self-Coup" in Tunisia (20220) 00(0) Journal of Asian and African Studies 1, 5.
59 'Tunisia Coup: Kais Saied Vows to Fights 'Traitors' and 'Mafia' in Incendiary Speech' Middle East Eye (15 Sept 2022) available at www.middleeasteye.net/news/tunisia-coup-kais-saied-speech-vows-fight-traitors-mafia accessed 11 May 2024.
60 Tamburini (n 58).
61 'Tunisia Country Report 2022' BertelsmannStiftung (2022) available at https://bti-project.org/fileadmin/api/content/en/downloads/reports/country_report_2022_TUN.pdf accessed 11 May 2024.
62 Marzouki (n 14) 120.
63 Tofigh Maboudi, 'Reconstituting Tunisia: Participation, Deliberation, and the Content of Constitution' (2020) 73(4) Political Research Quarterly 774, 785.
64 Hayat Alvi, 'The Human Rights and Development Impetuses for Tunisia's Jasmine Revolution' (2014) 1(1) Contemporary Review of the Middle East 25, 26.
65 Schoeberlein (n 35) 19.
66 ibid.
67 Lee-Jones (n 36) 3.
68 Coralie Pring, 'The State of Corruption: The Public's View: People and Corruption: Middle East and North Africa Survey 2016', *Transparency International* (2016) 13; Congressional Research Service, 'Tunisia in Brief' (16 March 2020) RS21666, 6.
69 Lee-Jones (n 36) 4.
70 See, 'Tunisian President Seizes Control of Electoral Commission' *Reuters* (22 April 2022) www.reuters.com/world/africa/tunisia-pres-appoints-electoral-commission-members-by-decree-latest-power-grab-2022-04-22/ accessed 11 May 2024; For an analysis of the role of election commissions, see, Barry Solaiman, 'Electoral Commission' in R. Grote, F. Lachenmann and R. Wolfrum (eds), *Max Planck Encyclopedia of Comparative Constitutional Law* (OUP 2021) https://oxcon.ouplaw.com/display/10.1093/law-mpeccol/law-mpeccol-e678 accessed 11 May 2024.
71 Constitution of Tunisia (adopted 26 January 2014).
72 ibid. art 11.
73 'Tunisia: Citizens Testing Right-to-Information Law' *Human Rights Watch* (15 Feb 2019) www.hrw.org/news/2019/02/15/tunisia-citizens-testing-right-information-law#:~:text=Tunisia%27s%20law%20requires%20all%20government,%2C%20statistics%2C%20and%20"any%20information accessed 11 May 2024.
74 On lobbying in healthcare see, Barry Solaiman, 'European Distinctions Between Private and Public Law in Health Care and the Emerging Influence of Private Lobbies' in I. Glenn Cohen and others (eds), *Health Law as Private Law: Pathology or Pathway?* (CUP 2024).

75 Lee-Jones (n 36).
76 Ibid. 7.
77 Ibid. 6.
78 Yerkes (n 1) 21.
79 Ibid.
80 Decree 2014–4030 Approving the Code of Conduct and Ethics of the Public Official (3 October 2014) *Official Gazette of the Republic of Tunisia*.
81 Ibid. art 2.
82 Ibid. 920.
83 Ibid.
84 Ibid. 920–21.
85 Ibid. 920.
86 Ibid. 921.
87 Ibid.
88 Ibid.
89 Ibid.
90 Ibid. 922.
91 Ibid.
92 Ibid.
93 Ibid.
94 Ibid.
95 Lee-Jones (n 36) 8.
96 Ibid.
97 Ibid. 8–11.
98 Melek Saral, 'The Protection of Human Rights in Transitional Tunisia: Capacity, Willingness and Capacity-Building' (2019) 16(1) Muslim World J Hum Right 1,18.
99 'Tunisian President Resists Parliament's Bid to Create Constitutional Court' *Reuters* (6 April 2021) www.reuters.com/article/uk-tunisia-politics-idUSKBN2BT1PF accessed 11 May 2024.
100 Laryssa Chomiak, 'What Tunisia's Historic Truth Commission Accomplished – and what went wrong?' *Washington Post* (16 Jan 2019) www.washingtonpost.com/news/monkey-cage/wp/2019/01/16/heres-what-we-can-learn-from-tunisias-post-revolution-justice-commission/ accessed 11 May 2024.
101 Ibid.
102 Saral (n 98) 18.
103 Yerkes (n 1) 30.
104 'Tunisia: Crackdown on Democracy and Transparency' Transparency International (10 June 2022) Available at: www.transparency.org/en/blog/tunisia-crackdown-on-democracy-and-transparency accessed 11 May 2024.
105 Ibid.
106 Open Government Partnership Tunisia (OGPT), 'Open Government Partnership National Action Plan 2018 – 2020' (2018–2020) *Republic of Tunisia Presidency of the Government*.
107 Ibid. 10.
108 Ibid. 13.
109 Ibid.
110 Ibid. 16.
111 Ibid. 29.

112 Ibid.
113 Although, it is acknowledged that the signing treaties or passing laws are of limited effect without accompanying measures to improve economic development and social justice. See, Nouioua (n 2) 15.
114 Lessig (n 20).
115 There is also legislation at the provincial level, but this chapter highlights federal legislation for simplicity. See, Nova Soctia Lobbyists' Registration Act s 2(1) (c) & (f); Québec Lobbying Transparency and Ethics Act 2002, c 23, s 2 & 4; Ontario Lobbyists Registration Act 1998, s 1; British Columbia Lobbyists Registration Act 2001, pt 1, s 1(1); Newfoundland and Labrador Lobbyist Registration Act 2004, s 2(1)(c) & (f); Province of Alberta Lobbyists Act 2007, s 1(1)(f) & (k); Manitoba Lobbyists Registration Act CCSM, c L178, s 1(1); Saskatchewan Lobbyists Act 2014, s 2(1)(i) & (p); New Brunswick, Bill 43, Lobbyists' Registration Act, s1.
116 Canada Lobbying Act (RSC 1985, c 44 (4th Supp)) as amended in 2008 (Canada Lobbying Act 2008), preamble.
117 Office of the Commissioner of Lobbying of Canada, 'Frequently Asked Questions' (*OCL-CAL*) https://lobbycanada.gc.ca/en/registration-and-compliance/frequently-asked-questions/ accessed 11 May 2024; Canada Lobbying Act 2008, s 5(1) & 7(1).
118 Canada Lobbying Act 2008, s 2(1).
119 Office of the Commissioner of Lobbying of Canada, 'A Guide to Registration' (*OCL-CAL*). https://lobbycanada.gc.ca/app/secure/ocl/lrs/do/rgstrtnGd accessed 11 May 2024.
120 Ibid.
121 Ibid.
122 Office of the Commissioner of Lobbying of Canada, 'A Significant Part of Duties ("The 20% Rule")' (*OCL-CAL*). https://lobbycanada.gc.ca/en/rules/the-lobbying-act/advice-and-interpretation-lobbying-act/a-significant-part-of-duties-the-20-rule/ accessed 11 May 2024.
123 Office of the Commissioner of Lobbying of Canada, 'A Guide to Registration' (n 117).
124 Office of the Commissioner of Lobbying in Canada, 'Lobbyists' Code of Conduct 2023' (*OCL-CAL*, 2023) https://lobbycanada.gc.ca/en/rules/the-lobbyists-code-of-conduct/lobbyists-code-of-conduct-2023 accessed 11 May 2024.
125 Ibid.

PART II
Corruption in the Economic and Social Sector

7
CORRUPTION AS AN INVESTMENT RISK

A Case Study on Anti-corruption Strategies in Djibouti

Wael Saghir

Introduction

With foreign direct investors constantly seeking new opportunities, one of the things they usually assess before venturing overseas is the potential risks associated with their potential investment. As such, investors are keen on finding means that would help them reduce their exposure to these risks. It is noted that each region carries its consortium of risks that foreign investors may encounter. Some African countries have managed to lure in foreign investors since the 1980s to various degrees due to the number of attributes these markets enjoy from their natural resources (Basu & Srinivasan, 2002; Odusola, 2018). Investors from the US, France, the UK and China were the top four investors in African markets, amounting to more than USD 155,000 million in 2019 alone (Madden, 2019). Notably, Djibouti attracted 182 million USD in Foreign Direct Investment (FDI) in 2019 (UNCTAD, 2020; Santander Online, 2021). Due to its location and heavy reliance on FDI to stimulate its economic growth and development of different sectors, Djibouti became particularly attractive to foreign investors in the service and industrial sectors, agriculture and infrastructure.

Djibouti is seen as a strategic partner of China in the Belt and Road Initiative (BRI), which aims to enhance connectivity and cooperation across Eurasia and Africa. China has invested heavily in Djibouti's infrastructure, such as ports, railways, airports, and free trade zones. China has also established its first-ever overseas military base in Djibouti, at the mouth of the Red Sea (Vertin, 2020). China's FDI offers significant opportunities and benefits for Djibouti's economic growth and development, as well as its regional integration and stability. Such partnership has resulted in China's increased direct investments in the state, including contributing to the construction of Obock International Airport.

With the magnitude of investments flowing in from foreign investors and in sectors that are somewhat crucial to the recipients' markets, one may wonder to what degree corruption plays a role in facilitating these investments. This is of particular importance since such practices could well be considered as an investment risk that foreign investors may encounter since it helps create an uneven playing field for investors and further raises operational costs (Shleifer & Vishny, 1993) (Wei, 1997) (Campo & Lien et al., 1999). Moreover, corruption could have severe implications for the host state. Such a practice could lead to a financial crisis since it weakens domestic financial supervision and contributes to the possible deterioration of the quality of the banking sector (Wei, 2000).

This chapter looks at how FDIs engagement in corrupt practices plays a role in facilitating these investments in Africa (particularly in Djibouti) and examines the measures undertaken to combat corruption. This will take place by probing the nature of corruption as an investment risk, focusing on how corruption played a role in facilitating several investments in Djibouti before looking at the different measures of combating corruption. It aims to establish the significance of Djibouti as a case study. The intricate interplay of Djibouti's society, politics, economy, and development trajectories paints a comprehensive picture of corruption's multifaceted effects on investment risks. These characteristics illuminate whether political or commercial risks are more pronounced and how various stakeholders respond to these challenges. The rationale behind choosing Djibouti as a case is to provide a singular example and offer insights into broader patterns and implications for addressing corruption in similar contexts across Africa.

Nature of Corruption Risk

Historically, one of the most prominent risks foreign direct investors encountered was political risk. Political risk is defined as "any threat encountered by foreign investors, in the host state, through any form of political intervention or political instability that would restrict these investors from benefiting from their property rights in part or in full" (Saghir, 2018). Corruption is seen as the "abuse of public or private office for personal gain" ("Corruption: A Glossary of International Criminal Standards", 2007).

The two notions, i.e., political risk and corruption, are connected. Understanding the components of *political intervention* would lead to understanding the true nature of corruption as an investment risk. This is especially true since corruption in FDI could likely involve political persons in the host state who may influence the decision of admitting or granting a given investor the right to enter the national market. Furthermore, political risk and corruption are connected where they both generally involve someone acting on behalf and for the benefit of the state.

Generally, political intervention could take many forms, from expropriating investors' property rights to instability in the host state that would affect their access to property rights.

Moreover, the influence of culture cannot be underestimated, where corruption may perhaps be a culturally acceptable practice rather than frowned on. Such practices may be a culturally accepted practice in some FDI-exporting states. For example, the concept of *guanxi*, originating from China, revolves around the intricate network of interpersonal relationships used by individuals to exchange favours, information, and resources (Harding, 2014). While *guanxi* is not inherently corrupt, it can inadvertently facilitate corruption when employed to bypass established rules and regulations or gain undue benefits. The dynamic nature of guanxi is further influenced by factors such as transparency, accountability, and supervision within the organisational environment. Consequently, *guanxi* is not a fixed cultural norm but a situational practice that varies among contexts and individuals. In contrast, Africa's practices, such as dash and zawadi, involve gift-giving and favour-granting (Munyai, 2020). *Dash*, rooted in West Africa, involves offering a small amount of money or goods as tokens of appreciation. Similarly, *zawadi*, originating from East Africa, denotes gifts exchanged to show respect and friendship (Fadiman, 1986). Although these practices are not intrinsically corrupt, they have the potential to be misused for influencing individuals in positions of authority or creating unequal relationships.

When looking deeper into these practices, it is crucial to understand that they are not universally regarded as corrupt or wholly accepted. Their ethical implications vary across circumstances and are subject to norms and judgments. Moreover, practices like *guanxi*, *dash*, and *zawadi* are not exclusive to China or Africa; they manifest differently in other regions and cultures, often under different names. For instance, practices resembling these are found in Western countries through networking, tipping, or donations, illustrating the multifaceted nature of these social interactions.

Comparatively, *guanxi* and *zawadi* share commonalities and distinctions. *Guanxi* encompasses an intricate web of relationships used for favours and resource exchange. It can indirectly facilitate corruption by circumventing formal regulations. On the other hand, *zawadi* from East Africa represents a gift given to signify respect and friendship. Although not inherently corrupt, *zawadi* can inadvertently foster corruption by maintaining imbalanced relationships. Social expectations of reciprocity, gratitude, and generosity further influence its nature.

Cultural influence plays a pivotal role in shaping perceptions of corruption. *Guanxi*, for instance, is an accepted practice in China, particularly prominent in one of Africa's most significant Foreign Direct Investment (FDI) investors.

Similarly, Africa's widespread familiarity with practices like *dash* and *zawadi* showcases cultural norms of gift-giving and favours. These practices are not isolated to their regions; they offer insights into how cultures may accept certain practices within their context.

On the other side of the spectrum, the practice of corruption, particularly in developing states, is seen by civil servants as a means to help them become more prosperous and for that, they opt for public policies aimed at generating personal benefits rather than ones that would benefit the society at large (Mbaku, 2010).

To properly understand the nature of corruption, it is essential to probe the different parties involved briefly. The principal-agent model is one of the leading theories for studying corruption. Generally, the principal-agent model assumes that the "interests of principal and agent diverge, that there is an informational asymmetry to the advantage of the agent, but that the principal can prescribe the pay-off rules in their relationship" (Groenendijk, 1997). Thus, it assumes that the relationship exists between public officials with power and private individuals or firms seeking to benefit from such access (Rose-Ackerman).

Involvement of these main parties in corrupt practices may be streamlined and limited if these practices are not regarded as typical or widely accepted by a particular society. This view highlights the role of another party that may have a role in either discouraging or encouraging corruption. This view is called the collective action approach (Marquette & Peiffer, 2018).

Attributed to be the root cause of numerous economic hardships (Argandoña, 2006), for some, corruption is one of the many forms of political risk (Rubins & Kinsella, 2005; Busse & Hefker, 2005). The reasoning behind such attribution is that in most cases of corruption, government officials demand personal benefits (ibid.). Although this may be true in theory, the distinction still needs to apply between situations when a corrupt individual is a person representing the government, i.e., a government official, and cases where the corrupt person is a non-government official who is directly or indirectly connected to a government official who would facilitate the investment in the prospective host state. This type of corruption is indirect bribery (Bray, 2007). Such distinction would result in either attributing corruption as a commercial risk or would regard it as a political risk. Others view corruption as an answer to a broader social problem and are instead derived from the "self-conception of the actor in a concrete socio-historic situation" (Tanzler et al., 2012). Such a view is known as the Problem-Solving approach (Sanz, 2016).

In general, one of the most prominent forms of corruption is bribery. It involves exchanging money, gifts, favours, or other benefits to influence the actions or decisions of individuals in positions of power. It may also involve small-scale, everyday instances of bribery where individuals pay bribes to officials for services they are legally entitled to receive. That said, corruption may take other forms. It could take the form of monetary incentives, reciprocal service provision, embezzlement, misappropriation, or even gift-giving, to name a few.

Extortion and coercion commonly involve forcing individuals to pay bribes under threat or duress. This type of bribery highlights the power dynamics between the bribe giver and the recipient, often exploiting vulnerabilities in socio-economic contexts. It was observed that extortion and coercion are more likely to occur when public officials have discretionary power over contract awards when bidders have high sunk costs, and when there is a lack of transparency and accountability.

Another prominent form of corruption involves high-level officials and significant sums of money, known as Grand Corruption. It includes acts of bribery that have far-reaching consequences on public policy, contracts, and government decisions. Grand corruption often undermines the integrity of institutions and can have severe socio-economic repercussions. It may also influence political decisions, policies, or elections.

Moreover, a subset of corruption is known as grease or facilitation payments. These are typically small bribes given to expedite routine administrative tasks. These payments blur the line between corruption and a legitimate fee for expedited services, raising questions about their ethical implications.

However, the most prominent in the African continent is conventional corruption, where the official is offered and receives an illicit incentive for their personal use. Unconventional corruption occurs when the official aims to attain personal advantages, disregarding public interest.

For corruption to be considered a political risk, the parties involved in the transaction should involve at least one government official with the power or influence to make decisions on behalf of the state or government. The principal-agent model is simple, and the parties involved are clear. When discussing FDI and corruption, the parties involved are the investor, the bribe giver, and the government official or representative, the bribe taker. Here, the bribe taker is also the influencer in admitting the foreign investment.

On the other hand, for corruption to be regarded as a commercial risk, the parties directly involved should not include any state representative. The principal-agent model here would not necessarily be applicable as one more party would be involved in the transaction. As such, the parties involved would be the investor, the bribe giver, and an influencer, the primary bribe recipient. This influencer is not a government official or one acting in the name of the state; instead, he is someone directly or indirectly connected to a state representative with the power and authority to make decisions in favour of the investor. In this transaction, the government official is an indirect party to the primary transaction between the investor and the mediator. However, it is a direct party to a subsequent transaction between them and the mediator where the latter shares financial gains or incentives with the former.

It may be argued that since corruption involves official roles and powers in various ways, it is a commercial risk reflecting more fundamental political dynamics. This may be true. However, the distinction, particularly to investors, is essential. Both types of corruption, the one identified as a political risk and the other regarded as a commercial risk, have the same purpose and are initiated to gain the same results; the distinction between them as political and commercial is essential. Generally, distinguishing between political and commercial risks is vital when probing FDI protection and factoring and calculating the costs associated with a particular investment.

Political and commercial risks have different sources and drivers, implying different levels of predictability and controllability. Political risk is often driven by human decisions and actions, which can influence various factors, such as ideology, interest, emotion, or culture. Commercial risk is often driven by market forces and cycles, which various factors, such as supply, demand, competition, or innovation, can influence. Therefore, political risk is generally more unpredictable and uncontrollable than commercial risk.

Both types of risks have different effects and consequences, implying different severity and reversibility levels. Political risk can directly and immediately affect FDI projects, such as expropriation, nationalisation or confiscation. Commercial risk can have indirect and delayed effects on FDI projects, such as reduced revenues, increased costs, or lower returns. Therefore, political risk is generally more severe and irreversible than commercial risk.

Given the difference in nature, both types of risks have different measures to reduce foreign investors' exposure to them. Each of these solutions or measures has different levels of effectiveness. For example, Political risk can be mitigated by various solutions and instruments, such as political risk insurance (PRI), bilateral investment treaties (BITs), multilateral investment guarantees (MIGs), or dispute resolution mechanisms (DRMs). On the other hand, commercial risk can be mitigated by various solutions and instruments, such as conducting business thorough market research and analysis, insurance, or a myriad of contractual clauses like exclusion clauses and stabilisation clauses, among others. Therefore, political risk is generally more available and effective than commercial risk.

Corruption cannot be entirely regarded as a standalone *risk* in the traditional sense, nor can it be regarded as a *cost of doing business*. It is a subset action that negatively impacts foreign investors and host states. Thus, probing its nature becomes essential to understand the levels of protection available to both parties.

Probing the nature of corruption as a risk for FDIs may not necessarily be for examining protection available but rather as a means for potential FDIs to factor in their risk management strategy and understand the mechanisms available to minimise their exposure to such practice. This becomes particularly important as corruption could expose FDIs to non-political risks, such as technology leakage (Smarzynska & Wei, 2000).

Moreover, mapping the risk management strategy requires a proper understanding of the type and nature of the particular risk being mapped, calculated and analysed. As part of the risk mapping, FDIs have their strategy and approach to factor in corruption risk (Škrbec, 2016). Understanding the variable nature of corruption as an investment risk and how it may have its roots embedded within the host state's culture, probing the current practices in Djibouti is paramount before examining the measures enacted to curb corruption in these states.

FDI and Corruption in Djibouti

It is observed that many commercial risk rating agencies consider African states as risky destinations (Haque et al., 2000). For example, according to the latest statistics conducted by Euler Hermes on Zambia's investment environment, the country's political risk, economic risk and financial risk were all high according to the further dive into debt being projected for the country (Ozyrut). In addition to these risks, corruption was blamed for the drop in the overall numbers of inward FDIs to Zambia and the quality of these investors (Sakala, 2019). This is particularly evident as US companies cited corruption as an obstacle to their prospective investments in Zambia ("Djibouti", 2021).

Djibouti was considered less risky than Zambia, with the projection of business-related risks being the most prominent, followed by political risk. Such a high-risk risk rating may be related to Djibouti's rank on the corruption index, which came higher than that of Zambia.

To properly assess how host governments and investment exporters may be exposed to corruption, it is essential to examine the investment exporter's attitudes in the region in general by probing how one of the most significant capital-exporting states, China, is behaving in the region the one side and then probe the Djiboutian government's attitudes towards corruption on the other.

One of the most prominent investors in the African region is China. The magnitude of Chinese FDI in Africa can be seen in reports that suggest up to 10,000 Chinese companies operate across the African continent (Solomon & Frechette, 2018). Chinese regional investments were spread across numerous sectors, including transportation, port construction, and management. The aggressive investment strategy in the region is directly linked to China's Belt and Road Initiative, whereby East Asia will be connected to Europe via a network of highways, energy pipelines, railways and streamlined border crossings (Chatzky & McBride, 2020).

This led the African region to be regarded as a lucrative investment destination by Chinese companies. Notably, the attractive investment climate and market opportunities Zambia and Djibouti offered attracted foreign investors from states that do not necessarily have bribery or corruption-related codes of conduct -- states like India and China, whose investors have been reported to engage in bribery practices in the form of political party financing and providing what they refer to as *facilitation fees* (OECD, 2012).

Djibouti attracted FDI across different sectors and from all parts of the world. Notably, Chinese investments flooded Djibouti. One of the main modes of entry of Chinese investment into Djibouti was the investment made in the Obock International Airport, the construction of the international free trade zone and the Doraleh port, among other projects amounting to more than $14 billion in loans and investments (Siebt, 2021). Moreover, the Chinese tech giant Huawei is linking East Africa with South Asia via an undersea fibre-optic cable financed by the China Construction Bank ("Huawei Marine and Tropical Science Commences Work", 2017). China also holds over 70% of Djiboutian debt (ibid). Such magnitude of Chinese investment has been regarded as one of Djibouti's weaknesses, where it was seen as a state dependent on Chinese investments (COFACE on Djibouti, 2021). Such dependence can be observed through the list of infrastructure projects financed by China's Export Credit Agency (ECA), the Export-Import Bank of China.

Several foreign investors reported instances where they were expected to meet some non-financial requirements, including hiring certain employees to receive government procurement contracts ("2020 Investment Climate Statements: Djibouti", 2020).

Perhaps the case of the multinational telecom giant Ericsson in Djibouti is one of the prominent examples involving corruption and FDI. Several employees of the giant's subsidiaries in Egypt were recorded to have bribed government officials and the Attorney General of Djibouti to win a contract with the country's telecommunication operator Telecom SA (*United States of America v Ericsson Egypt LTD*; 2019) (Rolander, 2021). This particular case presents the perfect example of how investors from what are regarded as developed states with low corruption rates could still engage in corrupt practices to help facilitate their investments if presented with the opportunity.

Another controversial case that allegedly probed state corruption was that of DP World, a UAE port operator, and Port de Djibouti S.A. (PDSA), the Djibouti Port company that the China Merchant Port Company partially owns. In the agreement between the two companies, DP and PDSA, DP was granted the right to operate the Doraleh Container Terminal through a Joint Venture. However, the government of Djibouti decided to seize DP World's shares, leading to several arbitral proceedings filed against PDSA in the UK and Hong Kong. The arbitral decisions in London's LCIA were ruled in favour of DP World. The notable thing in these cases, filed by DP World, was that the counterparty has always been PDSA. However, in the lawsuit filed by DP World in Hong Kong, the counterparty was China Merchants Port rather than PDSA. The significance of this particular court case was the allegations made by DP World that the Djiboutian government engaged in corrupt practices whereby China Merchants Port caused, according to DP World, the Djiboutian government to take control over Doraleh Container Terminal and nationalise it ("Legal Battle for Control of Djibouti Ports Comes to Hong Kong", 2019).

As the African Development Bank estimated, such practices by Djiboutian and African politicians and elites resulted in an estimated loss of over 300 billion dollars (Nduku and Tenamwenye, 2014).

Upon sampling these corruption-related examples from Djibouti, it is essential to examine the measures both states are undertaking to combat corruption and to probe the role played by the investment exporting country in the fight against such practices, whether through codes of conduct or conditions imposed on investors by their public investment loan or insurance providers.

Combating Corruption

The notion of combating corruption has been regarded as a top priority for governments across the globe, both in the context of countries attracting Foreign Direct Investment (FDI) and those dispatching it. Various strategies and measures have been introduced, ostensibly falling into two overarching categories: legal and non-legal approaches.

Among the non-legal approaches to curbing corruption are initiatives like education, accountability mechanisms, merit-based appointments, and ongoing audits ("Anti-corruption in developing countries"). These strategies promote ethical behaviour, enhance transparency, and ensure responsible decision-making. On the legal front, governments have crafted laws and regulations that criminalise corrupt practices, incentivise whistleblowers to come forward, and underscore the gravity of corruption involving government officials.

However, it is vital to analyse the effectiveness of these measures critically. While legal mechanisms are crucial, their enforcement often hinges on political will, institutional capacity, and adherence to the rule of law. Merely enacting laws is not enough; they must be effectively implemented and consistently enforced to deter corrupt practices. Additionally, non-legal measures like education and accountability mechanisms often require cultural shifts and changes in societal norms, which can be challenging and time-consuming to achieve.

On the other hand, legal measures come in the form of laws and regulations that criminalise corrupt practices and encourage whistleblowers to come forward with any information they may have on corrupt practices involving government officials.

FDI-importing states and FDI-exporting states have enacted laws and regulations to reduce and combat corruption. For example, regarding FDI-importing states, Djibouti has recently enacted Law No. 03/AN/13/7L to implement the UN Convention against corruption. Articles 15, 16, 18 and 21 of the new law aim to criminalise and combat corruption. These anti-corruption laws do not only target state officials but their family members as well. However, the country still lacks effective mechanisms to combat corruption despite these measures. For example, when defining Public Officials, the United Nations Convention Against Corruption (UNCAC) covers persons who hold a legislative, executive, administrative, or judicial office, perform a public function or provide a public service, regardless of their status, level, or nationality. On the other hand, Djibouti does not define who public officials are according to its new anti-corruption law; instead, it relies on those available in the Penal Code, which is loose in comparison.

The country, which ranked 128th internationally by Transparency International in 2021 compared to 94th in 2013 (Corruption Perceptions Index, 2019; Transparancy, 2018), has required that public and private companies in Djibouti design codes of conduct which prohibits bribery of public officials (Articles 18–19; Law No. 03/AN/13/7L).

In its fight against corruption, Djibouti established the National Anti-Corruption Commission, which is entrusted with evaluating the state's anti-corruption measures and their effectiveness (The Commission was established by Act No. 03/AN/13/7 L of 16 July 2013).

Perhaps some of the main criticisms of Djibouti's measures to clamp down on corruption are the lack of definition of the public officials, the lack of State liability and the lack of targeted regulations to counter conflict of interest, particularly in government procurement (Conference of the States Parties to the United Nations Convention Against Corruption, 2017) (2018 Investment Climate Statements: Djibouti, 2018). Notwithstanding, the only available definition for public officials is found in the Penal Code, whereby public officials, according to the law, hold public authority or are entrusted with public service (Code Penal de Djibouti, Paragraphs 2 and 6, Articles 200 and 206). Furthermore, the lack of consistent prosecution or punishment for corrupt practices is another main hurdle curtailing the development of effective anti-corruption measures in the country. Such practice whereby corruption was enabled without significant repercussions may be attributed to bad governance. For that, and in light of the new anti-corruption laws, nationwide campaigns promoting ethical behaviour and condemning corruption and corrupt practices are the best way to complement these laws.

Through such mechanisms, the general public can become more aware of corruption's damage to society. Furthermore, the newly established agencies entrusted with combating corruption should be given more liberty, enabling them to chase corruption and corrupt individuals. These are some of the internal measures that Djibouti can undertake. Some external measures exporting states started implementing to fight corruption.

Measuring the effectiveness of these measures undertaken by Djibouti may prove somewhat challenging. This may be attributed to a lack of available data or how reliable it is, which may lead to inaccurate measurement of the overall effectiveness of these measures. According to data from 2020 and 2021, Djibouti had no recorded bribery-related investigation cases (UK Government, 2021).

Regarding FDI-exporting countries, the US and the UK were ranked 23rd and 12th internationally in 2020 (Corruption Perceptions Index, 2019) and enacted laws that have extraterritorial effects aimed at combating corruption and restricting illicit practices by their investors. For example, the UK enacted the Bribery Act 2010, which criminalises bribery and corruption undertaken by UK investors or persons close to the UK (Section 12, UK Bribery Act 2010). This Act has an extraterritorial effect and particularly applies to offences cited under its 1st, 2nd, 6th, 7th and 12th sections.

Like the UK, companies investing overseas are bound by the Foreign Corrupt Practices Act (FCPA) in the United States. This Act makes it unlawful for investors to pay foreign government officials if they affect the official's decision-making (US Foreign Corrupt Practices Act 15, 1977, USC § 78dd-1). Additionally, US legislation applies to companies listed in US Stock exchanges and companies using US correspondent accounts to facilitate US dollar transactions ("SEC Enforcement Actions: FCPA Cases", 2021; Diamant at al., 2019).

China, which came in 80th on the Corruption Perception Index, does not have a dedicated law, statute or code to oversee its investors' conduct overseas. Instead, their move to combat engaging in corrupt practices overseas by its companies or any of its individuals for commercial purposes is criminalised in Chinese Criminal Law and under the Anti-unfair Competition Law (Law Against Unfair Competition of the People's Republic of China, 1993) (Chinese Criminal Law of the People's Republic of China, 1997, Article 164) (ibid., Article 7).

On a broader level, international movements were directed at combating corruption, like the United Nations Convention against Corruption. This landmark instrument, adopted by the UN in 2003, recognised the cross-border nature of corruption and included a list of punitive and preventive measures to counter corruption (United Nations Convention Against Corruption, 2004, Articles 5–14 and 15–44). Perhaps one of the main recommendations this instrument makes, which Djibouti is a party to, is calling for adequate access to public information (United Nations Convention Against Corruption, 2004, Articles 10 & 13).

Another critical international effort to combat corruption is the Convention on Combating Bribery of Foreign Public Officials in International Business Transactions, otherwise known as the OECD Anti-Bribery Convention. This legally binding Convention exclusively focuses on the bribe grantor rather than the bribe recipient. Thus, the signatory member states to this Convention have contributed to two-thirds of the world's exports (*Stocktaking of Business Integrity and Anti-Bribery Legislation*, 2012).

In addition, FDI-exporting states typically encourage their investors to expand their operations and export their goods and services overseas. This is done through the export credit programmes offered domestically to their businesses. Export credit providers facilitate FDI through such programmes through their loans to investors. Export Credit Agencies (ECAs) also provide insurance against several risks these investors may encounter.

One of the prominent examples of Export Credit Agencies is that of the United Kingdom. The UK Export Finance (UKEF) is regarded as one of the oldest programmes and offers services to UK investors wanting to invest overseas (Saghir, 2018). This ECA requires any investors seeking their support not to engage in practices breaching UK policies, including those related to corruption and money laundering (UK Export Finance: Financial Crime Compliance, 2021). Similarly, the US Export-Import Bank also conditions that the US companies seeking its services and intending to operate overseas be familiar with the FCPA (EXIM Bank Policies).

Such measures undertaken by loan and insurance providers were thought to help further limit instances in which investors engage in corrupt practices in their overseas ventures.

With that in mind, combating corruption should be seen as a multifaceted challenge that extends beyond legal frameworks and involves complex cultural, institutional, and systemic aspects. While the efforts to combat corruption through legal and non-legal means are noteworthy, the effectiveness of these measures varies significantly based on the political landscape, the level of governance, and the commitment of involved parties. It is imperative to recognise that addressing corruption requires a holistic approach that encompasses legal reforms, robust enforcement, cultural changes, and comprehensive international collaboration.

Conclusion

The endemic of corruption can be found worldwide, and individuals and investors alike may be exposed to it. Understanding the root causes of corruption and its true nature would help investors looking to expand their operations overseas understand the type of corruption risk encountered in the various investment destinations and its actual cost.

When foreign investors look for new markets, they factor in several considerations to help understand the cost involved in entering this market. In the risk management strategy, foreign investors encounter several risks, including corruption. However, corruption as a risk has a variable nature. It is a political risk, mainly because it involves bribing government officials to influence their decision-making to admit the investor or to award the foreign investor the right to supply the local government. It could also be a commercial risk once an intermediary is involved who is, in return, connected to a government official to influence their decision-making. In both scenarios, corruption remains an illegal and unethical practice. However, understanding what it truly is would help investors properly factor in their investments' costs and risks.

The African continent remains attractive to foreign investors (UNCTAD, 2019). With its richness of natural resources, the region offers lucrative investment potential to investors. This has led many foreign investors, particularly from India and China, who may not have comprehensive codes of conduct, to criminalise corruption and regulate how their investors conduct their operations overseas.

Despite being a risky investment destination, Djibouti has attracted many investors in different sectors. Like many other African states, Djibouti suffered from corruption. It introduced movements to combat such practices, mainly because corruption could potentially deter new investors from entering their markets. However, The country's efforts are insufficient, requiring a more robust response to corruption and better deterrence mechanisms. One main area that still requires attention is state liability for corruption and properly tackling conflict of interest through dedicated comprehensive legislation. These are a few ways to improve the country's current initiative further. The new anti-corruption legislation is a good starting point, but the importance lies in the legislation's applicability. The effectiveness of such measures lies in changing the cultural perception of corruption.

On the other hand, the collaborative approach to combat corruption has resulted in capital-exporting countries imposing rules of engagement for their investors while going overseas.

In that sense, one of the first mentions of transnational bribery was presented in the OECD Declaration on International Investment and Multinational Enterprises of 1976. This was followed by the International Chamber of Commerce's Recommendations to Combat Extortion and Bribery in Business Transactions of 1977, where the report stated how corruption does not "constitute a fundamental problem" in matters related to international trade development. However, the report regarded this act as a "social evil".

Perhaps the first comprehensive effort directed at regulating how investors and businesses engage overseas is that of the US. The FCPA of 1977 has criminalised corrupt practices that American businesses and investors may engage in overseas. Though this is a national law directed at US citizens and US-registered businesses, it had an extraterritorial effect, allowing the States to prosecute any citizen, US business, US-listed company and even foreign companies using US corresponding banks to facilitate US-dollar transactions that have engaged in corrupt practices overseas under Act. This was followed by the OECD's new initiative to combat corruption in 1994, which handled commercial transactions exceptionally well.

Though not all capital-exporting states had a detailed approach to combating corruption, like the US and the UK, they still covered transnational bribery and corruption within their existing legislation, similar to the Chinese approach. Alongside this international effort in combating bribery and corruption, these have been complemented by national initiatives of host states. Djibouti has enacted legislation that restricts and criminalises the acceptance of bribery by public officials.

Moreover, capital-exporting states have undertaken further actions to reduce corruption. Through the loans and insurance policies offered by Export Credit Agencies of capital-exporting states, companies seeking these services undertake to refrain from engaging in corrupt practices while venturing overseas. As such, these agencies clarified in their policies that companies should not breach anti-corruption laws while investing overseas. Such an approach can be seen in the UK through the UK Export Finance (UKEF) and in the US through the US Export-Import Bank (Exim Bank). The UKEF, for example, in addition to the due diligence it conducts on applicants, assesses the applicant and the state where the applicant will invest. Furthermore, exporters using UKEF's facilities must disclose fees or commissions paid to intermediaries facilitating investment/business transactions. Similarly, the US ExIm Bank conducts thorough due diligence on applicants, assessing applicants and states where the applicants are interested in investing. Additionally, the ExIm Bank provides exporters training on how to comply with anti-bribery laws and regulations.

Though both the US ExIm Bank and UKEF have similar measures and cooperate on anti-corruption practices, ExIm Bank applies extra rigorous measures. ExIm Bank may cancel the policy of an exporter if they found the exporter was involved in an act of bribery.

With these national and international efforts directed at combating corruption, the question yet to be answered is how effectively these initiatives have reduced corrupt practices in Djibouti. So far, it seems to be ineffective. However, whether this will change or not is a different question.

References

Laws, Statutes and International Conventions

Code Penal de Djibouti [1995] (Djibouti Criminal Law) [French Language]. Found at: www.presidence.dj/PresidenceOld/LES%20TEXTES/decr0038pr95.htm Accessed on the 19th of November 2021.

Convention on Combating Bribery of Foreign Public Officials in International Business Transactions. Found at: www.oecd.org/corruption-integrity/explore/oecd-standards/anti-bribery-convention/ Accessed on the 19th of November 2021.

Criminal Law of the People's Republic of China [1997]. Found at: www.fmprc.gov.cn/ce/cgvienna/eng/dbtyw/jdwt/crimelaw/t209043.htm Accessed on the 19th of November 2021.

Law Against Unfair Competition of the People's Republic of China [1993] (Chinese et al. Law). Found at: www.wipo.int/edocs/lexdocs/laws/en/cn/cn011en.pdf Accessed on the 19th of November 2021.

Law No. 03/AN/13/7L (Anti-Corruption Law of Djibouti) [French Language]. Found at: www.droit-afrique.com/upload/doc/djibouti/Djibouti-Loi-2013-03-corruption.pdf Accessed on the 19th of November 2021.

OECD Declaration on International Investment and Multinational Enterprises [1976]. Found at: www.oecd.org/daf/inv/investment-policy/ConsolidatedDeclarationTexts.pdf Accessed on the 19th of November 2021.

UK Bribery Act [2010]. Found at: www.legislation.gov.uk/ukpga/2010/23/contents Accessed on the 19th of November 2021.

United Nations Convention Against Corruption [2004]. Found at: www.unodc.org/documents/brussels/UN_Convention_Against_Corruption.pdf Accessed on the 19th of November 2021.

US Foreign Corrupt Practices Act 15 USC § 78dd-1 (FCPA) [1977]. Found at: www.law.cornell.edu/uscode/text/15/78dd-1 Accessed on the 19th of November 2021.

Cases

United States of America v Ericsson Egypt LTD (December 2019). Found at: www.justice.gov/opa/press-release/file/1272156/download Accessed on the 15th of June 2021.

Books

Haque, N. U., Nelson, M., and Matheison, D. J. (2000). Rating Africa: The Economic and Political Content of Risk Indicators. In P. Collier and C. Pattillo (Eds.), *Investment and Risk in Africa* (pp. 33–70). New York: St Martin's Press.

Mbaku, J. (2010). *Corruption in Africa: Causes, Consequences, and Cleanups*. Lexington Books.

Munyai, A. (2020). *Overcoming the Corruption Conundrum in Africa: A Socio-legal Perspective*. Cambridge et al.

Nduku, E. and Tenamwenye, J. (ed.)., (2014) *Corruption in Africa: A Threat to Justice and Sustainable Peace*, (Globethics.net Focus 14, December 2014).

Rubins, N. and Kinsella, S. (2005). *International Investment, Political Risk, and Dispute Resolution: A Practitioner's Guide*. USA: Oxford University Press.

Saghir, W. (2018). *Foreign Direct Investment Risks and Export Credit Agencies: A Practitioner's Guide*. Willdy et al.

Tanzler, D., Maras, K. and Giannakopolous. (2012). *The Social Construction of Corruption in Europe*, Law, Crime and Culture Series. Ashgate Publishing.

Wei, S. J. (2000). *Corruption, Composition of Capital Flows and Currency Crises*. World Bank.

Articles

Argandoña, A. (2006). *The United Nations Convention against Corruption and its Impact on International Companies*, IESE Business School – University of Navarra Working Paper no 656. Found at: https://papers.ssrn.com/sol3/papers.cfm?abstract_id=960662 Accessed on 9th of December 2020

Basu, A. and Srinivasan, K. (2002). "Foreign Direct Investment in Africa Some Case Studies" IMF Working Paper WP/02/61 (IMF,), 4.

Busse, M. and Hefker, M. (2005). Political Risk, Institutions and Foreign Direct Investment. *SSRN Electronic Journal*. https://dx.doi.org/10.2139/ssrn.704283

Campos, J. E., Lien, D. and Pradhan, S. (1999). The Impact of Corruption on Investment: Predictability Matters. *World Development*, 27 (6), 1059–1067.

Diamant, M. S., Sullivan, C. W. H. and Smith, J. H. (2019). *FCPA Enforcement against U.S. and Non-U.S. Companies* (8 Mich. Bus & Entrepreneurial L. Rev 353. Found at: https://repository.law.umich.edu/mbelr/vol8/iss2/5 Accessed on the 20th of November 2021

Groenendijk, N. (1997). "A Principal-Agent Model of Corruption" *Crime, Law & Social Change*, 27, 207–229.

Harding, J. (2014). Corruption or Guanxi? Differentiating Between the Legitimate, Unethical, and Corrupt Activities of Chinese Government Officials. *UCLA Pacific Basin Law Journal*, 31(2). Found at: https://escholarship.org/uc/item/0p8650mm Accessed on 20th of June 2021.

Marquette, H. and Peiffer, C. (2018). Grappling with the "Real Politics" of Systemic Corruption: Theoretical Debates Versus "Real-World" Functions. *Governance*, 31(3), 499–514.

Rose-Ackerman, R. "The Political Economy of Corruption" Institute for International Economics. Found at: www.piie.com/publications/chapters_preview/12/2iie2334.pdf Accessed on the 10th June 2021.

Sanz, N. (2016). The Moral Dimension of Corruption: A Theoretical Framework. *Journal of Business Ethics*, 138(1), 65–74.

Shleifer, A. and Vishny, R. (1993). Corruption. *Quarterly Journal of Economics*, 108(3), 599–617.

Smarzynska, B. and Wei, S. J. (2000). "Corruption and Compensation of Foreign Direct Investment: Firm-Level Evidence" *(National Bureau of Economic Research)*, 2. Found at: www.nber.org/system/files/working_papers/w7969/w7969.pdf Accessed on the 2nd of February 2021.

Vertin, Z. (June 2020). "Great Power Rivalry in the Red Sea: China's Experiment in Djibouti and Implications for the United States", *Global China & Brookings Institute Doha*.

Wei, S. (1997). "Why is Corruption so much more Taxing than Tax? Arbitrariness Kills. NBER Working Paper 6255. Cambridge, MA.

Other Publications

Conference of the States Parties to the United Nations Convention against Corruption (UN, 23 January 2017). Found at: https://uncaccoalition.org/files/Cycle1-Executive-Summary-Djibouti.pdf Accessed on the 20th of November 2021.

Corruption: A Glossary of International Criminal Standards (OECD, 2007). p 19. Found at: www.oecd.org/corruption/anti-bribery/39532693.pdf Accessed on 20th of January 2021.

Recommendations to Combat Extortion and Bribery in Business Transactions [ICC 1977].

Stocktaking of Business Integrity and Anti-Bribery Legislation, Policies and Practices in Twenty African Countries (OECD, AFDB 2012) p. 22.

Online Sources and Website

2018 Investment Climate Statements: Djibouti (US Department of State) Found at: https://2017-2021.state.gov/reports/2018-investment-climate-statements/djibouti/index.html Accessed on the 20th of November 2021.

2020 Investment Climate Statements: Djibouti (US Department of State) Found at: www.state.gov/reports/2020-investment-climate-statements/djibouti/ Accessed on the 20th of May 2021.

2021 Investment Climate Statement: Djibouti, US Department of State. Found at: www.state.gov/reports/2021-investment-climate-statements/djibouti/ Accessed on the 20th of June 2022.

Anti-corruption in developing countries (Canadian Government Online) Found at: www.international.gc.ca/world-monde/issues_development-enjeux_developpement/human_rights-droits_homme/anti_corruption-lutte_corruption.aspx?lang=eng Accessed on the 10th of June 2021.

Bray, J. (2007). "Facing up to Corruption 2007: A Practical Business Guide" (Simmons & Simmons) p. 5–6 Found at: www.criticaleye.com/inspiring/insights-servfile.cfm?id=170 Accessed on the 10th of May 2021.

Chatzky, A. and McBride, J., "China's Massive Belt and Road Initiative" (Council on Foreign Relations Online, January 28, 2020). Found at: www.cfr.org/backgrounder/chinas-massive-belt-and-road-initiative Accessed on the 19th of November 2021.

COFACE on Djibouti (COFACE Online, February 2021) Found at: www.coface.com/Economic-Studies-and-Country-Risks/Djibouti Last Accessed on 19th November 2021.

Corruption Perceptions Index 2019 (Online). Found at: www.transparency.org/en/cpi/2019/index/zmb Accessed on the 10th of May 2021.

"Djibouti" (Euler et al.) Found at: www.eulerhermes.com/en_GL/economic-research/country-reports/Djibouti.html Last accessed on the 19th of November 2021.

EXIM Bank Policies (US Ex-Im Bank Online). Found at: www.exim.gov/policies Accessed on the 15th of June 2021.

Fadiman, J. A. (1986). "A Traveler's Guide to Gift and Bribes" *Harvard Business Review*. Found at: https://hbr.org/1986/07/a-travelers-guide-to-gifts-and-bribes Accessed on the 15th of May 2021.

Huawei Marine and Tropical Science Commences Work on constructing the PEACE Submarine Cable Linking South Asia with East Africa (Huawei Online, November 2017). Found at: www.huawei.com/en/news/2017/11/PEACE-Submarine-Cable-SouthAsia-EastAfrica Accessed on 19th November 2021.

Legal Battle for Control of Djibouti Ports Comes to Hong Kong (Bloomberg Online, February 13th, 2019). Found at: www.bloomberg.com/press-releases/2019-02-13/legal-battle-for-control-of-djibouti-ports-comes-to-hong-kong Accessed on the 20th of November 2021.

Madden, P. (October 2019). "Figure of the week: Foreign direct investment in Africa" Brookings Institute Online.

OECD. (2012). International Drivers of Corruption: A Tool for Analysis. www.oecd.org/dac/international-drivers-of-corruption-9789264167513-en.htm

Odusola, A. "Investing in Africa is Sound Business and a Sustainable Corporate Strategy". UNDP Regional Bureau for Africa. Found at: www.un.org/africarenewal/web-features/investing-africa-sound-business-and-sustainable-corporate-strategy Last accessed on the 9th of May 2021.

Rolander, N. "Sweden Charges Four Former Ericsson Employees With Bribery" (Bloomberg Online, 26 May 2021). Found at: www.bloomberg.com/news/articles/2021-05-26/sweden-charges-four-former-ericsson-employees-with-bribery Accessed on the 15th of June 2021.

Sakala, N., "Heightened corruption perception influencing drop in FDI – Saasa" (Diggers News Online, December 2019) Found at: https://diggers.news/local/2019/12/09/heightened-corruption-perception-influencing-drop-in-fdi-saasa/ Accessed on the 9th of May 2021.

Santander Online (May 2021). "Djibouti: Foreign Investment". Found at: https://santandertrade.com/en/portal/establish-overseas/djibouti/investing-3?url_de_la_page=%2Fen%2Fportal%2Festablish-overseas%2Fdjibouti%2Finvesting-3&&actualiser_id_banque=oui&id_banque=0&memoriser_choix=memoriser Last accessed on the 9th of May 2021.

"SEC Enforcement Actions: FCPA Cases" (SEC Online, September 29th, 2021) Found at: www.sec.gov/enforce/sec-enforcement-actions-fcpa-cases Accessed on the 20th of November 2021.

Siebt, S. "Djibouti-China Marriage 'Slowly Unravelling' as Investment Project Disappoints" (France24 Online, 9 May 2021). Found at: www.france24.com/en/africa/20210409-djibouti-china-marriage-slowly-unravelling-as-investment-project-disappoints Accessed on 1st of June 2021.

Škrbec, J. (2016). *Corruption Risk Management: Addendum to the Risk Management Guidelines*, (European Union) Found at: www.dksk.mk/fileadmin/user_upload/1_CORRUPTION_RISK_MANAGEMENT_-_Adendum.pdf Last accessed on the 9th of May 2021.

Solomon, S. and Frechette, C. "Corruption is Wasting Chinese Money in Africa" (Foreign Policy Online, 13 September 2018). Found at: https://foreignpolicy.com/2018/09/13/corruption-is-wasting-chinese-money-in-africa/ Accessed on the 15th of May 2021.

Transparancy. (2018). www.transparency.org/en/cpi/2018/index/dji Accessed on the 10th of May 2021.

Transparency International's website: www.transparency.org/en/cpi/2013/index/dji Last accessed on the 21st of October 2022.

UK Export Finance: Financial Crime Compliance (April 2021). Found at: www.gov.uk/guidance/uk-export-finance-financial-crime-compliance Accessed on the 30th of May 2021.

UNCTAD (2019). Foreign direct investment to Africa defies global slump, rises 11%. Found at: https://unctad.org/news/foreign-direct-investment-africa-defies-global-slump-rises-11 Accessed on the 10th of January 2021.

UNCTAD (2020). *World Investment Report 2020: International Production Beyond Pandemic*. United Nations.

UK Government (2021). UK Sanctions Relating to Global Anti-Corruption [online]. Found at: www.gov.uk/government/collections/uk-sanctions-relating-to-global-anti-corruption Accessed on the 5th of August 2021

US Export-Import Bank (2021). Policies. Found at: www.exim.gov/policies Accessed on the 5th of August 2023.

8
DEBUNKING THE DEMAND-DRIVEN MYTH OF CORRUPTION

The Case of the Saint Louis Scandal in Mauritius

Sanjeev Narrainen

Introduction

Mauritius is a small island state with a population of 1.3 million (Rahardja and Swaroop, 2024). The country's economy has made great strides since its independence in 1968 and was classified as the upper-middle income in 2021. Mauritius performs well on various political and economic indicators relative to many African countries. It has retained its first position in 54 African countries in the 2022 Mo Ibrahim Index on African Governance. The economy is projected to grow by 5% in 2023 and 4.2% in 2024, thanks to its blossoming tourism industry (Africa et al., 2023). Over the past few decades, Mauritius has built a glowing international reputation. It is regarded as one of the best-managed democracies in Africa, as a place to do business, and as a country where the rule of law is upheld. However, recent reports have begun to challenge this "picture-perfect" image. Corruption in Mauritius appears to be ubiquitous and takes many forms: from petty bribery involving public officials to massive contract fraud; straight-up embezzlement to complicated money laundering schemes; from privileges for politicians to award of state lands to cronyism.

Recent scandals reported in the media during the COVID-19 pandemic have highlighted serious concerns about transparency, accountability and integrity in public administration. A series of recent scandals had caused public outrage and threatened to harm the country's reputation as an African model of good governance. In the Betamax case the Board of the Privy Council (July 2021) showed corruption using high political connections. Betamax was awarded the contract for fuel transportation for the State of Mauritius when the Labor Party was in power. The contract was rescinded under the present government. In addition to the Rs 5.68 billion in damages paid to Betamax, the government must find the necessary funds to pay legal costs before the Supreme Court and the Privy Council. The recent nominations of the Director-General of the Anticorruption Agency, the Governor of the Central Bank, and the CEO of the State Bank of Mauritius to crucial government institutions have been much criticised (L'Express, 2021).

Mauritians view their country as marred with corruption, one where political corruption dominates daily occurrences. However, famous – and even official and academic – narratives about corruption in Mauritius lack a common framework for understanding an expansive and varied topic. In the last two decades, Mauritius was referenced as an African country with innovative laws to fight corruption and money laundering. Unfortunately, this seems to be the case no longer. Citizens have a negative opinion of the effectiveness of the anticorruption agency and its poor prosecutorial performance (Sihombing et al., 2023; Peerthum et al., 2020). Some highly politically connected Mauritians have developed savvy but unethical methods to adapt to the government's approach to fighting corruption. Those who adopt such means in the local dialect are commonly called *chatwas*.

This article explains how Mauritius's corruption works in a public contract to construct a power station (Saint Louis Power Station). It also shows why it is essential to focus on the internal dynamic of the private sector (the contractor in this case), as the corruption can flow from the supply side given that there are already anti-corruption mechanisms/laws to deal with public-sector corruption. It categorises how corruption occurs, stipulating the many different types of behaviours, techniques, and tactics corrupt actors use in line with Nwozor et al. (2023), who echo the need to create an intolerant public attitude towards corruption to be able to monitor it and respond to the development and improvement of criminal techniques. This chapter builds upon the existing Mauritian-focused corruption literature and the work done by scholars and practitioners seeking to define and categorise different types of corruption. It analyses the context of corruption in Mauritius and debunks the myth that corporations are demand-driven.

The challenges of corruption in development projects

Corruption represents a significant risk in international development projects (Diallo & Thuillier, 2010; Leiderer, 2012), as it has the potential to compromise desired development outcomes (Kramer, 2007; U4, 2016). Several opinion polls worldwide have shown widespread public concern that some development assistance is wasted due to corruption (World Bank, 2003; KPMG, 2015; TI, 2017). While these projects greatly assist countries in meeting their development goals, unfortunately, studies reveal that they may also be lightning rods for corruption (World Bank, 2009; ADB, 2017; AfDB,

2018). Unfortunately, the risks of corruption and malpractices are more prevalent in development assistance projects because of their complexities and uncertainties (Khang & Moe, 2008). The energy sector is not an exception. Moreover, it can increase business costs (Tekin-Konu, 2006). This can be a severe issue as these MDBs are mobilising funds to address country-level infrastructural gaps.

Corporate corruption essentially refers to corruption facilitated by the contracting firms representing the private sector. In this scenario, the contracting firms seek opportunities to engage in corrupt activities with high-level public officials for advantages and benefits in the long run. The perpetrators of these corrupt acts are from the supply side, the contracting firms supplying to public officials, or other intermediaries.

Why is corruption a problem in development projects?

According to the World Bank (2015), corruption can increase the cost of projects by 20% to 25%. Undoubtedly, the cost of corruption in international development projects is significant (Gyimah-Brempong, 2002; World Bank, 2015). With the sanctioning of prominent corporations such as Siemens, Alstom, and SNC Lanvalin by Multilateral Development Banks (MDBs) in recent years, it is imperative to address the issue of corruption from the supply side. Corruption, in any form, is detrimental to the effectiveness of humanitarian aid. Isopi and Mattesini (2008, p. 37) examine the relationship between aid and corruption. According to Isopi and Mattesini, corruption depends upon the 'political and institutional environment of the recipient country', and more hazards arise from corrupt bureaucracies, which divert aid from its intended source.

The duality of corruption

Literature has classified corruption as a public-sector problem (Rose-Ackerman, 1996; World Bank, 1997). However, some studies have also argued that corrupt practices are a significant feature of private-sector activities (Harsh, 1993; Bakre, 2007; Sikka, 2008; Otusanya, 2010). There needs to be both a receiver and a supplier for corporate corruption to occur. In development projects, the demand side deals with corrupt institutions and public officials who, for instance, demand bribes to conduct business transactions, whereas the supply side deals with those who instigate or facilitate corrupt practices. Thus, the two perpetuate a corrupt system. Government interventions in private organisations significantly cause corruption (Donahue, 1989; Gillespie & Okruhlik, 1991; Lambsdorff, 2006).

In the dominant International Business (IB) domain, the common assumption is that governments are instigators of corruption to which multinational corporations (MNCs) may have to comply (Habib & Zurawicki, 2002; Rodriguez et al., 2005; Uhlenbruck et al., 2006; Brouthers et al., 2008; Cuervo-Cazurra, 2016; Petrou & Thanos, 2014). For this reason, corruption is treated as exogenous to the MNCs. It is viewed more as a feature of the host-country environment in which the MNCs' decision-makers face the dilemma between risks and opportunities. Admittedly, much of the focus is on the impact of host-country corruption on the MNCs, with bribes and kickbacks demanded by public officials being the only dimension of corruption examined.

While from a public-sector perspective, corruption is often portrayed as an individual-driven phenomenon (Banfield, 1975), on the other hand, from a business perspective, it is supply-side. Such corruption transactions are either unavoidable for a firm's operations or as an investment for privileged treatments from the public sector (Banfield, 1975; Martin et al., 2007). Nevertheless, few studies have examined corruption at a broad corporate level as acts committed on behalf of the corporate and for corporate benefits (for example, Baucus and Near, 1991; Brief et al., 2001; Hill et al., 1992; Sonnerfeld & Lawrence, 1978; Pinto et al., 2008; Voliotis, 2017). However, the corporate perspective remains an area that has been underexplored (David-Barrett, 2017) simply due to the ignorance that these corporations can be instigators or facilitators of corruption for their corporate benefits.

Understanding the 'how' and 'why' of corruption

A fundamental question preoccupying academic research into corruption is how corrupt relationships arise between the parties involved (Button et al., 2018; Hock, 2018). This research was influenced by the lack of insight into how corporate corruption evolves. While the conspiratorial relationship may not be difficult to establish for petty corruption involving individuals (Fletcher & Herrmann, 2012; Graycar & Sidebottom, 2012), this may not be so for corporations (United Nations, 2013; Graycar & Prenzler, 2013; Button, Shepherd and Dean, 2018). Legal and cultural variations further compound the problem in the international context (Melgar et al., 2010).

Methodological approach

In order to empirically investigate the determinants of corporate corruption, it is imperative to have a research design that will capture the multidimensionality and complexity of the phenomenon. In order to grasp the challenges posed by the research, a mixed-method approach is most appropriate to capture the different perspectives of the phenomenon under study. Using the research methods used in this article has enabled us to understand better the dynamic of corruption occurring from the supply side.

In a similar vein, it is essential to understand the different individuals, third parties, agents and organisations that connive in orchestrating these corrupt schemes (Button et al., 2018; Hock, 2018; Tillman, 2009) in order to conjure up the whole scheme of corporate involvement in corruption.

The quantitative survey targets sanctioned firms cross-debarred by the MDBs that have not entered into a negotiation agreement process before being sanctioned. The survey was conducted in 2020, and the author collected data as part of his doctorate thesis. Forty-three out of 125 respondents responded to the survey questionnaire, representing 34.4%. With the survey questionnaire, there is an opportunity to investigate the perception of sanctioned corporations and better understand their motivations for corporate corruption. Using real case scenarios, a case study method is used to understand the 'how' and 'why' firms engaged in corrupt practices (Yin, 1994). The cases involve development projects.

Justifications for using mixed methods

The mixed-method approach has the merit of providing an analytical framework to uncover the micro-level interactions of individuals while considering macro-level institutional embeddedness (Bandelj, 2012). The principles and rationale for using the qualitative and quantitative tools are outlined below. A mixed method is broadly defined as:

> Research in which the investigator collects and analyses data integrates the findings and draws inferences using both qualitative and quantitative approaches or methods in a single study or a program of inquiry.
> *(Tashakkori and Creswell, 2007, p. 4)*

The Saint Louis Gate

In June 2020, a corruption scandal dubbed St Louis Gate came to light and involved political appointees of the government, board members of the Central Electricity Board (CEB) and the Danish firm Burmeister & Wain Scandinavian Contractor (BWSC). In 2014, a tender package was issued by the CEB which was cancelled and reissued in 2015 for a significant upgrade of an existing diesel power station at St. Louis, on the outskirts of the capital city of Port Louis. BWSC was awarded the contract, but a whistleblower alerted the financier African Development Bank (ADB) about the bribes received by several CEB employees through an intermediary. ADB investigated the claims and excluded BWSC from all future work for 21 months. In June 2020, after this was raised in Parliament, the entire Management Team of CEB was replaced. By the end of June 2020, Prime Minister Pravind Jugnauth dismissed the Deputy Prime Minister from his Cabinet. The Deputy PM also held the portfolio of Minister of Energy. The dismissal came after the PM received a report from the ADB alleging that bribes had been paid to various parties via an intermediary during the tendering process.

In July 2020, the contracting firm PAD & Company Limited (PAD & Co. Ltd.) was placed under voluntary administration for revelations of fake bank guarantees for a civil works contract of Rs 210 Million, as well as revelations of the firm's involvement in the BWSC-CEB-ADB St Louis gate scandal. ICAC investigators have also interrogated Shamshir Mukoon (former director of CEB) and Alain Hao Thyn Voon (former director of contracting firm PAD & CO).

On 5 September 2020, Bertrand Lagesse, consulting engineer for Burmeister & Wain Scandinavian Contractor (BWSC), was arrested in Mauritius for contravening Articles 3 (1) (b), 6 and 8 of the Financial Intelligence and Anti-Money Laundering Act over a period beginning in May 2016. He is suspected of having acquired a property worth 212,948 Euros (Rs 10 Million) and holding Rs 8.17 Million in a bank account using proceeds of this corruption. Bertrand Lagesse had also erased his telephone and computer records during his arrest.

The AfDB also debarred the company for 21 months for engaging in 'sanctionable practices', which included 'financially rewarding members of the Mauritian administration and others, through the intermediary of third parties to access confidential tender-related information'. In other words, they bribed their way into obtaining insider information to give them an advantage in the pre-tender procurement phase.

Using qualitative methods – the interview schedule

In answering the research questions, the most appropriate participants for the qualitative interviews are professionals with vast working experience at the AfDB. Twenty-three interviews were conducted. These professionals have a wealth of experience in procuring aid-financed projects in Africa. This fits the view that the only way to discover the lived realities of crime, deviance and social control is to talk to the people who have experienced and understood it (Caless, 2011). A semi-structured questionnaire was designed. These questions examined the experiences of firms sanctioned by MDBs and their perception of corruption emanating from the supply side.

Key findings

The corporate set-up

In the case study mentioned above, the firm pleaded guilty to corruption and corruption offences and voluntarily agreed to negotiate with the AfDB.

Also, it was noted that the top management of the contracting firms was well aware of the scheme at the outset. The bribes offered were disguised in the form of consultancy fees or simply as average monetary payments. This fact was even concealed in the books and records of these companies. It is noted that the scheme is well-orchestrated between representatives of the corporates (bribe suppliers) and the bribe receivers. The corporate actors act as the assertive bribers.

The corrupt network

The case study reveals that the corporate actors initiated the initiative to engage in corruption schemes. It is also revealed that in order to perpetuate corruption, long-standing relationships were built over some time. A common characteristic of a corrupt network is confidentiality within the relationship and secrecy towards outsiders. In order to build trust within the network, it was observed that the firm indirectly channelled bribes through an agent to deliver pecuniary benefits to officials. Corruption tends to become endogenous (situations are created that facilitate its existence), tending to grow and becoming organised and institutionalised.

Corporate benefit

It is clear from the case study that the BSWC were effectively trying to gain a competitive advantage.

The schema below depicts the trend and pattern that emerged based on the St Louis case. It provides insights into how the benefits obtained from corrupt transactions can incentivise corporate and receiving actors to participate in the transactions. It helps to have an improved understanding of corporate corruption dynamics. The corruption scheme developed by these firms is apparent. They deal primarily with public officials close to the political elites through secretive schemes to siphon facilitation money to those in positions of power to influence future decisions. This corruption scheme is instigated from the supply side, whereby the firms engaged in development projects prospect the environment and are willing to pay facilitation money for its corporate benefits. In all cases, cooperation between public and private actors is critical, reflecting that bribery and corruption are typically based on an exchange between these actors (David-Barrett, 2017).

Analysis

The case study, the qualitative and quantitative methods provide essential insights into the roles and activities of the different actors and the causal mechanisms the corporate actors employ for corporate corruption. The

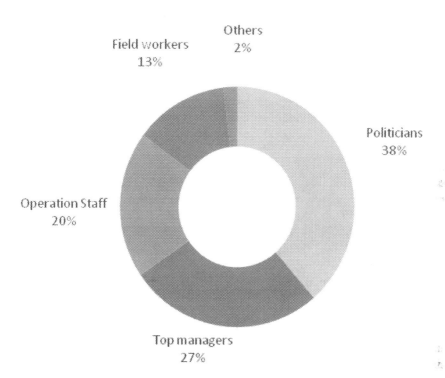

FIGURE 8.1   Percentage of corrupt officials.

synthesis of information performed through the case study allows not only for learning about the paths of corruption but also the involvement of the actors, both at corporate and institutional levels, in allowing the corrupt transactions to go undetected. The case study provides the *how* and *why* of corporate involvement through the presentation of the bribery scheme, as illustrated in Figure 8.1. Corporate corruption has been demystified, and key themes have been extrapolated from the case studies describing the phenomenon under review.

Analysis of survey questionnaires

This survey captures the perceptions of corruption in corporations that MDBs have debarred. The quantitative survey employs a Likert scale, using a five-point ordinal scale to rate the degree to which the respondents agree or disagree with a statement (1 = disagree; 2 = mostly disagree; 3 = neutral; 4 = mostly agree; 5 = agree). Forty-three (43) questionnaire responses were received out of 125 questionnaires sent out, representing a response rate of 34.4%. The essential characteristics of the responses are outlined below. The tables and graphs illustrate the results and trends, together with discussions. Given the challenges faced in attaining research participants in corruption research and research generally, the final sample (representing 34.4%) is considered an adequate response for this research. A response rate above 20% is considered satisfactory and acceptable (Comfort & Smithson, 1996; Fowler, 2002). Recent studies have demonstrated that a low response rate in survey research does not necessarily produce a non-response bias (Keeter et al., 2000; Karahanna et al., 1999).

Corrupt actors involved

Respondents were asked to enumerate, based on their experience, the most corrupt actors during project implementation. Politicians came top of the list, representing 38% of responses, followed by top managers (27%) and operations staff (20%). Politicians or politically exposed persons (PEPs) are essential in the corruption exchanges between the business actors paying bribes and the bribe receivers (represented by the public sector).

Based on these figures, the high percentage of 65% representing politicians and top managers combined have the propensity to engage in supply-driven corruption schemes. While not ignoring the fact that these projects can also attract corruption from the demand side, involving operational staff and field workers, the high percentage of 65% of politicians/top managers is a strong indication that corporate corruption is mainly facilitated by contracting firms, for their corporate benefit, through the networking of influential actors. The results of the case studies also confirm this scheme.

Political connections

It is not surprising that 88% of respondents claimed that political instability had undoubtedly been a cause for the indulgence of corporations in malpractices. According to Kew (2006), political instability in a country is the failure of the political class to adhere sufficiently to the basic tenets of democracy and constitutionalism. Harriman (2006, p. 2) asserts that political stability 'has given rise to abuse of power, brazen corruption, disregard for due process and the rule of law, intolerance of political opposition, abuse of the electoral process and the weakening of institutions'.

These MDB-financed projects are directly linked to the government of the day, even though the government requests these investments. The ruling party decides whether to extend the projects or not. Corporations working on existing projects will undoubtedly take advantage of this political instability to set up networking with influential actors, as illustrated through the case studies, for the ultimate corporate benefits.

One interviewee also revealed how political connections encourage corporations to engage in corruption through the privileged contacts they engage in. He commented as follows:

> MDBs encourage development irrespective of the countries. If the countries are receptive to development, these MDBs will be ready to invest in developmental projects. Political instability may be why these countries want to engage in development projects with MDBs to have an upper hand in the procurement process. – Interviewee 11.

Another interviewee highlighted how political connections can encourage corruption emanating from the business side.

> These development projects are the governments' initiatives for development. Political connections encourage the political agents, and all those that revolve around the influenced politicians, to establish good contacts with contractors. These contractors are on the lookout for such opportunities. They are well-connected and can influence the process by providing competitive advantages to the contracting firms. This is how the corrupt transactions take place. It is not necessary for there to exist a demand side. The business side represents the active corruptor while the public sector represents the positive corruptor by accepting the bribes. – Interview 10.

Based on the above findings, it is clear that political connections affect the propensity of these corporations to become corrupt. Cingoano and Pinotti (2013) assert that corporations gain market power when politically connected. Empirical evidence is based on the findings that political connections increase the market value of corporations engaged in development projects. These findings confirm that politically connected firms have a competitive advantage over non-politically connected firms. Researchers made similar observations (Faccio et al., 2006; Igan & Mishra, 2014).

Analysis – themes and categories

The first cycle was 'process coding' (Miles et al., 2013, p. 75), focusing on the causes of corruption and explaining 'how' and 'why' the corporate actors engaged in corrupt practices. The initial coding process emerged from the data while deliberately avoiding abstract notions. The second phase was 'pattern coding' (Miles et al., 2013, pp. 86–87), whereby codes describing similar behaviours were grouped into more general and abstract units of analysis. This enabled large amounts of codes to be placed into smaller categories.

The sweetening process

Corruption does not always start with a direct bribe. Usually, it starts with a sweetening process, which serves as an enticement of the bribe-receiver/s. If required, the grooming phase of the corruption process involves building rapport and pushing the boundaries of a relationship down the 'slippery slope' towards the final act (Köbis et al., 2016). The corruptors manipulate the relationships so that effective bonds minimise rejection risks (Free & Murphy, 2015). At the same time, they are constantly watching out for the target's weaknesses. To the question of how these corporations engage with the target in instigating corrupt transactions, interviewees explained how these firms identified their prey.

> Through their wide field experience, these firms know exactly where the weaknesses are and who has the powers to influence the procurement process. They will identify the persons and entice them into the bribery scheme. They are experts in it – Interviewee 14.

Another interviewee was more explicit in elaborating how firms approach their targets in elaborating on corrupt schemes.

> Their bribery scheme has evolved; it is no longer the traditional, under-the-table money. It has become a well-orchestrated scheme, where these firms try to deceive the existing safeguards in their own companies to escape detection – Interviewee 11.

Corporate benefits

The interviews and case study review cover the 'top management' involvement in corruption. Top management involvement was identified as necessary in orchestrating the corrupt transaction in the four cases. Selected verbatim quotations from the interviews are highlighted below to support this argument.

> I would say that, though these multinational firms might have robust codes of conduct/codes of ethics in place, it does not prevent them from committing a corrupt act which would ultimately benefit the whole firm - Interviewee 15.

This aligns with , whoAnand, Ashford, and Joshi (2004) , who assert: 'While adopting such codes is a positive development, it is not sufficient as it can sometimes be used as a badge of morality'. To the question of why these types of funded projects are vulnerable to corporate corruption, one interviewee explained:

> These multinationals are operating in different jurisdictions. They must struggle to remain in business as obtaining a contract is competitive. The competition is fierce, and they have to protect the interests of their companies. They will look for ways to lubricate the wheels of the business in order to secure future contracts – Interviewee 13.

Another interviewee was more explicit in describing how these multinationals are ready to do business:

> The firms which have already won contracts will do their best to secure future contracts and the funding mechanisms to influence decision-makers – those who have close contacts with politicians – to secure future contracts. In all circumstances, these firms take risks to obtain corporate benefits – Interviewee 17.

The above responses are consistent with Passas (1998), who asserts that globalisation multiplies, intensifies and activates 'criminogenic asymmetries' that lie at the root of corporate crime. In fact, according to the rational choice approach, organisations are continuously assessing their costs and benefits. They tend to favour actions that increase their profit margin. Van de Bunt (1994) posits that this can occur even if firms have no problems achieving their objectives.

Scholars have identified two perspectives of organisational corruption by referring to the 'bad apples' and 'bad barrels' dichotomy (Ashford et al., 2008; Pinto et al., 2008; Wheeler & Rothman, 1982). Organisational corruption can arise due to individual greed (Treviño, 1986; Treviño & Youngblood, 1990) for private benefit (Aguilera & Vadera, 2008). This is a form of corruption against the corporation and is represented by the 'bad apples'. Based on the 'bad barrel' perspective, corrupt behaviours, where organisations are the primary beneficiaries, occur according to organisational goals (Baker & Faulkner, 1993). This is reflected in the statements of the following interviewees, who emphasised the notion of corporate benefit:

> I sincerely believe no individuals within the organisation will have the guts to engage in a corrupt act, committing the organisation. The risks are too high. Those in positions of power could act only with the blessing of the company's stakeholders – Interviewee 7.

They will never tell you the corrupt behaviour is part of the firm's strategy even though the primary beneficiary of the corruption scheme is the company. I think it is more the issue of loyalty that explains this – Interviewee 5.

According to researchers, there are multiple factors to explain the bad barrel perspective on corruption (Kish-Gephart et al., 2010) and the secretive actions surrounding it (Vaughan, 1996; 1999). In line with what Baker and Faulkner (1993) posit, organisational goals may dictate the corrupt behaviour in which the organisation is the primary beneficiary.

The game of power

Corrupt actors use corporate resources to engage in corruption (Jávor & Jancsics, 2016). According to Bourgeois (1981), opportunities for corruption within a corporation arise when there are surplus or unexploited opportunities in the system. One interviewee explicitly mentioned the modus operandi employed by top managers:

These firms operate in different jurisdictions; they have to be competitive. Moreover, they have to thrive to survive and have future contracts. Representatives of these firms use organisational resources in the corrupt exchange – Interviewee 5.

Another interviewee highlighted how the resources for corruption can be created:

It is not difficult. They know how to find the resources. Low-quality materials and poor artistry provide cost savings. This provides the necessary resources in the corruption exchange, and the corrupt exchanges allow them to look the other way – Interviewee 9.

The allocation of resources in an organisation is typically very unequal and often determined by power relations (Hills & Mahoney, 1978; Pfeffer & Leong, 1977; Rajan & Zingales, 2000). According to Dahl (1971), power includes resources, opportunities, acts, and objects that can be exploited to affect others' behaviour.

One interviewee explained how the game of power is crucial in the corrupt exchanges:

The higher the hierarchy, the higher the corporate representatives have more power. They are like the commander of an aeroplane. They will act to the uttermost benefit and interest of the organisation. In most cases, they are obliged to do so – Interviewee 17.

The above aligns with Bacharach and Lawler's (1981, p. 45) claim: 'Outcome is a crucial implicit element of power. Power must be an impelling influence. Therefore, power that is not impelling is not power at all. This power element is essential'. According to Jávor and Jancsics (2016), the more powerful a corporate actor is, the higher the propensity to engage in corruption on behalf of the corporation. This research proves them correct.

Corrupt networks

The first insight into corrupt networks appeared in the interviews. In trying to understand how linkages are built between corporations and other stakeholders to complete corrupt transactions, one interviewee revealed the following:

> These high-level executives know very well the weaknesses in the system. They try establishing secret networks with main stakeholders and engage in a sweetening process – Interviewee 3.

One interviewee explicitly identified the main stakeholders that the executives of the contracting firms will try to network with:

> They aim higher up the hierarchy because the higher they go, the lower the risks of being detected. They target state-owned firms, governmental institutions, political nominees, and even political parties – all high-level public officials – Interviewee 1.

The above findings illustrate how networking is built and aligns with what Javor and Jancsics (2016) call the 'professionalised' corrupt networks. Under such networks, the actors acting on the corporations' behalf can achieve their objectives. Buckley and Casson (1976, p. 75) explain: 'These actors in these networks have meta-power'. Powerful actors from the supply side of the corruption scheme trigger the willingness to engage in these corrupt networks. This is clearly illustrated in the political nexus identified in the case study.

It is argued in this research that corporate resources are essential elements in facilitating corporate corruption used by the corrupt actors in the corruption schemes. As confirmed by the research findings, these corrupt networks have strong links to political parties, public officials and oversights. This finding corroborates with Nielsen (2003), who posits that the characteristics of these corrupt networks are strong links with branches of government, watchdogs, auditing, and journalistic organisations. This research confirms this nexus. Furthermore, Jansics and Javor (2012) highlight such networks' secretive nature and power as an essential element in forming such networks. The findings corroborate this assertion.

Corporate actors

The predominant sentiment expressed by respondents confirmed the cover-up of corrupt practices at the management level. Respondents used words and phrases such as 'intentionally turned off organisational control', 'turning blind eyes', 'control deactivation', 'authorised malpractices to go undetected', and 'ability to control and manipulate information'.

A respondent noted the following:

> Top management within organisations are those who have power. They can make malpractices go undetected by turning off internal and external control mechanisms . . . This happens in corporate corruption – Interviewee 5.

Another interviewee emphasised how top management strives to embed the malpractices:

> When corruption occurs at the organisational level, top executives ensure that practices are concealed in the internal procedures and processes of the organisation. In this way, there is no risk that divergences are detected – Interviewee 9.

Capture

The essential element of corporate corruption is 'capture.' Capture is the result or process by which public decisions over laws, regulations or policies are directed away from the public interest at the expense of a narrow interest group (Carpenter & Moss, 2014; OECD, 2017). It is, in fact, contrary to lobbying, which is more transparent and open (Boehm, 2007). Public procurement is the area most captured (Boas et al., 2014; Bromberg, 2014; Hyytinen et al., 2008; Fulmer & Knill, 2013; Slinko et al., 2004). Actors from both the public sector and the private sector are involved in capture (Gournev & Bezlov, 2010; Szanto et al., 2012; Wedel, 2003).

Policy capture has pervasively negative impacts on the economy and society. It can misallocate public and private resources, resulting in rent-seeking activities, inappropriate influence peddling, and corrupt practices. Studies show that companies that are politically connected gain in market power and have a competitive edge over those that are not politically connected (Cingano & Pinotti, 2013; Faccio, 2006; Faccio et al., 2006; Goldman, Rocholl and So, 2013). Companies not part of a capture network face economic disadvantages (OECD, 2016). Conversely, it facilitates access to more business opportunities than conventional business strategies. Surprisingly, capture affects democracies with solid public institutions. Johnston (2014) used the term 'influence market corruption' to describe the scenario where private wealth interests seek influence in solid public institutions. In many instances, the interviews explained this notion of capture. One interviewee explained as follows:

> These corporates establish strategic contacts with high-level officials – Interviewee 17.

Another interviewee elaborated further.

> Networking involving public officials/ private actors is an important vehicle for capture to occur, creating a sense of reciprocity where illegal payments and future contracts are linked – Interviewee 5.

Determinants of corporate corruption

The main categories were defined according to the research questions. Transcripts for relevant quotes from the interviews were assigned to the main categories. In the second step, the codes were grouped into subcategories. Data obtained through the quantitative and qualitative data analysis were integrated and merged to capture insights regarding the dynamics of corporate corruption. Different approaches exist to integrate qualitative and quantitative data (O'Cathain et al., 2010; Creswell & Plano Clark, 2011). For this research, a separative approach was undertaken. Data were collected and analysed separately and then integrated through themes to elaborate the results (Fetters et al., 2013). Integration through data merging occurs when the two databases are brought together for analysis and comparison.

The qualitative themes were compared with the survey results to assess concordance (Moseholm & Fetters, 2017). The quantitative data was also used to explain findings from the qualitative data. Quantitative and qualitative findings were synthesised through narrative in the results and discussions through triangulation. The results were combined in a table format, where the frame of the analysis was the four overarching themes. The themes represent the four primary determinants that encourage corporate corruption. The findings concurred with studies conducted by Gregory (1999) and de Graaf and Huberts (2008), who posit that the private sector's management style undermines the 'ethics infrastructure' in the public sector because their goals are focused on results. Furthermore, the empirical findings obtained confirm the assertion made by Pinto, Leana, and Pil (2008) that these corporations, rather than the individuals, are the principal beneficiaries of corporate corruption.

For corrupt transactions, the different actors must inevitably have a goal, and consequently, they act to achieve it. For the actors to achieve their goals, they should inevitably have power, as confirmed by the analysis of the cases. The actors from the corporation are predominantly from the top management level, as confirmed by the case studies and the interviews conducted. Notably, specific forces encourage the actors from the supply side to engage in corrupt transactions. For the corrupt mechanism to be established, inevitably, there should be a communication channel between the instigators and the targets of the transactions. This has been echoed in the interviews and the case study.

An empirical approach starting with the set of determinants and then identifying the most relevant of them seems to be the most optimal solution. The critical determinants for corporate corruption are identified in Table 8.1. The framework below is presented to conceptualise the understanding surrounding the determinants of corporate corruption. By synthesising the findings through the different research methods, a matrix can be used to explain the phenomenon of 'corporate corruption' in development projects. From these findings, it is clear that the corrupt practices involving corporations are not mere coincidence but are calculated risks taken by these corporations.

As the main themes evolved, it was tested extensively with each interviewee during the semi-structured interview in order to gauge their accuracy based on their extensive experience. The four significant determinants that represent the predisposition for corporate corruption were identified:

- Minimising competition
- Institutional blindness
- Addressing uncertainty
- Maximising profit

Corporations engaged in MDB-financed projects are highly likely to engage in corporate corruption. The four significant determinants represent

TABLE 8.1 Attributes of corporate corruption

Attributes	Descriptions based on findings from the research
Collective action	Involvement of top managers/executives.
Key actors involved	Top executives, directors, managers, and high-level public officials.
Victims	States, bidders and users.
Beneficiaries	Firms are winning the contracts. High-level political parties.
Types of violations	Bribery, corruption, fraud, misrepresentations.
Intentionality of behaviour	To gain a competitive advantage for the benefit of the organisations.
Reputational intermediaries	Internal controllers, internal auditors, external auditors.

the drivers that instigate these corporations to corporate corruption. The public officials represent the targets that facilitate corrupt transactions. They may not necessarily represent the demand side as they may be just the receivers of the bribes. The four main determinants that encourage corporate corruption to occur are explained below.

Minimising competition

Regardless of what assets a company owns and how much cash it holds, loss over extended periods will eventually weaken its asset positions and decrease the amount of its cash holdings. When companies can operate consistently and with low costs, they will be better positioned to absorb any price decline or market downturn and stay profitable. The lower the cost, the larger the profit margin. If the cost rises to a level resulting in a thin profit margin, companies become vulnerable to price shock or sales deterioration and can sustain significant losses. To minimise loss, companies must aim to achieve the break-even sales volume by maintaining a satisfactory level of market share. With increasing competition, MNCs are thriving in the international market. These corporations look for survival strategies. They are on the constant lookout for the market while minimising competition. Their objective is to secure the market without going to completion. Corporate corruption seems to be the quick and strategic instrument for achieving this.

Institutional blindness

These MNEs respond to the institutional weaknesses and fall into the vicious trap of corruption by supplying corruption. Studies have shown that the strength of institutions and the prevalence of corruption (Cuervo-Cazurra, 2008; Doh et al., 2003). Boddewyn and Doh (2011) explained that this institutional void lured corporations into engaging in unethical behaviour. According to Khanna and Palepu (2010), MNCs adapt their business model to address the cost of institutional voids. MNCs further entrench host-country corruption by institutionalising it as a norm, thus reinforcing the cycle (Luiz & Stewart, 2014). Ultimately, they become accomplices in generating conditions within the country of operation. The findings of this research converge to this assertion.

Luiz and Stewart (2014) argue that MNCs either can reinforce the vicious cycle of underdevelopment, institutional weakness, and corruption or can, through their influence on institutions, create a virtuous reinforcing cycle that promotes good corporate policy and development. MNCs are competing for markets globally. This study provides empirical evidence to show that corporations lack a systematic framework for generating insights about the future consistently and reliably. The results point to the fact that these corporations are fully aware of their involvement in corruption schemes but, due to their institutional blindness, are ignorant that they are taking inappropriate risks and developing competitive vulnerabilities.

Addressing uncertainty

Randomness and uncertainty play increasingly significant roles in determining business success, mainly because of rapidly evolving social networks. It is human nature to want to know everything. Knowledge is central to how human beings work and interpret the world around them, hence the need to address uncertainty by ensuring that corporations get a competitive advantage. Companies may take different approaches to maximise profit or minimise loss based on their organisational strengths. While product differentiation and low price can be critical to maximising profit, controlling cost and maintaining market share may be more important in minimising loss. The corporate world is full of uncertainties. These corporations indulge in corporate corruption to ensure stability and obtain future contracts.

Profit maximisation

Profit maximisation is the firm's capability to produce maximum output with limited input or by using minimum input to produce its stated output. It is termed the foremost objective of the company. It has been traditionally recommended that the apparent motive of any business organisation is to earn a profit, as it is essential for the company's success, survival, and growth. Profit is a long-term objective but has a short-term perspective – one financial year. Profit can be calculated by deducting total cost from total revenue. A firm can ascertain input-output levels through profit maximisation, which gives the highest profit. Profit maximisation is a short-term objective of a firm, while the long-term objective is wealth maximisation. Profit maximisation ignores risk and uncertainty, unlike wealth maximisation, which considers both.

Integration of findings

What are the challenges facing corporations involved in international development projects?

The data relating to this question was identified through a detailed survey, interview and case study. Ethics experts and organisation theorists often associate diverted behaviours in corporations with the responsibility of individuals. This study shows that senior managers/top managers involved

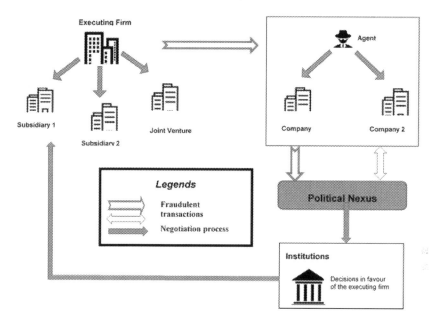

FIGURE 8.2 Corruption scenario from the supply-side.

in corporate corruption do it for corporate benefit; hence, these corporations become responsible for their actions. Rich empirical materials were obtained based on the different methods used, confirming this.

As illustrated in Figure 8.2, the findings show that the benefits generate rationalisations for corruption. This claim is supported by Paternoster and Simpson (1996), Pinto et al. (2008) and Whyte (2016), who assert that organisations adopt corrupt behaviours to gain a corporate advantage. The above illustration provides insights into how actors are incentivised in corrupt transactions.

This study considered the corporate perspective towards corruption and deconstructed corporations' mechanisms in instigating corruption in development projects. The findings show that corrupt transactions result from the prevalence of profitability objectives over the corporate and societal value of ethics. The findings prove that these MNCs have a high propensity to indulge in corrupt practices because of obstacles to their business development. Luo (2004) and Blundo et al. (2006) also highlight this point.

This study illustrates that corporations engaged in development projects financed by MDBs try to establish or improve their positions by acquiring or controlling larger shares or taking other actions to gain an advantage over competitors. Corporate corruption represents a deliberate means of gaining a competitive advantage. However, it does not occur inadvertently as corporate actors work towards achieving these corporate benefits. This research demonstrates that corporations attempt to control or adapt to uncertain environments. Consequently, corporate corruption may emerge in the quest of these corporations to seek corporate benefit. This finding aligns with similar observations by researchers of the causes of wrongdoing by firms (Aldrich, 1979; Pfeffer & Salanickm, 1978).

Corporations respond to their corporate environment by developing strategic instruments counteracting their challenges. Consequently, these corporations become instigators of corporate corruption for their ultimate corporate benefits. This research identified four main determinants encouraging corporate corruption, namely (i) minimising competition, (ii) institutional blindness, (iii) addressing uncertainty, and (iv) profit maximisation.

Conclusion

Few studies have considered the role of the private sector in facilitating corruption (Harsh, 1993; Hellman et al., 2003; Otusanya, 2010; Sikka, 2008; You and Khagram, 2005). The central question raised by this research was 'What are the determining factors encouraging corruption from the supply side?' The findings of this research using triangulation illustrate how contractors and consultants working on development projects would be considered vehicles of corruption, facilitating corruption from the supply side. While there is scant research on the causes of corruption in development projects, it is clear that recipient countries should not be solely blamed for it. The interactions between private organisations and government institutions can be conducive to corrupt practices.

The particular nature of corruption by contracting firms creates several obstacles to enforcement responses. Such types of corruption whereby the contracting firms (representing the supply side) are facilitating the corruption may cause serious social, economic, political and environmental harms. As depicted in the case, corporate corruption is inherently a market phenomenon involving legitimate corporations operating in legitimate areas but in illicit activities. This article elaborated on the mechanisms emerging within the control landscape of contracting firms doing business in Mauritius. The findings of this article also dispel the myth that for corruption to flourish, the demand side (representing the public sector) needs to be active. Corruption will flow irrespective of whether it is from the demand side or the supply side. This research confirms that corruption initiated by the supply side is possible even if the recipients remain passive. Another finding was the symbiotic relationship between the private and the public sectors' corruption. It shows that private-sector enterprises in Mauritius cannot stand independent of the public sector.

A good knowledge of the nature and characteristics of corruption prevalent in the public sector of Mauritius will no doubt help establish reforms tailored towards curbing the risk factors and enablers of corruption. Corruption in Mauritius's public sector takes many forms, shapes and sizes that can be narrowed down to financial and non-financial – occurring in political and bureaucratic corruption.

For Mauritius to bring corruption under control, the institutions vested with the capacity to fight against corruption and economic crime must be reviewed and assessed after more than twenty years of operations. It will also help to restore the negative perception of the public of the institutions as being biased and unfair in the investigation of corruption involving high-level public officials. The national strategies involving all stakeholders, including politicians, civil society organisations, and institutions, in countering corruption should be built to enhance the fight against corruption.

The government of the day must pay more attention to the warning signs to avoid sliding down the slippery slope of corruption (Serebrennikova et al., 2023). The recent corruption scandals involving public officials have caused severe reputational damage to the running government. The case study used in this study deconstructed the mechanism employed by corporations in instigating corruption in development projects with the involvement of high-level public officials. The findings show that corrupt transactions result from the prevalence of profitability objectives over the corporation and the societal value of ethics. The findings prove that these multinational corporations tend to indulge in corrupt practices because of obstacles to their business development. It seems that it is a way for these corporations to gain a competitive advantage.

Corporations respond to their corporate environment by developing strategic instruments counteracting their challenges. Consequently, these corporations are becoming instigators of corruption from the supply side for their ultimate corporate benefits. This study identified four main determinants encouraging corporate corruption, namely (i) minimising competition, (ii) institutional blindness, (iii) addressing uncertainty, and (iv) profit maximisation.

This case study illustrates how corporate actors employ the scheme to bribe public officials and politicians. This study also illustrates how a robust anti-corruption law is not enough to discourage corporations from bribing schemes from the supply side. Political will is critical. This chapter serves as a clarion call to African countries that are building or enhancing their governance structures at the institutional level to be aware of the dynamic nature of corruption. Closing the door of corruption from the demand side of the public sector by having a rigorous system to counteract corruption is not an end. The supply side of corruption from the private side should not be underestimated.

Moving forward, actors involved in public procurement must be aware of these challenges and how to address them. For example, there is a need for greater transparency within the procurement process in the public sector. The public should have access to the bidding documents as far as legally possible. In the present situation, were it not for unsuccessful bidders challenging the contract awarding to BWSC, the public would not have had access to some of the bidding information. In addition to providing training and capacity building to the public officials involved in the procurement process, civil society organisations could be called on to play a monitoring role in the process under the establishment of a civilian oversight committee mechanism (Serebrennikova et al., 2023).

There is little doubt that Mauritius's image of clean governance has taken a knock due to corruption scandals plaguing the country. Unless processes are implemented to address corruption risks as Sihombing et al. (2023) recommended and hold the culprits accountable, the country may be on a slippery slope down the corruption hill.

References

ADB (2017). *Act for integrity and respect. Office of anticorruption and integrity.* 2017 Annual Report. Manilla, Philippines: Asian Development Bank.

AfDB (2018). *Annual Report 2015-2016, Office of Integrity and Anti-corruption.* Abidjan, Cote D'ivoire: African Development Bank Group.

AfDB (2023). African economic outlook. www.afdb.org/en/knowledge/publications/african-economic-outlook

Aguilera, R. V and Vadera, A. K. (2008). The dark side of authority: Antecedents, mechanisms, and outcomes of organizational corruption. *Journal of Business Ethics*, 77(4), 431–449.

Aldrich, H. E. (1979). *Organizations and environments.* Englewood Cliffs, NJ: Prentice-Hall.

Anand, V., Ashford, B. E., and Joshi, M. (2004). Business as usual: The acceptance and perpetuation of corruption in organisations. *Academy of Management Perspectives*, 18(2), 39–53.

Ashforth, B. E., Gioia, D. A., Robinson, S. L., and Treviño, L. K. (2008). Re-viewing organisational corruption. *Academy of Management Review*, 33, 670–684.

Bacharach, B., and Lawler, E. J. (1980). *Power and politics in organizations.* Hoboken, NJ: Jossey-Bass.

Baker, W. E., and Faulkner, R. R. (1993). The social organization of conspiracy: Illegal networks in the heavy electrical equipment industry. *American Sociological Review*, 58, 837–860.

Bakre, O. M. (2007). The unethical practices of accountants and auditors and the compromising stance of professional bodies in the corporate world are evidenced by corporate Nigeria. *Accounting Forum*, 31(3), 277–303.

Bandelj, N. (2012). Relational Work and Economic Sociology. *Politics and Society*, 40, 175–201.

Banfield, E. C. (1975). Corruption as a feature of governmental organisation. *Journal of Law and Economics*, 18, 587–605.

Baucus, M. S. and Near, J. P. (1991). Can illegal corporate behaviour be predicted? An event history analysis. *Academy of Management Journal*, 34, 9–36.

Blundo, G. & J. P. Olivier de Sardan, eds., with N. Bako-Arifari & M. T. Alou. (2006). *Everyday corruption and the State: Citizens and public officials in Africa*. London: Zed.

Boas, T., Hildalgo, D. and Richardson, N. (2014). The spoils of victory: Campaign donations and government contracts in Brazil. *Journal of Politics*, 76(2), 415–429.

Boddewyn, J., and Doh, J. (2011). Global strategy and the collaboration of MNEs, NGOs, and governments to provide collective goods in emerging markets. Global Strategy Journal, 1(3), 345–361.

Boehm, F. (2007). Regulatory capture revisited – Lessons from Economics of corruption. Internet Center for Corruption Research (ICGG) Working paper no. 22. Passau, Germany.

Bourgeois, L. J. (1981). On the measurement of organizational slack. *The Academy of Management Review*, 6(1), 29–39.

Brief, A. P., Buttram, R. T., and Dukerich, J. M. (2001). Collective corruption in the corporate worldf: Toward a process model. In M. E. Tuner (Ed.), *Groups at work: Theory and research*. Mahwah, NJ: Lawrence Erlbaum Associates, pp. 461–499.

Bromberg, D. (2014). Can vendors buy influence? The relationship between campaign contributions and government contracts. *International Journal of Public Administration*, 37(9), 556–567.

Brouthers, L. E., Yan, G., and McNicol J. P. (2008).Corruption and market attractiveness influences on different types of FDI. *Strategic Management Journal*, 29(6), 673–680.

Buckley, P. J. and Casson, M. (1976). *The future of the multinational enterprise*. London: MacMillan.

Button, M., Shepherd, D., and Dean, B. (2018). Co-offending and bribery: The recruitment of participants to corrupt schemes and the implications for prevention. *Security Journal*, 31(4)(12.10), 882–900.

Caless, B. (2011). *Policing at the top: The roles, values and attitudes of chief police officers*. Bristol, UK: Bristol University Press.

Carpenter, D and Moss, D. (2014). *Preventing regulatory capture: special interest influence and how to limit it*. Cambridge University Press, New York.

Cingano, F., and Pinotti, P. (2013). Politicians at work: The private returns and social costs of political connections. *Journal of the European Economic Association*, 11(2), 433–465.

Comford, T., and Smithson, S. (1996). *Project research in information systems: a student's guide*. London: Macmillan.

Creswell, J. W., and Plano Clark, V. L. (2011). *Designing and conducting mixed methods research* (2nd ed.). Thousand Oaks, CA: Sage.

Cuervo-Cazurra, A. (2008). Better the devil you do not know. Types of corruption and FDI in transition economies. *Journal of International Management*, 14(1), 12–27.

Cuervo-Cazurra, A. (2016). Corruption in international business. *Journal of World Business*, 51(1), 35–49.

Dahl, R. A. (1971). *Polyarchy: Participation and opposition*. New Haven: Yale University Press.
David-Barrett, E. (2017). Business unusual: Collective action against bribery in international business. *Crime, Law and Social Change*, 71(3), 1–20.
de Graaf. G and Huberts. J (2008). Portraying the Nature of Corruption using an explorative case study design. *Public Administration Review*. 68(4), 640–653.
Diallo, A., and Thuillier, D. (2010). The success of international projects, trust, and communication: An African perspective. *International Journal of Project Management*, 23(3), 237–252.
Doh, J. P., Rodriguez, P., Uhlenbruck, K., Collins, J., and Eden, L. (2003). Coping with corruption in foreign markets. *Academy of Management Executive*, 17(3), 114–127.
Donahue, A. M. (1989). *Ethics in politics and government*. New York: N. W. Wilson.
Faccio, M. (2006). Politically connected firms. *American Economic Review*, 96369–96386.
Faccio, M., Masulis, R., and McConnell, J. (2006). Political connections and government bailouts. *Journal of Finance*, 61, 2597–2635.
Fetters, M. D., Curry, L. A., and Creswell, J. W. (2013). Achieving integration in mixed methods designs-principles and practices. *Health Services Research*, 48, 2134–2156.
Fletcher, C., and Herrmann, D. (2012). *The Internationalisation of corruption*. Farnham: Gower.
Fowler, F. J. Jr. (2002). *Survey research methods*. London: SAGE.
Free, C., and Murphy, P. R. (2015). The ties that bind: The decision to co-offend in fraud. *Contemporary Accounting Research*, 32(1), 18–54.
Fulmer, S., and Knill, A. M. (2013). Political contributions and the severity of government enforcement, in *AFA 2013 San Diego Meetings Paper, American Finance Association*. San Diego.
Gillespie, K., and Okruhlik, G. (1991). The political dimensions of corruption cleanups: A framework for analysis. *Comparative Politics*, 24(1), 77–95.
Goldman, E., Rocholl, J. and So, J. (2013). Politically connected boards of directors and the allocation of procurement contracts. *Review of Finance*, 17(5), 1617–1648.
Gounev, P., and Bezlov, T. (2010). *Examining the links between organized crime and corruption*. Sofia: Centre for the Study of Democracy.
Graycar, A., and Prenzler, T. (2013). *Understanding and preventing corruption*. Houndsmill, UK: Palgrave MacMillan.
Graycar, A., and Sidebottom, A. (2012). Corruption and control: A corruption reduction approach. *Journal of Financial Crime*, 19(4), 384–399.
Gregory, R. (1999). Labour market institutions and the gender pay ratio. *The Australian Economic Review*, 32(3), 273–278.
Gyimah-Brempong, K. (2002). Corruption, economic growth, and income inequality in Africa. *Economics of Governance*, 3(3), 183–209.
Habib, M., and Zurawicki, L. (2002). Corruption and foreign direct investment. *Journal of International Business Studies*, 33(2), 291–293.
Harriman, T (2006). Is there a Future for Democracy in Nigeria? Text of a public lecture delivered at the Department of International development, Oxford University.
Harsh, H. C. (1993). Accumulators and democrats: Challenging state corruption in Africa. *The Journal of Modern African Studies* 31(1), 31–48.

Hellman, J. S., Jones, G., and Kaufman, D. (2003). Seize the state, seize the day: State capture and influence in transition economies. *Journal of Comparative Economic*, 31(4), 751–773.

Hill, C. W. L., Kelly, P. C. Agle, D. R., Hitt M. A and Hoskisson, R. E. (1992). An empirical examination of the causes of corporate wrongdoing in the United States, *Human Relations* 45, 1055–1076.

Hills, F. S. and Mahoney, T. A.(1978). University budgets and organizational decision making. *Administrative Science Quarterly*, 23, 3, 454–465.

Hock, B. (2018). The bundling of foreign bribery cases. TILEC Discussion Paper No. 2018–012.

Hyytinen, A., Lunberg, S., and Toivasen, O. (2008). Politics and procurement evidence from cleaning contracts. Helsinki Center of Economic Research Discussion paper no. 233, Helsinki.

Igan, D., and Mishra, P. (2014). Wall Street, Capitol Hill, and K Street: Political influence and Financial Regulation. *Journal of Law and Economics*, 57(4), 1063–1084.

Isopi, A., and Mattesini, F. (2008). Aid and corruption: do donors use development assistance to provide the 'right incentives?' Tor Vergata, *Research paper*, Vol. 66, Centre for Economic and International Studies, University of Rome, Rome.

Jancsics, D., and Jávor, I. (2012). Corrupt governmental networks. *International Public Management Journal*, 15, 62–99.

Jávor, I., and Jancsics, D. (2016). The role of power in organizational corruption: An empirical study. *Administration and Society*, 48(5), 527–558.

Johnston, M. (2014). *Corruption, contention, and reform, the power of deep democratisation*. Cambridge: Cambridge University Press.

Karahanna, E., Straub, D. W., and Chervany, N. L. (1999). Information technology adoption across time: A cross-sectional comparison of pre-adoption and post-adoption beliefs. *MIS Quarterly*, 23 (2), 183–213.

Keeter, S., Miller, C., Kohut, A., Groves, R. M. and Presser, S. (2000). Consequences of reducing nonresponse in a national telephone survey. *Public Opinion Quarterly*, 64 (2), 125–148.

Kew, D. (2006). Nigeria in Sanja Tatic (Ed.) *Countries at the crossroads*. New York: Freedom House.

Khang, D.B., and Moe, T.L. (2008). Success criteria and factors for international development projects: a life-cycle-based framework. *Project Management Journal*, 39(1), 72–84.

Khanna, T., and Palepu, K. (2010). *Winning in emerging markets: A road map for strategy and execution*. Boston: Harvard Business Press.

Kish-Gephart, J. J., Harrison, D. A., & Treviño, L. K. (2010). Bad apples, bad cases, and bad barrels: Meta-analytic evidence about sources of unethical decisions at work. *Journal of Applied Psychology*, 95(1), 1–31.

Köbis, N. C., van Prooijen, J.-W., Righetti, F., and Van Lange, P. A. M. (2016). Prospection in individual and interpersonal corruption dilemmas. *Review of General Psychology*, 20, 71–85.

KPMG (2015). Current of changes-The KPMG Survey of Corporate Responsibility Reporting.

Kramer, R. C. (2007). Corporate Crime: An Organizational Perspective. In Wickman, P. and Dailey, T. (Eds). *White collar and economic crime, multidisciplinary and cross-national perspectives*. Lexington: Lexington Books, pp. 75–95.

L'Express. (2021). *The disease of the subservience explained.* https://lexpress.mu/amp/396409

Lambsdorff, J. G. (2006). Causes and Consequences of Corruption: What Do We Know from a Cross-Section of Countries? In: Rose-Ackerman, S. (Ed.). *International handbook on the economics of corruption*. London: Edward Elgar, pp. 3–51.

Leiderer, S. (2012). Fungibility and the choice of aid modalities. *WIDER Working Paper Series* wp-2012-068, World Institute for Development Economic Research (UNU-WIDER).

Luiz, J. M., and Stewart, C. (2014). Corruption, South African multinational enterprises and institutions in Africa. *Journal of Business Ethics*, 124, 383–398.

Luo, Y. (2004). An organisational perspective of corruption. *Management and Organisation Review*, 1(1), 119–154.

Martin, K. D., Cullen, J. B., Johnson, J. L., and Parbooteah, K. P. (2007). Deciding to Bride: A cross-level analysis of firm and home country influences on bribery activity. *Academy of Management Journal*, 50(6), 1401–1422.

Melgar, N., Rossi, M., and Smith, T. W. (2010). The perception of corruption in a cross-country perspective: Why are some individuals more perceptive than others? *Economia Aplicada*, 14(2), 183–198.

Miles, M. B., and Huberman, A. M. (2013). *Qualitative data analysis: An expanded sourcebook*, 2nd Edition. Thousand Oaks, CA: Sage.

Moseholm, E., and Fetters, M. D. (2017). Conceptual models to guide integration during analysis in convergent mixed methods studies. *Methodological Innovations*, 10(2), 205979911770311.

Nielsen, R. P. (2003). Corruption networks and implications for ethical corruption reform. *Journal of Business Ethics*, 42, 125–149.

Nwozor, A., and Afolabi, O. (2023). Are you keeping up your appearance? Nigeria's anti-corruption crusade and image dilemma in the global arena. *Journal of Financial Crime*, 30(3), 813–827.

O'Cathain, A., Murphy, E., and Nicholl, J. (2010). Three techniques for integrating data in mixed methods studies. *BMJ*, 341.

OECD (2016). *Preventing corruption in public procurement*. OECD Publishing.

OECD (2017). *Preventing policy capture. Integrity in public decision-making*. OECD Publishing.

Otusanya, O. J. (2010). *An investigation of tax evasion, avoidance and corruption in Nigeria*, Unpublished Doctoral Thesis, University of Essex, UK.

Passas, N. (1998). Structural analysis of corruption: The role of criminogenic asymmetries. *Transnational Organized Crime*, 4(1), 42–55.

Paternoster, R., and Simpson, S. (1996). Sanction threats and appeals to morality: Testing a rational choice model of corporate crime. *Law and Society Review*, 30(3), 549–584.

Peerthum, S., Gunputh, R., and Prasad, R. (2020). Assessing the effectiveness of the fight against public-sector corruption in Mauritius: Perception v reality. *International Journal of Law Crime and Justice*. www.sciencedirect.com/science/article/abs/pii/S1756061619303830?via%3Dihub

Petrou, A. P., and Thanos, I. C. (2014). The 'grabbing hand' or the 'helping hand' view of corruption: Evidence from bank foreign market entries. *Journal of World Business*, 49(3), 444–454.

Pfeffer, J., and Leong, A. (1977). Resource allocation in United Funds: An examination of power and dependence. *Social Forces*, 55, 775–790.

Pfeffer, J., and Salancik, G. R. (1978). *The External control of organizations: A resource dependence perspective*. New York: Harper and Row.

Pinto, J., Leana, C.R., and Phil, F, K. (2008). Corrupt organisations or organisations of corrupt individuals? Two types of organisation-level corruption. *The Academy of Management Review*, 33(3), 685–709.

Rahardja, S and Swaroop, V. (22 March 2024). What can Sub-Saharan Africa learn from Mauritius's successful development? https://blogs.worldbank.org/en/africa can/what-can-sub-saharan-africa-learn-from-mauritius-s-successful-afe-0324

Rajan. R. G., and Zingales, L. (2000). *The Governance of the New Enterprise*. NBER Working Paper No. w7958.

Rodriguez, P., Uhlenbruck, K. and Eden, L. (2005). Government corruption and the entry strategies of multinationals. *Academy of Management Review*, 30(2), 383–396.

Rose-Ackerman, S. (1996). Democracy and grand corruption. *International Social Science Journal*, 48, 365–380.

Serebrennikova, A., Minyazeva, T., Dobryakov, D., Shiyan, V., and Afanasieva, O. (2023). Countering Corruption in the context of digitalisation: Criminal and criminological aspects. *Journal of Financial Crime*, 30(1), 130–142.

Sihombing, R, Soewarno, N., and Agustia, D. (2023). The mediating effect of fraud awareness on the relationship between risk management and integrity systems. *Journal of Financial Crime*, 30(3), 618–634.

Sikka, P. (2008). Enterprise culture and accountancy firms: New masters of the universe. *Accounting, Auditing and Accountability Journal*, 21(2), 268–295.

Slinko, I., Yakovlev, E., and Zhuravskaya, E. (2004). Effects of state capture: Evidence from Russian Region. In Rothstein, B., Kornai, J., and Rose-Ackerman, S. (Eds). *Building a trustworthy state in post-socialist transition*. New York: Palgrave Macmillan, pp. 119–132.

Sonnenfeld, J., and Lawrence, P. R. (1978). Why do companies succumb to price fixing? *Harvard Business Review*, 56(4), 145–157.

Szanto, Z., Toth, I., and Varga, S. (2012). The social and institutional structure of corruption: some typical network configurations of corruption transactions in Hungary. In Vedres, B. and Scotti, M. (Eds). *Networks in social policy problems*. Cambridge: Cambridge University Press, pp. 156–176.

Tekin-Koru, A. (2006). Corruption and the ownership composition of the multinational firm at the time of entry: Evidence from Turkey. *Journal of Economics and Finance*, 39, 251–269.

Tillman, R. (2009). Making and breaking the rules: The political origins of corporate corruption in the new economy. *Crime Law and Social Change*, 51(1), 73–86.

Transparency International (TI). (2017). *Corruption perceptions index 2017*. Berlin, Germany.

Treviño, L. K. (1986). Ethical decision making in organisations: A personal-situation interactionist model. *Academy of Management Review*, 11: 601–617.

Treviño, L. K., and Youngblood, S. A. (1990). Bad apples in bad barrels: A causal analysis of ethical decision-making behaviour. *Journal of Applied Psychology*, 75, 378–385.

U4. (2016). *Multilateral development banks' integrity management systems*. U4 Anti-Corruption Resource Centre.
Uhlenbruck, K., Rodriguez, P., Doh, J., and Eden, L. (2006). The impact of corruption on entry strategy: Evidence from telecommunication projects in emerging economies. *Organization Science*, 17(3), 402–414.
United Nations. (2013). *A guide for anti-corruption risk assessment*. UN Global Impact. https://unglobalcompact.org/library/411#:~:text=Seeks%20to%20provide%20a%20practical,and%20develop%20an%20action%20plan.
Vaughan, D. (1996). *The challenger launch decision: Risky technology, culture, and deviance at NASA*. Chicago: University of Chicago Press.
Vaughan, D. (1999). Rational choice, situated action, and the social control of organisations. *Law and Society Review*, 32, 23–61.
Voliotis, S. (2017). Establishing the normative standards that determine deviance in organizational corruption: Is corruption within organizations antisocial or unethical? *Journal of Business Ethics*, 140(1), 147–160.
Wedel, J. R. (2012). Rethinking corruption in an age of ambiguity. *Annual Review of Law and Social Science*, 8, 453–498.
Wheeler, S., and Rothman, M. L. (1982). The organization as weapon in white-collar crime. *Michigan Law Review*, 80: 1403–1426.
Whyte, D. (2016). It's common sense, stupid! Corporate crime and techniques of neutralisation in the automobile industry. *Crime, Law and Social Change*, 66, 165–181
World Bank. (1997). *World development report 1997: The state in a changing world*. Washington, D.C.: World Bank.
World Bank. (2003). *The Global Poll multinational survey of opinion leaders 2002*. Washington, D.C: World Bank.
World Bank. (2009). *Fraud and corruption. Awareness handbook*. Washington D.C.: World Bank.
World Bank. (2015). Benchmarking Public Procurement 2015. Washington, D.C: World Bank.
Yin, R. K. (1994). *Case study research design and methods: Applied social research and methods series*. Second ed. Thousand Oaks, CA: Sage.
You, J. S. and Khagram, S. (2005). A comparative study of inequality and corruption. *American Sociological Review*, 70, 136–157.

Appendix – Interview Questionnaire

Causes of corruption
1   What are the common causes of corruption in bank-financed projects?
2   Why do you think the contractors are willing to corrupt?
2a   Probe – Who are the professionals working on the projects more likely to engage in corrupt activities?
3   Do you feel governments are doing much to discourage corruption in bank-financed projects?
3a   Probe – What are the key reasons that encouraged such inaction?

Nature of corruption
4   Do you think the culture of the country and the organisation's culture encourages a culture of corruption?

4a   Probe – Which one is predominant in a bank-financed project?
4b   Probe – To what extent do you think the culture of the country or the culture of the organisation is predominant? Why?
     Is it more the local culture or the imported culture?
5   Do you agree with the definition of corruption as using public office for private gain? Why?
6   According to you, what should be the most appropriate definition of corruption?
7   Do you think the mastermind behind the corrupt act is the employee or the corporate?

What are the consequences of corruption?
8   Why is corruption so prevalent in bank-financed projects?
9   How can corruption affect a project?
9a   Probe – What are the consequences of corruption in a bank-financed project?
10   Can we say that the allegations received by MDBs represent the tip of the iceberg?
11   Are the sanctionable practices in MDBs wide enough to cover all types of corruption?
11a Probe – What are prevalent corruption offences that are not covered?

Sanctions process
12   To what extent do you agree that Negotiated agreements with corrupt firms are appropriate?
12a Probe – How far does it act as a deterrent?
12b Do you consider it to be a fair process? And Why?

Deterrent measures
13   How far do you think the investigation strategy of MDBs is efficient in discouraging corruption? What can MDBs do differently?
14   Are Sanctions appropriate to bring an anti-corruption culture? How far are they effective?
14a Does it have a deterrent effect?

9
CHARISMATIC CHURCHES AND CORRUPTION IN GHANA

Feeding the Beast?

Riccardo D'Emidio

Introduction

Faith, religion and spirituality are firmly rooted in the public sphere and in the personal lives of most Ghanaians (Gifford, 2004a; Ellis & Haar, 1998; De Witte, 2003), often crossing public and private boundaries, leading some scholars to call Ghana "the most religious country in the world" (Beck & Gundersen, 2016). Despite the attempts of colonial rule to separate the language of power into political and religious idioms, these remain intimately intertwined. Religion is present in all state functions – from presidential elections to department meetings – and religious leaders are explicitly tasked in Ghana's ten-year anti-corruption plan to "take the anti-corruption message to the pulpit" and raise awareness against corruption (CHRAJ 2014:48).

Several scholars have flagged and explored how political and religious transformation in Ghana has been closely entangled (Shipley, 2009; Debrunner, 1967). It is in this light that some literature suggests that the structural and moral tensions around state privatisation during the structural adjustment programs of the 1980s and 1990s fostered the boom of Neo-Pentecostal and Charismatic churches in Ghana (Meyer, 2002; 2004; Gifford, 2004a). Pentecostalism is an American creation that has become the fastest-growing branch of Christianity across Africa, Latin America and Asia (Bonsu & Belk, 2010). In Ghana, neo-Pentecostals tend to identify as "Charismatic", emphasising using the Holy Spirit's spiritual gifts. This chapter uses the terms Charismatic and Neo-Pentecostal interchangeably to refer to Ghana's vast and diverse Christian movement.

While it is challenging to pinpoint an exact definition of the global – and Ghanaian – Neo-Pentecostal movements, there seems to be a consensus

DOI: 10.4324/9781003468608-12

across the literature that these new churches can be defined according to a set of core religious features such as the emphasis on wealth and success, the centrality of the Holy Spirit and the importance of being Born Again (Ellis & Haar, 1998; Gifford, 2004a; 2004b; Meyer, 2002; 2004).

Since the 1980s, this new kind of Christianity soared across the world and in Ghana; according to Gifford (2004b), between 1986 and 1992, membership of these churches grew at rates of up to 100%. Considering the explosion of the Charismatic movement in Ghana, this chapter explores the discursive linkages between the Neo-Pentecostal movement's focus on wealth and prosperity and the overall "corruption complex" in Ghana. How do this movement's discourses of wealth and prosperity interact with corruption discourses in Ghana? What are this religious movement's social practices and discourses, and how do they interact with national discourses and social practices of corruption? How are anti-corruption institutions represented and articulated in Charismatic discourses? Building on the work of Blundo et al. (2006) and Olivier de Sardan (1999), this chapter offers an interpretation of how particular Neo-Pentecostal churches develop and reinforce a set of discourses, norms and practices that feed into the overall Ghanaian "corruption complex".

Methodologically, this chapter uses Critical Discourse Analysis (CDA) to analyse a selection of sermons delivered in leading Charismatic churches and a set of twenty semi-structured interviews with representatives of anti-corruption actors. This methodological choice allows the analysis to uncover the discourses on wealth, poverty and corruption and how they are articulated in social and religious practices, institutions and social identities.

The analysis contained in this chapter has at least two significant implications for anti-corruption theory and practice. First, the findings of this research highlight the added value in analysing corruption narratives and framings within broader social and cultural processes, moving beyond the understanding of African countries as monolithic societies. Secondly, this research calls further into question liberal expectations – often underpinning many anti-corruption campaigns and awareness-raising initiatives – that citizens need more information or an increased awareness not to engage in corrupt behaviour. Instead, the findings contained in this chapter indicate that discourses and norms embedded in relationships of power and patronage constrain citizens' engagement and action against corruption.

The chapter is divided into six sections: I first outline some current anti-corruption theory and practice paradoxes, positioning the analytical framework used for the analysis. The second section provides a brief overview of the rise of Neo-Pentecostal and Charismatic churches, while section three presents some of the methodological choices made. Section four discusses discursive constructions emerging from the analysis of the selected sermons, while section five links these insights into broader social processes. The final section concludes by discussing the implications of the findings for further research and anti-corruption interventions.

The paradoxes of anti-corruption and the "Corruption Complex"

Corruption remains among African citizens' most pressing issues, and Ghana is no exception. According to Afrobarometer, more than half of the population of Ghana believes that corruption is on the rise and that the government is performing poorly in its fight against it, with over 30% of Ghanaians exposed to bribery to obtain any public service (Keulder, 2021).

The endemic nature of corruption in Ghana persists despite the wealth of public sector reforms of the past 30 years: there are laws in place for public service management, public financial management, public procurement, auditing and anti-corruption, and all the relevant organisations tasked with implementing these have been constituted (Adadevoh, 2014). Ghana's overall anti-corruption framework is made up of an integrated ten-year plan, the National Anti-Corruption Action Plan (NACAP), aligned to the recommendations of the United Nations Convention Against Corruption (UNCAC) and coordinated by the Commission for Human Rights and Administrative Justice (Ghana's anti-corruption agency).

Despite the significant increase in anti-corruption interventions and decades of institutional reform in Ghana and across the African continent, many scholars argue that anti-corruption efforts today remain a "huge policy failure" (Heywood, 2017; Menocal & Taxell, 2015; Amukowa, 2013; Disch et al., 2009). In this regard, Mungiu-Pippidi (2018) contends that among the several factors that have led to the failure of anti-corruption, three critical interlinked misconceptions have compounded the "depressingly thin" anti-corruption success stories (Hough, 2016). First, there is the common misguided assumption that public integrity and ethical universalism are global and affirmed norms, leading development partners and national governments to want to "restore" control of corruption as opposed to building it from the ground up (Mungiu-Pippidi, 2018:23). Second, there is a recurrent and problematic treatment of corruption in developing countries as a deviation instead of the norm. This, in turn, fosters state institutions and development partners to invest in norm-enforcing instead of *norm-building* instruments. Last, in many developing countries, corruption is not only a norm but "an institutionalised practice". It follows that anti-corruption agents need to understand corruption as such and "not just as a sum of individual corrupt acts" (Mungiu-Pippidi, 2018:23).

To unpack the idea of corruption as an "institutionalised practice", the notion of the "corruption complex" developed by Olivier de Sardan (1999) can be a helpful tool. When discussing corruption in Africa, Olivier de Sardan (1999:27) argued that the core of the sociological problem of corruption is situated in the distance between "juridical condemnation of certain practices and their frequency, their banalisation or indeed their cultural legitimacy".

According to Olivier de Sardan (1999:26), the notion of "corruption complex" encompasses all the different types of corruption, going beyond the strict juridical definition or the broader international definitions of corruption to include several illicit practices, technically distinct from corruption, all of which nonetheless have in common with corruption their association with state, parastatal or bureaucratic functions, and also contradict the official ethics of "public property" or "public service", and likewise offer the possibility of illegal enrichment, and the use and abuse to this end of positions of authority.

In his endeavour to map some of the reasons why corruption finds in contemporary Africa such a favourable ground for its extension and banalisation, Olivier de Sardan (1999) identifies several logics (which he then refers to as social norms) embedded in society, which, by exerting continuous pressure on social actors, contribute to "accord a cultural acceptability to corruption" (ibid.: 44). These logics underlie several common behavioural traits such as (1) the logics of negotiation – bargaining beyond the pricing of commercial transactions to include negotiation of the rules themselves. The practice of corruption benefits from this bargaining logic since the vagueness of the normative system widens the margin of negotiation. (2) The logic of gift-giving – in Sahelian countries, the practice of "kola" (or "dash" in Ghana) is a formally valued aspect of tradition. The general monetarisation of everyday life has transformed the giving of kola into the giving of money. (3) The logic of solidarity networks – which often cut across public and private spheres and systematically includes an almost general obligation of mutual assistance – generates considerable and sustained pressure from and to all network members. (4) The logic of predatory authority has to do with "the right that many persons holding positions of power accord themselves to proceed to various types of extortion" (Olivier de Sardan 1999:41). Lastly, (5) the logic of redistributive accumulation entails that anybody accessing a position of power is expected to share and spread the benefits of his or her privilege with their networks (Olivier de Sardan 1999:41).

These logics are driven by at least two kinds of "facilitators" eroding and dissolving the "separation between the legal and illegal everyday practices", namely "over-monetarization" and "shame" (Olivier de Sardan 1999:45–47). By over-monetarization, Olivier de Sardan (1999) refers to that process whereby personal relations take on a monetary form: giving of "taxi fare" to a visitor, giving coins to friends' children, etc. This monetarization of everyday sociability is the object of much exertion of pressure, and several anti-corruption activists would argue that this process has "corrupted" many customary traditions.

Similarly, "shame" is, in most African cultures (but not only there), a powerful means of social control. Olivier de Sardan (1999) defines shame as a social morality based on other people's opinions rather than an individual examination of conscience. Shame relates to the disapprobation of others and, above all, of one's family circle or church congregation. So, for example, denouncing a fellow churchgoer guilty of embezzlement generates shame, or similarly, refusing a favour to a "recommended" person generates shame.

The Neo-Pentecostal and Charismatic movement in Ghana

Within Ghana's anti-corruption framework (NACAP), religious bodies, churches and faith-based organisations are listed as critical stakeholders at the par of civil society, political parties, the judiciary and other state institutions. As such, they are tasked to engage in awareness raising and "improve the quality of public ethics and morality" with an explicit request to take the "anti-corruption message to the pulpit" (CHRAJ 2014:48). While such a request might be at odds with a Western governance model, in a profoundly religious and spiritual country such as Ghana the intervention of 'Men of God – regardless of their faith – in development and democratic processes is standard practice and is well documented (Okyerefo et al., 2011). There are daily accounts in national media of pastors and churches pledging their commitment to fight corruption together. The prominent role given to churches and religious leaders in the fight against corruption in Ghana and the concomitant rapid rise of the Neo-Pentecostal churches calls for a more nuanced review of the Ghanaian Charismatic movement.

While it is beyond the scope of this paper to provide a complete account of this thriving movement (for an overview, see Meyer 2004 and Gifford 2004a), the following pages outline the Charismatic movement using Lincoln's (2003) framework of the four domains of religion. These include (1) a discourse or a set of themes with transcendental concerns above the human, temporal and contingent world; (2) a set of practices that embody the religious discourse; (3) a community whose members construct their identity concerning the religious discourse and its practices; and (4) institutions which, through social relations, reproduce or modify religious discourse and practices, and which ensure the continuity of the religious community over time.

Themes and discourses

While reviewing the literature, sermons and services, three recurrent and crosscutting themes emerge distinctly. The first recurrent theme is the centrality given to wealth, success and status. Charismatic Christianity hinges upon the need for one to be "born-again" and experience the blessings, transformation, empowerment, success, and prosperity concomitant with the "born-again" experience (Benyah, 2018). It is worth noting that while success is to be experienced in every area of life, the main focus remains on financial and material matters leading to prosperity (understood not as sufficiency or adequate wealth but as abundant wealth).

The second recurrent theme of Charismatic Christianity – although emphasised to different extents – is the worldview in which spiritual forces are pervasive and dominant on this Earth. Something is wrong if a Christian is not wealthy and affluent: success and wealth are blocked by demonic influence (Bonsu & Belk, 2010).

The third and final recurrent theme is the repudiation of tribalism and chieftaincy and the embracing of modernity (Quayesi-Amakye, 2015:649), putting forward the church as the actual starting point for the modernisation of the country (Gifford, 2004a:126).

Practices that embody religious discourse

While many practices within Ghanaian Charismatic Christianity embody the religious discourse, for this chapter, three are relevant. First, being born-again is perceived as a radical rupture not only from one's sinful past but also from the wider family and village of origin, encouraging trust in the pastor and committing exclusively to the religious network (Meyer, 2004:457).

Second, reflecting the emphasis on wealth and success as a sign of divine blessing, pastors adopt flamboyant personal styles, driving expensive cars, addressing mass audiences in mega-churches, performing miracles in front of the eye of the camera, using high-tech media to spread the message, and celebrating their prosperity as a blessing of the Lord. Members believe that if a pastor is not rich or able to demonstrate God's material blessings, he is possibly a fake pastor who is not practising what he preaches (Bonsu & Belk, 2010:318).

Last, accounts of the 'prosperity gospel' have drawn attention to the quasi-gift economy these churches instantiate by insisting that their congregants pay generously – tithe – into church coffers (Zaloom, 2016; Van Wyk, 2014). The underlying logic here is that if you pay a tithe, others will come to bless you with other gifts. Central to this endeavour is testimonies, whereby "your healing only becomes permanent when you testify" in front of the congregation (quoted in Gifford 2004a:50).

The community

According to Meyer (2009:13), the actual base of these churches is the urban area, where they seek to build churches at prime locations (near shopping malls, bus stations and adjacent to main roads). The church employs socio-geographical segmentation to define potential converts – often targeting the upwardly mobile or the very poor (Bonsu & Belk, 2010:310). All churches have specific target groups, reflected in the themes and language used in sermons and services.

Institutions

The prominent institutions of this kind of Christianity are the churches, through which social relations reproduce or modify religious discourse and practices and ensure the continuity of the religious community over time. Nonetheless, Charismatic churches in Ghana are characterised by a broad range of services ranging from physical structures such as universities and religious camps to an extensive range of marketing channels such as publishing houses, TV channels, radio stations, CDs, DVDs, festivals, music videos, websites and social media. These kinds of commercial products and advertisements serve multiple functions of creating and managing positive social visibility and image for church owners and creating public awareness for church events. They also create product differentiation and shorten the searching time for religious seekers (Asonzeh, 2007).

Methods and data collection

The analysis undertaken in this chapter resides in a critical tradition rooted in poststructuralist discourse analysis (Foucault, 2002) and applied linguistics (Fairclough, 2013; van Dijk, 1993b). The articulation and interaction of the Neo-Pentecostal religion with the "corruption complex" in Ghana constitute this chapter's "object of research" (Bourdieu & Wacquant, 1992). In this regard, Critical Discourse Analysis (CDA) presents a set of valuable tools to analyse the relations between discourse and other social elements such as power, ideology, institutions and social identities.

Discourse is understood here as a form of social practice that allows people to make sense of and give sense to a set of phenomena (Fairclough, 2003). In this regard, discourse is intrinsically linked with its social and material context; it is socially constituted and constituting, thus contributing to (re) constructing specific identities, social relations and systems of knowledge (Breit, 2010).

Fairclough (2003; 2013) contends that CDA has three basic properties: relational, dialectical and transdisciplinary. It is a relational form of research in that its primary focus is not on entities or individuals but on social relations. These relations are dialectical, and the dialectical character of these relations makes it clear why simply defining "discourse" as a separate "object" is not possible. The social activity consists of complex articulations of these and other objects as its elements or moments; its analysis is an analysis of dialectical relations between them, and no object or element (such as discourse) can be analysed other than in terms of its dialectical relations with others. These relations cut across conventional boundaries between disciplines, making CDA a transdisciplinary analysis.

Within this context, Critical Discourse Analysis (CDA) is "critical" because it claims to expose connections between language, power and ideology (van Dijk, 2001) and as such, it is primarily concerned with the role of discourse in enacting, reproducing (or resisting) social power abuse, dominance and inequality (van Dijk, 2001:300). Discursive power is a crucial constituent of social power and a significant means of reproducing dominance and hegemony. Van Dijk (2001:356) highlights how teachers control educational discourse; professors control scholarly discourse, politicians policy discourse and so on. In this case, it is contended that pastors from the Charismatic movement control religious discourse and discourse related to wealth and poverty.

The added value of using CDA to analyse how religious discourses interact and articulate with the (anti)corruption complex is twofold. Firstly, by exploring the discourses of wealth, poverty and corruption and their dialectical relation with social and religious practices, CDA can shed light on some of the mechanisms that contribute to the "banalisation ... or cultural legitimacy" of corruption and the failure of anti-corruption reform (Olivier de Sardan 1999:27). Secondly, through CDA it is possible to sketch out the contours of what Mungiu-Pippidi (2018:23) called the "institutionalised practice" of corruption. By identifying particular discourses – and practices – CDA can illustrate how these become hegemonic or dominant and how they can cross structural boundaries and social fields (such as religion, politics and the organisation of the state).

The analysis in this chapter draws from the work of van Dijk (1993b; 1993a; 2001) and Fairclough (2003; 2013), adapting their framework for CDA (see Figure 9.1), using van Dijk's (2001:354) distinction between *micro-discourse* (specific study of language) and *macro-discourse* (study

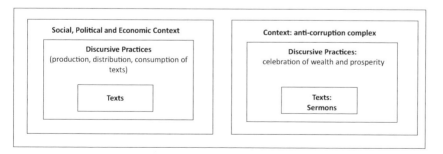

FIGURE 9.1 Text and context in discourse analysis (adapted from Fairclough 2013:133).

of power and dominance). The analysis here takes place at two different levels: first, through an analysis of the language, narratives and expressions contained in the selected sermons, discursive constructions are identified within the selected texts and linkages established with the overall context (i.e. the Ghanaian corruption complex). Particular attention is given to the *"structures of text and talk"* (van Dijk 2001:359, emphasis in the original), such as the choice of words and sentence structure used, highlighting the underlying assumptions and narratives used to establish and disseminate a set of meanings. The second level, through the analysis of a set of semi-structured interviews with representatives of the anti-corruption sector in Ghana, seeks instead to delineate the process through which discourses of wealth and poverty and their connection to corruption become naturalised and become an integral component of the context, *i.e.* they become "common sense". In this regard, among the many discursive constructs and narratives within the selected texts, there is an explicit focus on the ones that resonate with the "corruption complex" and its inherent logic.

Through CDA, this chapter seeks to explore and uncover the complex relationship between the discourses on wealth and prosperity preached in the Ghanaian Charismatic movement and the overall "corruption complex" in Ghana. The main contention in the following pages is that there is a significant relationship between the Charismatic quest for wealth and the banalisation, or "the cultural legitimacy" of corruption in Ghana (Olivier de Sardan 1999).

To investigate this hypothesis, three different sermons dealing with wealth and money have been selected, together with twenty semi-structured interviews with representatives of anti-corruption civil society organisations (CSOs) and representatives of public anti-corruption actors, such as the Ghana Police Service.

The choice of focusing on sermons as key "texts" for the analysis is determined by the role of preaching and sermons in the Charismatic movement: they embody the religious discourse and provide a framework for the congregation through which meanings are developed and established. It is essential to highlight here that the limited selection of these three sermons does not presume to represent the overall Charismatic movement in Ghana. However, it seeks to illustrate how these three churches develop and produce a set of discourses and social practices on richness and poverty that interact with the "corruption complex".

The sermons analysed have been selected because they capture the pivotal importance given to the wealth and prosperity of the Charismatic movement in Ghana. All three sermons are roughly one hour long, have been accessed from YouTube and transcribed by the author. Moreover, these sermons are delivered by three of the most influential pastors in Ghana, belonging to three different Neo-Pentecostal churches. These include Dr Mensa Otabil, head of the International Central Gospel Church (ICGC); Bishop Heward-Mills, heading the Light House Chapel International (LHCI); and Bishop Charles Agyin-Asare, head of the Perez Chapel International (PCI). While presenting nuances between them, they represent what Gifford (2004a) calls the "premier division" among Ghana's plethora of Charismatic churches. The three selected churches are all highly influential across the country (Gifford, 2004b; Meyer, 2009), and the three pastors are considered celebrities in the country and are consistently listed among the five wealthiest pastors in the country in various media.

The micro level: discursive constructions

When reviewing the selected sermons, four discursive constructions emerge that intimately resonate with some of the logic that characterises and feeds into the Ghanaian "corruption complex". While there are nuances and differences among the three sermons, the following section highlights the commonalities and how they reinforce each other.

1. Extreme wealth as an entitlement. All three pastors quote the same verse from the Bible, Deuteronomy chapter 8, verse 18, to argue that the entitlement to wealth and prosperity stems from the covenant that the Born Again Christian has established with God. Dr. Otabil explains, "Money is critical, important . . . It is foundational to your relationship with God". It is important to note that across all the analysed texts, there is a strong emphasis on extreme wealth, insufficient wealth for a good living, but affluence beyond necessity. Bishop Agyin-Asare preaches that "people will have five cars and three or four houses". There is a persistent mention of gold, silver, abundance and millionaires, and the preaching is often interrupted by prayers to bestow onto the believers' money and wealth. In different ways, all three preachers provide a set of "keys" and spiritual guidance to unleash the abundance of divine wealth onto the congregation. Interestingly, all pastors argue that God will grant richness and wealth to believers because "He trusts that [they] will put his money to good use" (Dr. Heward-Mills). When juxtaposing this entitlement to wealth and richness with the "logic of predatory authority" mentioned in the previous section, one cannot avoid asking how corruption is understood within this discursive field. In his sermon, Bishop Heward-Mills provides an answer when he argues that in terms of corruption, "Ghana is turning into Nigeria", and when "your leader is a thief . . . your options are minimal, you have to lie, you have to cheat otherwise you just die. You will die of honesty!"
2. The power of money and wealth. The almightiness of prosperity is flaunted throughout the sermons, evoking modernist ideas such as the Titanic

and millionaires like Rockefeller, but also evoking and establishing clear linkages to political power. The pastors mention the Presidents of Ghana, Israel and the USA in all three sermons. Moreover, Bishop Dag Heward-Mills contends that "prosperous people can recognise prosperity", while those "condemned to poverty . . . will never recognise it". All three sermons highlight the power and fundamental importance of money and wealth, especially in spreading the gospel. This emphasis illustrates the process of over-monetarization cited by Olivier de Sardan (1999), yet raising it to another level, whereby money can buy anything and will always be the only winner.

3. Wealth as a blessing and the grace of giving. One of the most recurrent discursive constructions throughout the sermons is the overlap between financial wealth and blessing. Once bestowed upon the believer, this can be shared with the people around them. To use the words of Bishop Agyin-Asare, "You cannot give what you do not have; you cannot be a blessing to anybody if you have not been blessed". These considerations chime deeply with the logic of gift-giving and redistributive accumulation that sustain the corruption complex in Ghana. All three pastors emphasise the power of giving, using the metaphor of sowing and reaping: you give to receive. You give to God (or to His closest representative, i.e. the man of God) through tithes and offerings, and you will receive back much more than what you have given. Blundo et al. (2006:126) have illustrated how often the language of religion in West Africa, particularly the word "blessing", can be used in corrupt transactions.

4. The curse of poverty. During the sermon, Bishop Heward-Mills prays: "May the Lord deliver you from the jaws of poverty, from the traps and snares of the curse of poverty!" The choice of words here clearly evokes the connection between poverty and the devil, trapping the believer into a painful existence. As Bishop Agyin-Asare says, "You can start poor, but you do not have to remain poor". Faith and giving to the Church is the only way to break this curse. It follows that if one continues to be in poverty, there is something incorrect: the believer, for instance, may not be giving enough tithes or offerings to the Church. The implication here is that being poor is something to be ashamed of because it is a way for God to punish the believer for doing something wrong or, even worse, to be the victim of a demonic curse. Once again, this resonates with the concept of shame as a social morality based on other people's opinions and disapproval, especially in the eyes of the congregation.

In his sermon, Dr. Otabil preaches that poverty arises from "evil agendas" in "high places", and he then breaks into a passionate prayer:

> We come against every spirit, every spirit of the Antichrist that comes against and opposes the prosperity of the righteous, we come against it in

the name of Jesus we bind it, we bind it, we bind it, we resist the devil, he flees out from us in the name of Jesus, agendas in boardrooms, agendas at the IMF, agendas at the World Bank, agendas at the UN, agendas at the AU, agendas at primary corporate headquarters . . . agendas set against the prosperity of the righteous we come against you in the name of Jesus.

What emerges in this prayer is an explicit binary opposition between the "righteous", who are entitled to wealth and riches and the evil agendas in high places. The question once again is: within this binary opposition, where does anti-corruption stand? This passage's choice of bodies and international institutions indicates their agendas do not sit with the righteous.

These four discursive constructions are key discursive "convergence points" within the Ghanaian corruption complex. While producing these sermons within churches during the specific preaching situation is a discourse at the micro level, it also acts as a constituent in reproducing the corruption complex at the macro level.

Bridging discourse with the context

According to van Dijk (2001:354), one of the ways to bridge the two different levels and arrive at a unified critical analysis is through "*actions-process*" (emphasis in original), whereby social acts of individual actors, in this case the preaching of pastors, are constituent parts of group actions and social processes, in this case, the banalisation or as Olivier de Sardain (1999) calls it, "the cultural legitimisation of corruption".

The resonance and influence of the Charismatic movement in Ghanaian public culture and the anti-corruption sector in Ghana has not gone unnoticed. As emphasised by one research participant when she says, "The church would talk about going to hell . . . But that message shifted, and now it is about enjoying the wealth". Another research participant is more categorical when discussing corruption in Ghana:

> Today, the attitude and mindset of Ghanaians do not make religion anything that will make anybody pious and keep the person ethical; therefore, the person may not want to delve into corruption and other activities. Religion has become associations; people belong to them, and it has become associations and businesses. See the issue of paying tithes, selling olive oil as spiritual and blessed oil, and selling some artefacts in churches at exorbitant prices? In Ghana, it happens; the church has become a marketing venture.

Across most interviews, celebrating wealth is not only flagged as problematic when discussing anti-corruption in Ghana but also increasingly recognised as crosscutting through all of society. Research participants working in anti-corruption feel at a loss as to how to deal with the pressure to gain wealth:

> There is so much regard for the rich or for the people who have and can give at home, at work, in the church, wherever, so people will have to find the means of getting more than they earn so that they can also get that recognition and respect, because the more you have, the more you are respected, regardless of where you obtain the wealth from.

The nexus between the praise of wealth, the Charismatic movement and the perceived pervasive corruption in the country is something that research participants recurrently put forward. To use the words of one participant: "Sometimes religion also leads people into corruption, especially in Africa". This research participant points to the enabling function of the Charismatic movement on corrupt behaviour, legitimising a range of corrupt practices.

This nexus is crystalised and strengthened through at least three enabling factors. The first has got to do with the sheer scale of churches (some can host up to 25,000 people), the extensive network that makes them up and the robust range of communication products and channels deployed by pastors (publishing houses, TV channels, radio stations, CDs, DVDs, festivals, music videos, websites and social media).

Second, pastors from leading Charismatic churches (including those delivering the sermons analysed in the previous section) are today considered among Ghana's most influential and wealthiest men; their sermons are broadcast on national radio and TV and are streamed on YouTube and other social media. Therefore, according to some scholars (Meyer, 2002; 2004; 2009; de Witte, 2002; 2003), Charismatic churches, such as those being discussed here, have become central actors in the country's public culture.

Last, Charismatic cultural productions, from the flourishing of gospel music to video films for sale on the streets and showing on TV, have become integral to Ghana's popular culture, giving rise to what some call a "*Pentecostalite* public culture" (Meyer 2002 emphasis in the original). This entails various popular expressions, from painting to posters, from theatre to video, from music to literature, adopting Pentecostal representation modes. This renewed Neo-Pentecostal public voice's political and cultural implication has led to a new "more Christian public culture" (Meyer, 2004). This public culture spills over other domains, such as the political one. John Atta Mills, for example, President of Ghana between 2009 and 2012, was a Charismatic Pentecostal and was outspoken in his desire to see the movement's prominence spread further (McCauley, 2013:15).

Conclusion

With its discourses and practices today, Charismatic Christianity in Ghana has broken the boundaries of religious discourse and has invaded public and political culture. The central contention in this chapter is that the "corruption complex" is a multifaceted system of social and political inequality reproduced by discourse in general and by elite discourses in particular. The author does not intend to suggest that corruption in Ghana is sustained exclusively by the rise of the Charismatic movement. Instead, this analysis has attempted to illustrate how a set of discourses and social practices within Charismatic churches also constitute and reproduce in the broader political and social context a set of discourses that feed into the Ghanaian "corruption complex". The main contention here is that there is a significant linkage between the Charismatic quest for wealth and the banalisation, or "the cultural legitimacy" of corruption in Ghana (Olivier de Sardan 1999). Specifically, this linkage is permissive, with ministers giving their blessing and enabling a set of corrupt behaviours feeding into the overall corruption complex.

These considerations are particularly relevant when considering the capacity of corruption to permeate many (if not all) societies and institutions in various forms, demonstrating their exceptional resilience to different kinds of institutional reform (Mungiu-Pippidi, 2018). In light of this, the argument put forward in this chapter has at least five profound implications for the anti-corruption sector, both in terms of scholarly research and practical interventions. First, in terms of research, this chapter illustrates the urgent need for (and potential of) multidisciplinary approaches to better understand and conceptualise corruption as an institutionalised practice. Drawing from the critical tradition rooted in poststructuralist discourse analysis and applied linguistics can provide insights into how constitutive dimensions of corruption, such as power, dominance and hegemony, relate and interact with broader social processes. Second, by analysing specific parts of society and their religious and cultural productions, this research uncovers how these spill over the broader public sphere and converge in the existing "corruption complex", debunking the often unquestioned treatment of African countries and societies as homogenous systems. Third, the argument put forward so far supports the considerations suggested by Mungiu-Pippidi (2018), whereby if in contexts of endemic corruption anti-corruption is to succeed, the relevant institutions (whether development partners or national states) should focus their efforts on *norm-building* instruments as opposed to *norm-enforcing* instruments. Fourth, from a practitioner's point of view, the sheer magnitude and pervasiveness of the Charismatic movement in Ghana should raise questions about the effectiveness and impact of anti-corruption awareness campaigns. While this area has recently started to be explored (Walton,

2018; Peiffer, 2017; Walton & Peiffer, 2017), further research is needed to understand better how these campaigns interact discursively with broader social, political and cultural processes. Last, in the past twenty years the anti-corruption sector and, more broadly, the development sector have engaged with faith communities to achieve the Sustainable Development Goals. This shift has taken place in light of the perceived closeness of churches and faith groups to poor communities (Alkire, 2006) but also because religion "deeply influences peoples' construction of meanings about the world ", shaping "believer's interpretations of social, economic, and political reality" (Deneulin & Rakodi, 2011:46). Several extensive studies have explored the nexus between corruption and religion (see Marquette 2012). Nonetheless, the positivist approach underpinning much of this research fails to grasp the significance of religion in public life and within the "corruption complex". In this regard, chiming with Deneulin and Rakodi (2011), further research is needed using more interpretive and contextual research methods, given that the roles of religion in development – and more specifically in anti-corruption – are mediated through socially and historically constructed meanings.

References

Adadevoh, E. A. (2014). 'New Wine in New Wine Skins: The Anti-Corruption Framework of Ghana'. *The Journal of World Energy Law & Business* 7 (3): 202–19. https://doi.org/10.1093/jwelb/jwu011

Alkire, S. (2006). 'Religion and Development'. In *The Elgar Companion to Development Studies*, edited by D. A. Clarke. Cheltenham: Edward Elgar.

Amukowa, W. (2013). 'The Challenges of Anti-Corruption Initiatives: Reflections on Strategies of the Defunct Kenya's Anti-Corruption Commission'. *Mediterranean Journal of Social Sciences*. https://doi.org/10.5901/mjss.2013.v4n2p481

Asonzeh, U. (2007). 'African Christianities: Features, Promises and Problems'. *Institut Für Ethnologie Und Afrikastudien, Johannes Gutenberg-Universität*, Working Paper 79.

Beck, S. V., and S. J. Gundersen. (2016). 'A Gospel of Prosperity? An Analysis of the Relationship Between Religion and Earned Income in Ghana, the Most Religious Country in the World*: Religion and Earned Income in Ghana'. *Journal for the Scientific Study of Religion* 55 (1): 105–29. https://doi.org/10.1111/jssr.12247

Benyah, F. (2018). 'Commodification of the Gospel and the Socio-Economics of Neo-Pentecostal/Charismatic Christianity in Ghana'. *Legon Journal of the Humanities* 29 (2): 116. https://doi.org/10.4314/ljh.v29i2.5

Blundo, G., J. P. Olivier de Sardan, N. Bako-Arifari, M. Tidjani Alou, and S. Cox. (2006). *Everyday Corruption and the State: Citizens and Public Officials in Africa*. New York: Zed. http://site.ebrary.com/id/10231405

Bonsu, S. K., and R. W. Belk. (2010). 'Marketing a New African God: Pentecostalism and Material Salvation in Ghana'. *International Journal of Nonprofit and Voluntary Sector Marketing* 15 (4): 305–23. https://doi.org/10.1002/nvsm.398

Bourdieu, P., and J. J. D. Wacquant. (1992). *An Invitation to Reflexive Sociology*. Chicago: University of Chicago Press.
Breit, E. (2010). 'On the (Re)Construction of Corruption in the Media: A Critical Discursive Approach'. *Journal of Business Ethics* 92 (4): 619–35. https://doi.org/10.1007/s10551-009-0177-y
CHRAJ. (2014). 'National Anti Corruption Action Plan'. Accra, Ghana: Commission for Human Rights and Administrative Justice (CHRAJ).
Debrunner, H. (1967). *A History of Christianity in Ghana*. Waterville publications.
Deneulin, S., and C. Rakodi. (2011). 'Revisiting Religion: Development Studies Thirty Years On'. *World Development* 39 (1): 45–54. https://doi.org/10.1016/j.worlddev.2010.05.007
De Witte, M. (2003). 'Altar Media's Living Word: Televised Charismatic Christianity in Ghana'. *Journal of Religion in Africa* 33 (2): 172–202. https://doi.org/10.1163/15700660360703132
Dijk, T. A. van. (1993a). *Elite Discourse and Racism*. Sage Series on Race and Ethnic Relations, v. 6. Newbury Park, Calif: Sage Publications.
———. (1993b). 'Principles of Critical Discourse Analysis'. *Discourse & Society* 4 (2): 249–83. https://doi.org/10.1177/0957926593004002006
Dijk, T. A van. (2001). 'Critical Discourse Analysis'. In *The Handbook of Discourse Analysis*, edited by Deborah Schiffrin, Deborah Tannen, and Heidi Hamilton, 20. New York: John Wiley & Sons.
Disch, A., E. Vigeland, and G. Sundet. (2009). 'Anti-Corruption Approaches: A Literature Review'. *Study* 2: 2208.
Ellis, S., and ter Haar, G. (1998). 'Religion and Politics in Sub-Saharan Africa'. *Journal of Modern African Studies* 36 (2): 175–201.
Fairclough, N. (2003). *Analysing Discourse: Textual Analysis for Social Research*. London; New York: Routledge.
———. (2013). Critical Discourse Analysis: The Critical Study of Language. Hoboken: Taylor and Francis. www.123library.org/book_details/?id=109941
Foucault, M. (2002). *Archaeology of Knowledge*. Routledge Classics. London; New York: Routledge.
Gifford, P. (2004a). *Ghana's New Christianity: Pentecostalism in a Globalizing African Economy*. Bloomington, Indiana: Indiana University Press.
———. (2004b). 'Persistence and Change in Contemporary African Religion'. *Social Compass* 51 (2): 169–76. https://doi.org/10.1177/0037768604043004
Heywood, P. (2017). 'Rethinking Corruption: Hocus-Pocus, Locus and Focus'. *The Slavonic and East European Review* 95 (1): 21. https://doi.org/10.5699/slaveasteurorev2.95.1.0021
Hough, D. (2016). *Analysing Corruption: An Introduction*. Newcastle upon Tyne: Agenda Publishing.
Keulder, C. (2021). 'Africans See Growing Corruption, Poor Government Response but Fear Retaliation If They Speak Out'. 421. Afrobarometer Dispatch.
Lincoln, Bruce. (2003). *Holy Terrors: Thinking about Religion after September 11*. University of Chicago Press.
Marquette, H. (2012). ' "Finding God" or "Moral Disengagement" in the Fight against Corruption in Developing Countries? Evidence from India and Nigeria: 'Finding God' or "Moral Disengagement" in the Fight against Corruption. *Public Administration and Development* 32 (1): 11–26. https://doi.org/10.1002/pad.1605

McCauley, J. F. (2013). 'Africa's New Big Man Rule? Pentecostalism and Patronage in Ghana'. *African Affairs* 112 (446): 1–21. https://doi.org/10.1093/afraf/ads072

Menocal, A. R., and N. Taxell. (2015). 'Why Corruption Matters: Understanding Causes, Effects and How to Address Them'. The UK.

Meyer, B. (2002). 'Pentecostalism, Prosperity and Popular Cinema in Ghana'. *Culture and Religion* 3 (1): 22.

———. (2004). 'Christianity in Africa: From African Independent to Pentecostal-Charismatic Churches'. *Annual Review of Anthropology* 33 (1): 447–74. https://doi.org/10.1146/annurev.anthro.33.070203.143835

———. (2009). 'Pentecostalism and Neo-Liberal Capitalism: Faith, Prosperity and Vision in African Pentecostal- Charismatic Churches'. *Journal for the Study of Religion* 20 (2). https://doi.org/10.4314/jsr.v20i2.47769

Mungiu-Pippidi, A. (2018). 'Seven Steps to Control of Corruption: The Road Map'. *Daedalus* 147 (3): 20–34. https://doi.org/10.1162/daed_a_00500

Okyerefo, M. P. K., D. Yaw Fiaveh, and K. T. Asante. (2011). 'Religion as a Tool in Strengthening the Democratic Process in Ghana'. *Journal of African Studies and Development* 3 (6): 7.

Olivier de Sardan, J. P. (1999). 'A Moral Economy of Corruption in Africa?' *The Journal of Modern African Studies* 37 (1): 25–52.

Peiffer, C. (2017). 'Message Received? How Messages about Corruption Shape Perceptions'. *Developmental Leadership Program* 46 (March).

Quayesi-Amakye, J. (2015). 'Pentecostals and Contemporary Church-State Relations in Ghana'. *Journal of Church and State* 57 (4): 640–57. https://doi.org/10.1093/jcs/csu033

Shipley, J. W. (2009). 'Comedians, Pastors, and the Miraculous Agency of Charisma in Ghana'. *Cultural Anthropology* 24 (3): 523–52. https://doi.org/10.1111/j.1548-1360.2009.01039.x

Van Wyk, I. (2014). *The Universal Church of the Kingdom of God in South Africa: A Church of Strangers*. The International African Library. New York, NY: International African Institute, London and Cambridge University Press.

Walton, G. (2018). *Anti-Corruption and Its Discontents: Local, National and International Perspectives on Corruption in Papua New Guinea*. Abingdon, Oxon; New York, NY: Routledge.

Walton, G., and C. Peiffer. (2017). 'The Impacts of Education and Institutional Trust on Citizens' Willingness to Report Corruption: Lessons from Papua New Guinea'. *Australian Journal of Political Science*, September 1–20. https://doi.org/10.1080/10361146.2017.1374346

Witte, M. de. (2002). 'Accra's Charismatic Screens'. *Etnofoor* 15 (1/2): 222–28.

Zaloom, C. (2016). 'The Evangelical Financial Ethic: Doubled Forms and the Search for God in the Economic World: The Evangelical Financial Ethic'. *American Ethnologist* 43 (2): 325–38. https://doi.org/10.1111/amet.12308

10

THE CAUSES AND CONSEQUENCES OF CORRUPTION IN ZAMBIA

Arthur Chisanga, Steven Daka, Victor Kaonga and Tambulani Chayima Nyirenda

Background on Zambia's Corruption Landscape

Zambia, a landlocked country in Southern Africa, has a complex historical, social, economic, political, and cultural fabric that helps us comprehend the dynamics of corruption within its borders. As we investigate the roots and effects of corruption in Zambia, it is critical to understand the underlying forces that have moulded the country. In 1964, Zambia gained independence from British colonial power. Its early years were filled with optimism and promise, as it was regarded as an example of a peaceful transition to self-government. These promising beginnings, however, were quickly eclipsed by a succession of challenges (Bratton & van de Walle, 2010). Given this context, Zambia's history of corruption can be traced back to the colonial era, when resource exploitation and unequal power dynamics paved the way for unethical behaviours. The transition to independence presented difficulties in adapting governing structures to the needs of a developing nation, allowing corrupt practices to flourish. Zambia was vulnerable to corruption due to its over-reliance on the copper sector and related economic woes. Revenue leakage, resource mismanagement, and a lack of efficient control in economic sectors presented opportunities for embezzlement and fraud. Political insecurity and power struggles have obscured the significance of open and accountable governance (Transparency International Zambia Chapter, 2015). The drive to retain power or obtain political advantage has occasionally resulted in personal gain by exploiting governmental resources and institutions. Recent high-profile corruption cases in Zambia highlight the issue's systemic character. Understanding Zambia's historical, social, economic, political, and cultural context is critical for understanding

DOI: 10.4324/9781003468608-13

the causes and repercussions of corruption in the country (Center for International Private Enterprise, 2016), such as the 2019 incident involving fraudulent contracts exposed corruption in public procurement procedures. The "cashgate 2016" scandal showed corruption at the highest echelons of government, exposing a breakdown in ethical behaviour among senior individuals. The 2018 incident exposed corruption in the mining sector through unlawful payments to gain contracts, highlighting the critical need for comprehensive changes to address systemic flaws and promote openness, accountability, and good governance. Despite the prevalence of corruption in Zambia, extraordinarily little documented empirical evidence of the causes and actual consequences exists. A few studies on corruption in Zambia have focused mainly on confirming its existence, not its actual causes and consequences. To paint a country-specific picture of the causes and consequences of corruption in Zambia, this chapter aims to look deeper into the elements driving corruption in Zambia and investigate alternative remedies to alleviate its negative consequences on its growth.

Conceptual Definition of Corruption

There is no universally accepted definition of corruption, as different people have defined it differently. Corruption is when a public office or entrusted power is abused for personal benefit. According to the Anti-Corruption Act No. 3 of 2012, Zambia defines corruption as soliciting, receiving, obtaining, providing, promising, or offering gratification through a bribe or other personal inducement. The World Bank's short definition of corruption is the most widely cited: "the abuse of public office for private gain" (World Bank, 2006). Although bribery and the exchange of favours are commonly linked with corruption, the above definition encompasses nonmonetary transactions, such as nepotism, influence peddling, and behaviours that do not involve trades, such as forgeries and open embezzlement. "The exploitation of public power, office, or authority for private gain – through bribery, extortion, influence peddling, nepotism, fraud, speed money, or embezzlement" is corruption, according to the UNDP definition (UNDP, 2005). These two different definitions by both the World Bank and UNDP have the flaw of limiting corruption to the public arena. Transparency International's (TI) definition expands to include private sector corruption: "the abuse of entrusted power for private gain" (TI, 2007).

Theories of Corruption in Zambia

The theories of corruption's causes in Zambia are the topic of this section. What is the theoretical framework for describing the causes of corruption? Understanding how different theories describe, conceptualise, and ultimately infer policy suggestions can help us better comprehend the complexities of corruption and highlight the range of analytical and practical options for dealing with it (de Graaf, 2010). The theoretical model used to study corruption significantly impacts the recommended solutions. Different causal pathways lead to various discourses on preventing and controlling corruption. This chapter seeks to illustrate that (i) each theory has strengths and flaws, and (ii) the most popular or hegemonic theory in practice and academia (such as the economics of corruption in the last two decades) is not always the analytically most vital or most beneficial.

Considering the disadvantages of various theoretical perspectives, such as structural functionalist theory, new institutional economics of corruption, criminological, postmodern, and systems theories, and others, could thus aid analysts and practitioners in identifying blind spots when developing anti-corruption policies and encourage researchers to engage in inter-conceptual analysis. The following theories have been chosen for this chapter because they provide a solid perspective on the Causes of Corruption in Zambia.

Utilitarian-Hedonistic Approach to Corruption

The Utilitarian-Hedonistic Approach to Corruption, which is based on utilitarianism and hedonism, provides a new viewpoint on the roots and consequences of corruption, particularly in the context of Zambia. This theoretical approach blends utilitarianism's emphasis on total well-being with hedonism's emphasis on pleasure-seeking as a fundamental human quest. It adds an emotional dimension to the assessment of societal norms and actions, emphasising the pursuit of pleasure and avoidance of pain. At its foundation, the Utilitarian-Hedonistic Theory of Corruption asserts that corruption emerges from an instinctive drive to embrace events, chances, places, and situations that promise personal value and pleasure while avoiding pain and adverse consequences. This lack of innate control over the pursuit of pleasure can lead people to engage in dishonest actions to acquire personal benefits and rewards. This theory is used in the specific context of Zambia by emphasising how the innate drive for pleasure and utility, paired with a lack of control, contributes to the prevalence of corruption. Several factors can demonstrate this link.

Disaffection and Loss of Possibilities can be triggered by the loss of opportunities for personal enrichment and acquiring positions of power. When people feel marginalised or excluded from growth opportunities, the pursuit of pleasure by unscrupulous methods may appear to be a feasible option. For example, if people believe that formal channels for socioeconomic advancement are limited, they may resort to bribery or embezzlement to meet their demands. Another factor is Recognition and Respect; corruption might be motivated by a need for social recognition and respect. Individuals who believe corrupt activity is linked to prestige and power may be likelier to engage in it. For example, suppose people observe that influential personalities frequently engage in corrupt acts without penalties. In that case, they may be driven to follow suit to earn respect and approval – additionally, instability and economic pressures. Zambia's economic woes and inadequate access to necessities can produce significant pressures. Individuals may prioritise short-term profits to alleviate immediate financial troubles in such circumstances, increasing the possibility of engaging in corrupt behaviours to protect their economic well-being.

The Utilitarian-Hedonistic Theory of Corruption has significant implications for the causes and consequences of corruption in Zambia. Policymakers and scholars may attack corruption at its base by understanding the interplay between the pursuit of pleasure, the avoidance of pain, and the absence of innate control. Creating opportunities for legitimate personal and societal growth, improving openness in government, and ensuring that the repercussions of corruption outweigh the potential advantages are all effective ways to combat corruption. Finally, the Utilitarian-Hedonistic Theory of Corruption is a valuable lens for examining the roots and consequences of corruption in Zambia. It explains how the innate pursuit of pleasure and utility, combined with a lack of control, leads to dishonest practices. Zambia can take essential strides toward minimising corruption and building a more transparent and ethical society by addressing the causes that drive individuals to corruption and implementing policies that fit with the insights of this theory.

Institutional Theory

Corruption cases are expected in Zambia, demonstrating the pervasiveness of the disease. A thorough understanding has arisen through the meticulous investigation of these cases, demonstrating the profound social, political, and economic repercussions they involve. The Institutionalism model provides a strategic framework for fighting corruption in the public sector. This strategy capitalises on a country's fundamental institutions and government, including features such as a firmly established rule of law, well-defined anti-corruption norms, and autonomous organisations endowed with effective enforcement capabilities. This theory investigates the processes and procedures through which structures, rules, and routines get established as authoritative guidelines Scott (2005). Although Institutional theorists consider corruption to be influenced by the character and transparency of the political system's institutions, they recognise the intricate relationship between corruption, institutions, and political systems to be highly complex. This means that while corruption may occur at the personal level, it could also be that institutionally provided institutions are designed in such a way that they are different from their intended purpose (Debski, 2018).

About the above scenario, Zambia provides a classic example of how extractive institutions existed in from the pre-colonial era throught years after its end. Acemoglu and Robinson's hypothesis of "extractive institutions" refers to those arrangements designed to extract incomes and wealth from one subset of society, in this case African populations, to benefit a different subset of elite colonisers (Acemoglu & Robinson, 2012). According to this theory, the colonial institutions have changed current institutions, and existing institutions affect present economic development. To illustrate this point in the case of Zambia, the country's abundant natural resources, including minerals like copper, have continued to attract global interest and investments. However, the management and extraction of these resources have often been stained by corrupt practices, leading to resource mismanagement and rent-seeking opportunities. For example, the nationalisation of copper mines a few years after independence (1964), and their subsequent privatisation at the turn of the century have greatly improved public revenue from mining in Zambia. Nonetheless, the size of public revenue produced from mining in Zambia has fluctuated significantly, both during the nationalised period and under the ownership of privately owned companies. One of the critical mining companies (KCM) was closed due to a high level of indebtedness and threats of insolvency, lack of investment in developing new ore sources, and failure to adopt cost-effective production methods. This showed that exploiting mining resources did not contribute to the Zambian economy's positive structural transformation and diversification. This explains how extractive the institutions have been in Zambia.

Social Learning Theory (SLT)

Some scholars have employed social learning theory to explain criminal behaviour (Sandholtz & Taagepera, 2005). The thesis is founded on the idea that deviance and conformity can be produced through a comparable learning process. Definitions, differential association, modelling, and reinforcement were thought to influence social behaviour. When these elements interact, one is predisposed to conforming or deviant behaviour (Singer & Hensley, 2004; Tittle, 2004). According to social learning theory, legal and unlawful conduct standards, peers, and positive or negative reinforcement all influence behaviour. Differential association, or peer influence, is a crucial variable. The defined deviation is formed through interactions with peers and reinforced, either positively or negatively, by rewards and penalties (Ezeh, Leonard & Etodike, 2016). These concepts impact attitudes and behaviour in various domains, including sexual conduct, substance abuse, and white-collar crime (Akers & Sellers, 2009).

According to Bernard, Snipes, and Gerould (2010), social learning theory acknowledges that environmental, behavioural, and cognitive factors influence learning. As a result, in Zambia, criminal or deviant behaviour stems partly from observing the repercussions of certain activities on others (Akers & Sellers, 2009). Although social learning theory considers potential implications for criminal behaviour, it ignores the specific contexts that lead to such behaviour. According to Bernard, Snipes, and Gerould (2010), the social structure impacts crime because it influences one's exposure to norms and the repercussions of breaking them.

Social Disorganisation Theory

Dysfunctional behaviour has cultural, political, and economic origins, according to social disorganisation theory (Akers & Sellers, 2009). When a community's way of life and the established order change, there is a rise in deviance and crime. Informal social controls break down in disorganised communities, resulting in the growth of deviance and criminal cultures. Such communities cannot work together to combat crime and disorder (Hochester & Copes, 2008; Vito et al., 2007). According to the hypothesis, neighbourhoods with unravelling social institutions, such as failed schools, vacant or defaced buildings, changing ethnicity, and significant unemployment, will increase crime (Steenbeek & Hipp, 2011).

Johnson (1998) used social disorganisation theory to argue that corruption is ingrained in the culture of many countries. In Zambia, corruption is perpetuated rather than combated because of economic and political systems. Corruption can be decreased by improving criminal justice and political, social, and economic institutions, which will lead to social empowerment, according to the assumptions of social disorganisation theory (Collier, 2009; Johnson, 1998). Corrupt habits and behaviour in Zambia are transferred in a learning process. For example, while many civil servants carry out their duties according to the law at the grassroots, Zambia has failed to curb corruption because even recruits in the civil service have come to learn the unprofessed corrupt practices in the corridors of their work environments. The social learning theory has critical implications in the Zambian context as it illuminates that the risk of punishment influences Zambian citizens' decisions of whether to engage in corrupt acts. According to the hypothesis, corrupt practices among government employees in Zambia are the product of a corruption subculture that allows people to learn about corruption and deviant behaviour.

Theoretical Adoption of Corruption Theories in Zambia

The authors argue that considering the studied theoretical frameworks, the utilitarian-hedonistic social disorder theory of corruption and the Institutional theory, as optimised in this chapter, have been adopted to explain both the internal and external causes of corruption in Zambia. The social disorder theory emphasises the external factors that contribute to corruption, such as inequities in income distribution. In contrast, the utilitarian-hedonistic theory considers internal and personal factors contributing to corruption under natural conditions. At the same time, the Institutional theory focuses on institutionalism and the complex relationships between institutional logic, the resources and efforts required to sustain corruption elimination mechanisms in Zambia. The authors anticipate that the proposed dyadic theoretical model would provide sociologists, psychologists, and criminologists with concrete insights into what to expect when they analyse the subject matter – corruption in Zambia, its causes, and consequences.

The Institutional Framework for Fighting and Preventing Corruption in Zambia

To further understand the concept of Institutionalism and illustrate how it can combat corruption in the public sector by leveraging a country's and government's institutional qualities such as an established rule of law, a well-defined anti-corruption tradition, and autonomous institutions with strong enforcement capacity, this section will critically highlight the following two institutions that are key in driving the anti-corruption agenda in Zambia. It shall examine their background, legal mandates and some of the potential strengths and limitations:

The Anti-Corruption Commission (ACC)

The Anti-Corruption Commission (ACC) has been tasked with leading Zambia's fight against corruption. It comprises a board of five commissioners and a directorate chosen by the president and must be approved by Parliament. The ACC is responsible for investigating and prosecuting corruption cases and any other criminal offences under any written law that may come to the Commission's attention during a corruption investigation. It also promotes public awareness, education initiatives, and a free hotline for reporting corruption concerns. The ACC receives long-term donor support but has limited capacity and an ambitious mandate, jeopardising its ability to perform its tasks efficiently (Freedom House, 2013; NORAD, 2011). Donor money has aided the ACC's efforts in improving management and operational capacity and helping it accomplish institutional goals, including developing strategic plans to strengthen its investigation, prosecution, and prosecution ability. However, the Commission has several structural flaws, including budget sustainability, understaffing (it is anticipated that the Commission should have 318 employees, up from 217 in 2011), and geographic outreach (NORAD, 2011).

Partnerships with civil society organisations have helped to mitigate these flaws to some extent. The Drug Enforcement Commission's Anti-Money Laundering Unit also aids with investigations into charges of misbehaviour. Despite these challenges, the Commission has investigated several instances and participated in high-profile grand corruption investigations. While some investigated cases have resulted in several convictions, prominent officials sometimes remain free throughout lengthy appeal processes with unpredictable outcomes, fueling Zambian residents' scepticism of the ACC (Freedom House, 2011 and 2013). Many cases involving high-ranking officials have also gone unpunished, leading some to assume that anti-corruption measures are purely political (Bertelsmann Foundation, 2014). Civil society organisations such as TI Zambia have criticised the ACC's investigations into public money theft for being too slow. For example, the ACC announced to the public in 2013 that only forty-seven of the sixty-two cases it was investigating stemming from the 2011 Auditor General's reports on alleged malpractices had been investigated, and only three had been resolved, while the rest had been referred to other institutions (*Lusaka Times*, 2014). On the plus side, the ACC has launched investigations of serving cabinet officials and MPs from the ruling Patriotic Front, a move hailed by civil society organisations, including TI Zambia, in a press release on April 9, 2014 (*Zambia Daily Mail*, 2014).

The Judiciary

While the law guarantees the judiciary's independence, its judicial independence and integrity history is varied, and it is not immune to political meddling (Freedom House, 2011). While the Judicial Service Commission chooses magistrates in a fair procedure, the president can dismiss judges in subordinate courts. The president appoints Supreme Court and High Court judges, who must be approved by parliament. For example, when the President took office in 2012, he replaced most top judges and judicial personnel. He suspended three top judges for misconduct, which some critics saw as payback for an unfavourable judgement against the president's loyalists. As a result, while the judiciary acts with reasonable independence, on the whole, politics can influence court decisions when they are politically sensitive (Bertelsmann Foundation, 2014). The judiciary is understaffed, lacking resources and court facilities to function as it should, and judicial officers' low salary encourages corruption (Freedom House 2013, Bertelsmann Foundation (2014). According to Transparency International's 2013 Global Corruption Barometer data, Zambian citizens consider the judiciary to be one of the country's most corrupt institutions, with 13% of respondents to the 2011 Global Corruption Barometer survey admitting to paying a bribe to obtain judicial services (NORAD, 2011).

Causes of Corruption in Zambia

Although Zambia has made some progress in the battle against corruption over the past decades, the country remains deep-rooted in pervasive corruption and persistent governance challenges. The prevailing governance and corruption metrics underscore this claim. However, understanding the root causes and catalysts behind Zambia's corruption predicament is lamentably limited. This section will highlight several pivotal factors that contribute to this problem:

Low Media Freedom

Although the Constitution guarantees freedom of speech and press, it still contains measures that can and have been used in the past to restrict the media (US Department of State, 2013; Freedom House, 2013). The Official Secrets Act and the State Security Act can be misapplied against the media. Zambia needs to open the media environment, mainly by removing government control of public media editorial boards, but little progress has been made in promoting press freedom. The political elite has not shied away from utilising libel and defamation actions against independent media, and critical journalists suffer intimidation from law enforcement authorities, harassment, and legal action whenever corruption issues are raised against them (Freedom House, 2013). On claims of non-compliance, governmental organisations (such as the Zambia Revenue Authority and the Independent Broadcasting Authority) have closed media giants such as the *Post* newspaper and Prime Television during the last seven years. However, many saw such moves as a ploy to stifle press freedom. Additionally, as of 2023, Zambia has not yet enacted the Freedom of Information Bill.

Political and Economic Environment

Another of the primary causes of corruption in Zambia is poor governance. The more a country's economic activity is restricted and constrained, the greater the authority and power of officials in making decisions becomes, and the greater the risk of corruption because people are prepared to pay or offer money to avoid limits. Economic freedom, or the ability to choose how to produce, sell, and use your resources, should be linked to lower levels of corruption in theory. With fewer economic regulations, such as permission requirements, corrupt behaviour is less likely to be perceived as vital for doing business. Early empirical investigations backed up this theory, demonstrating that greater economic independence leads to lower levels of corruption (Paldam, 2002).

Higher Levels of Bureaucracy and Inefficient Administrative Structures

Further, public administration's effectiveness dictates whether corruption can find healthy soil and flourish. Ineffective and unclear regulations help to enhance the level of corruption in at least two separate ways; first, the system's artificially manufactured monopoly of power allows civil workers to obtain bribes based on their superior position, and second, inefficient and imprecise regulations generate inhibition and so motivate citizens to pay bribes to speed up the bureaucratic process. For example, in Zambia, bribes and irregular payments are sometimes exchanged when applying for public utilities (GCR, 2015–2016). One in ten companies reports expecting to give gifts to public officials "to get things done", including obtaining an operating licence.

Scapegoating Failed Corruption Reforms to a Lack of Political Will

There has been a microscopic thorough examination of the notion of "political will", with some scholars doubting it as a concept in policy literature, even though others insist on its empirical relevance. However, in this chapter, "political will" will be described as political leaders' commitment to take action to address a particular problem. In the case of Zambia, despite the civil society organisations such as Transparency International and the country's corruption perception index recently confirming the reports of public servants' corruption involving various senior government public officials (Transparency International, 2023), the existing government anti-corruption program has not been effective. It does not show results (ibid). Many arrests have ended in bail, with defendants denying the charges and investigations not always well-founded. Therefore, it can be observed that when there is inadequate support and strong leadership from institutional and political leaders in questions of accountability and corruption (political will), the effective functioning of accounting institutions is hampered (Schacter, 2005). Similarly, Schedler also contends that "there is no way to ignore or bypass the centres of state power," noting that "unless they consent to institutionalise "self-restraint" the road to anticorruption is blocked" (Schedler, 1999, pp. 338–339).

The saying "examples are tempting!" indicates corruption's political power. Suppose the top of politics is corrupt (government, political parties, and senior politicians). In that case, corruption will spread to all levels, and this evil will spread to the general population since no one respects institutions or the rule of law. However, the authors argue that the "political will" concept is an old story that can no longer be used to analyse corruption in Zambia. "Will" is a question of intentions or dispositions, and we cannot tell whether it is present until after reforms fail (Brinkeroff, 2000). Zambia has long been mired in circular arguments: reforms failed due to a lack of political will, and we know reforms failed due to a lack of political will. Zambia has had no shortage of political will over the last two decades; instead, patterns of corruption have revealed that corruption has been held and exercised by corrupt and venal officials and their clientele rather than reformers. For example, the fire tender scandal (2012–2015) involved the alleged corrupt purchase of 48 fire tenders for more than $30 million, and the Luapula Province road scandal (2020–2021) involved the alleged awarding of a contract to a company with no experience in road construction to build a road in Luapula Province, Zambia. It is then necessary to consider which constituencies and interests might and should have a stake in corruption control, why they have not been effectively mobilised, and how this situation might change if Zambia is to alter its current corruption trajectory.

Weak legislation and lack of enforcement

Regarding the effectiveness of anti-corruption regulations, it has been argued that reforms should not only be about compliance and control mechanisms, such as establishing anti-corruption agencies. They should also focus on reducing the incentives to engage in corrupt practices. For Zambia, despite having made anti-corruption legislative tools for the public sector, the challenge has been the inefficient sanctioning of corruption. This has increased the chance of those implicated to continue their corruptive behaviours while also producing a strong impact and likelihood that others will join in the corruption due to this inefficient sanctioning. The ineffectiveness also stems from the fact that the Anti-Corruption Act (2012) as a law is not regularly enforced, and officials frequently engage in corrupt behaviour without consequence. Transparency International Zambia (TIZ) says the average conviction rate for corruption prosecution is between 10% and 20%. Also, in the recent past, various senior public officials in the country have been accused of using anti-corruption legislation to pursue political opponents (ICS, 2017). Parallel to the existing challenges of enforcement and legislation, Zambia and countries like Singapore present an excellent example of how to make effective regulations. A classic case is how the CPIB, a government agency, does not "hesitate to bring whoever is corrupt to court, irrespective of his status, creed or rank" and that anybody "who offers, accepts or obtains a bribe can be fined up to $100,000 or imprisoned up to five years or both". Also, the number of years is even extended if the corruption involves government contracts and members of parliament (CPIB, 2014, p. 10). The agency is also autonomous, and its fight against corruption targets all irrespective of political affiliation or position in society, unlike in

Zambia; this approach, over time, improves enforcement approaches. As a result, when a country has practical enforcement tools, the public perceives corruption as a high-risk, low-reward venture. Consequently, it proves that good enforcement is crucial in changing people's beliefs to refrain from acting corruptly when they know that anti-corruption organisations make corruption extremely costly.

Low Levels of Education

Higher levels of knowledge should, in theory, lessen the amount of corruption in a society. Higher education tends to make people more committed to civil liberties and less tolerant of government repression (Truex, 2011). Furthermore, higher education leads to a greater understanding of international standards, which should lessen a person's tolerance for corruption. According to preliminary research, higher levels of education are associated with lower levels of corruption (Glaeser & Saks, 2006). There is no emphasis on education attainment in Zambia, especially for our political elites whose required entry level to be a candidate is a high school certificate (G12 certificate).

Unemployment

Unemployment is one of Zambia's fundamental problems, and it does not need much explanation because it has shattered many people's hearts. As a result of the high unemployment rate, people are forced towards corrupt practices. Unemployed people can use corruption to generate money and improve their lives. High levels of unemployment motivate people to offer bribes in return for a job. In 2020, Zambia's unemployment rate was approximately 11.41 per cent.

Consequences of Corruption in Zambia

Corruption has many consequences, impacting service availability, use, and expense. Inefficient public spending is often a result of corruption activities associated with the abuse of available resources in resource-constrained settings and increased financial pressure on the poorest. If a bribe is requested or an informal payment is made in addition to the official payment, corruption may raise the cost of care for patients, reducing demand for services and worsening health outcomes (Naher et al., 2020). Quite recently, some medical personnel at the University Teaching Hospital in Lusaka were caught on camera taking bribes for a COVID-19 test. Even though they were punished for the act, medical service providers can be costly for poor Zambian citizens if corruption continues to thrive. It has now become a norm that people would prefer to pay someone in public hospitals for efficient service delivery. If someone does not have money, they often have to wait and follow inefficient procedures, which in most cases undermine equal access to health services and quality health outcomes.

Certain top political officials in Zambia have used their political positions to amass vast sums of money from the country's coffers, and this is not without controversy (Mlambo et al., 2019). According to Heywood (2015), corruption enriches the wealthy while impoverishing the poor. Corrupt governments have less money to spend on social services. Politicians take money from the Treasury and put it in their pockets, leaving less money for schools, hospitals, and highways. People lose confidence in their representatives when governments fail to provide essential services, and they are less likely to entrust them with their tax money, leaving even less money for essential services. Corruption is a part of what Uslaner called the "inequality pit" (Uslaner, 2008). Zambia is at the point where inequality in accessing opportunities and resources has led to low confidence among the citizens in government institutions. As a result, we have more corruption because citizens do not trust the systems, leading to more inequality (the rich getting richer and the poor getting poorer). Inequality breeds corruption by making ordinary Zambian citizens believe the system is stacked against them, creating a sense of dependency and pessimism for the future, which undermines the moral imperative of treating your neighbours fairly and distorting the leading institutions of fairness in society, the courts, which ordinary citizens see as their defenders (Ariely and Uslaner, 2016; and Jong-Sung and Khagram, 2005). Corruption diverts money from needy people and restricts foreign direct investment (FDI).

According to economic theory, corruption could minimise economic growth by lowering investment incentives (for domestic and foreign entrepreneurs). From a political standpoint, on the other hand, it includes corrupt political leaders who exploit their influence for their gain. Furthermore, from a societal perspective, corruption has far-reaching implications for the social system, eventually affecting the public that has lost or does not have confidence in the democratic system. Corruption acts as a tax in cases where entrepreneurs are asked for bribes before their businesses can be launched, or corrupt officials later request shares in the profits of their investments. Given the need for privacy and the confusion about whether bribe-takers can keep their end of the bargain, corruption acts as an especially pernicious tax in Zambia. It is widely acknowledged that corruption affects the composition of government spending: corrupt governments spend less on education and health and potentially more on public investment. Corruption further slows economic growth, breeding poverty over time. At the same time, poverty can be a source of corruption, as poor countries may be unable to commit adequate resources to establish institutions. People in need are more likely to abandon their moral values and the legal system.

Concluding Remarks

In this chapter, we used secondary data sets and widely acknowledged corruption measures to explore the causes and consequences of corruption in Zambia. Our study identifies the adverse effects of corruption on national development observed in the data. As in other studies, we note that corruption reduces economic growth and service provision to people experiencing poverty who look to the government for help. Unlike prior research, we have compelling evidence of corruption's causes, consequences, measurements, institutional framework, successes, failures, prospects, and opportunities. The impact of corruption found in the literature necessitates using novel ways based on theoretical frameworks addressed in this chapter. In Zambia, corruption impacts income distribution, an integral part of economic development. Furthermore, corruption in Zambia is changing the impact of business transparency on procurement bidding on government tenders.

The authors investigated the subject's conceptual and theoretical assumptions. Following an in-depth but condensed analysis of the conceptual and theoretical background, a utilitarian-hedonistic theory of corruption was suggested based on Merton's (1938) strain theory and deviance topology, which gave rise to the social learning theory of corruption and social disorder corruption theory. The authors hope that the suggested utilitarian-hedonistic theory's intrinsic and extrinsic insights will assist stakeholders in comprehending the unique character of corruption among Zambians and, as a result, better equip them to devise measures to combat the issue. Our work broadly sheds new insight into corruption's causes and repercussions, particularly in developing countries like Zambia. It serves as a valuable complement to prior research on the causes and consequences of corruption.

References

Acemoglu, D., & Robinson, J. (2012). *Why nations fail: The origins of power, prosperity, and poverty*. London: Crown Publishers.

AfroBarometer Working Paper No. 148. http://afrobarometer.org/publications/wp148-why-do-some africans-pay-bribes-while-other-africans-dont

Akers, R. L., & Sellers, C. S. (2009). *Criminology theories* (5th ed.). NY: Oxford University Press.

Ariely, G., & Uslaner, E. M. (2016). Corruption, fairness, and inequality. *International Political Science Review*, 38 (3). doi: 10.1177/0192512116641091

Bernard, T. J., Snipes, J. B., & Gerould, A. L. (2010). *Vold's theoretical criminology* (6th ed.) York, NY: Oxford University Press.

Bertelsmann Foundation. (2014). Bertelsmann transformation index (2014). Zambia country report, www.btiproject. Org/fileadmin/Inhalte/reports/2014/pdf/BTI%202 014%20Zambia.pdf
Brinkerhoff, D. (2000). Assessing political will for anti-corruption efforts: An analytic framework. *Public Administration and Development*, 20(3), 239–252. DOI:10.1002/1099-162X (200008)20:3<239: AID-PAD138>3.0.CO;2-3
Business Anti-Corruption Portal, Zambia country profile, www.business-anti-corrupt ion.com/countryprofiles/ sub-Saharan-Africa/Zambia/snapshot.aspx
Center for International Private Enterprise. (2016). *Zambia's corruption crisis: Causes, consequences, and solutions.*
Collier, P. (2009). *War guns and votes: Democracy in dangerous places.* New York, NY: Harper.
CPIB. (2014). *Annual report 2014.* Singapore: Corrupt Practices Investigation Bureau.
Debski, J. (2018). Gender and corruption: The neglected role of culture. *European Journal of Political Economy*, 55, 526–537.
De Graaf, G. (2010). Causes of corruption: Towards a contextual theory of corruption. *Public Administration Quarterly*, 31, No. One-half (SPRING 2007-SUMMER 2007), 39–86 (48 pages) SPAEF.
Ezeh, A. C., Leonard, L. C., & Etodike, C. E. (2016). Corruption in Nigeria organizations: Theories and implications. *International Journal in Management and Social Science*, 5 (7).
Freedom House. (2013). Freedom in the World: Zambia country report, www.freed omhouse.org/report/freedomworld/2013/Zambiahttp://www.u4.no/publications/ combating-illicit-financialflows-and-related-corruption-in-Africa-towards-a-more integrated-and-effective-approach/
Glaeser, E. L., & Saks, R. E. (2006). Corruption in America. *Journal of Public Economics*, 90 (6-7), 1053–1072.
Global Competitiveness Report (GCR). (2015–2016). Zambia. www3.weforum.org/ docs/gcr/2015-2016
Heywood, P. M. (2015). *Routledge handbook of political corruption.* New York, NY: Routledge.
Hochester, A., & Copes, H. (2008). *Where I am from, Criminal predators and their environment.* Boston, MA: Jones and Bartlett.
International Crisis Group (ICS). (2017). Zambia: The Need for Genuine Reform. www.emerald.com/insight/content/doi/10.1108/IJOTB-03-03-04-2000-B013/ full/pdf?title=beyond-african-humanism-economic-reform-in-post-independent-zambia
Johnson, M. (1998). Fighting systemic corruption: Social foundations for institutional reform. *European Journal of Research*, 10(1), 85–105.
Jong-Sung, Y., & Khagram, S. (2005). A comparative study of inequality and corruption. *American Sociological Review*, 70(1), 136–157.
Lusaka Times. (2014). "Zambia's 2012 Auditor general report under PF Government is now available", www.lusakatimes.com/2014/01/16/zambias-2012-auditor-gene ral-report-pf-government-now-available/
Merton, R. K. (1938). Social structure and anomie. *American Sociological Review*, 3(5), 672–682.

Mlambo, D. N., Mubecua, M., Mpanza, S. E., & Mlambo, V. H. (2019). Corruption and its implications for development and good governance: A perspective from post-colonial Africa. *Journal of Economics and Behavioral Studies*, 11(1), 39–47, February 2019. ISSN: 2220–6140

Naher, K., Hoque, R., Hassan, M. S., Balabanova, D., Adams, A. M. & Ahmed, S. M. (2020). The influence of corruption and governance in the delivery of frontline health care services in the public sector: A scoping review of current and prospects in low and middle-income countries of South and Sout-east Asia. *BMC Public Health*, 20(1), 880.

NORAD. (2011). Joint evaluation of support to anticorruption efforts – Zambia, www.oecd.org/countries/tanzania/48912843.pdf

Paldam, M. (2002). The cross-country pattern of corruption: Economics, culture and the seesaw dynamics. *European Journal of Political Economy*, 18, 215–240. https://doi.org/10.1016/S0176-2680(02)00078-2

Sandholtz, W., & Taagepera, R. (2005). Corruption, culture, and communism. *International Review of Sociology*, 15(15), 109–131.

Schacter, M. (2005). A framework for evaluating institutions of accountability. In A. Shah (Ed.), *Fiscal management* (pp. 229–245). Washington, DC: World Bank.

Schedler, A. (1999). Restraining the state: Conflicts and agents of accountability. In A. Schedler, L. Diamond, & M. F. Plattner (Eds.), *The self-restraining state: Power and accountability in new democracies* (pp. 333–350). Boulder, CO: Lynne Rienner Publishers.

Scott, R. (2005). Institutional theory: Contributing to a theoretical research programme. *Great Minds in Management: The Process of Theory Development*, 2(37), 460–484.

Singer, S. D., & Hensley, C. (2004). Applying social learning theory to childhood and adolescent fire-setting: Can it lead to serial murder? *International Journal of Offender Therapy and Comparative Criminology*, 48, 461.

Steenbeek, W., & Hipp, J.R. (2011). A longitudinal test of social disorganisation theory: Feedback effects among cohesion, social control, and disorder. *Criminology*, 49(3), 833–871.

The Republic of Zambia. (2012). Anti-Corruption Act No. 3 of 2012. https://parliament.gov.zm/

Tittle, C. R. (2004). Social learning theory and the explanation of crime: A guide for the new century. *Contemporary Sociology: A Journal of Reviews*, 33(6), 716.

Transparency International. (2007). "Global Corruption Report 2007: Corruption and Judicial Systems". Berlin.

Transparency International. (2023). What is corruption? Retrieved from www.transparency.org/en/what-is-corruption

Transparency International Zambia Chapter. (2015). Causes, consequences, and remedies of corruption in Zambia.

Truex, R. (2011). Perception of political corruption as a function of legislation. *Journal of Economic Behavior & Organization*, 78(2), 351–364.

UNDP. (2005). *Institutional arrangements to combat corruption: A comparative study*, United Nations Development Programme Democratic Governance Practice Team UNDP Regional Centre in Bangko.

U.S. Department of State. (2013). Zambia 2013 Human Rights Report [Country Reports on Human Rights Practices]. https://2009-2017.state.gov/j/drl/rls/hrrpt/2013humanrightsreport/

Uslaner, E. (2008). Economic inequality and the quality of government (July 2, 2005). Available at SSRN: https://ssrn.com/abstract=82446 or http://dx.doi.org/10.2139/ssrn.824466

Vito, G., Maahs, J., & Homes, R. (2007). *Criminology: Theory, research, and policy* (2nd ed.). Boston, MA: Jones and Barrlett.

World Bank. (2006). The abuse of public office for private gain. Retrieved from www.worldbank.org/en/home

Zambia Daily Mail. (2014, April 9). Press release [Newspaper]. Retrieved from www.daily-mail.co.zm/

CONCLUSION: THE WAY FORWARD

Deconstructing the Many Faces of Corruption in Africa

Ina Kubbe, Emmanuel Saffa Abdulai and Michael Johnston

This book has explored how corrupt practices manifest in African societies, categorising them under political and socio-economic themes. It seeks to help understand how and why corruption has prevailed in these spheres by focusing on the following significant questions that guided the studies:

1. What are the specific corruption issues facing ten selected African countries?
2. How do those issues resemble and differ from each other and those assumed in the mainstream anti-corruption literature and reform playbooks?
3. What broader lessons can be learned from a detailed study of those cases?

To answer these questions, we have presented chapters addressing theoretical and empirical gaps in our literature on corruption's causes, manifestations and consequences. While part one of the volume deals with corruption in the political sphere in South Africa, Nigeria, Sierra Leone, Uganda, Cameroon and Tunisia, the second part covers socio-economic activities marked by corruption in Djibouti, Mauritius, Ghana and Zambia.

Two issues – bureaucratic and institutional decay – often listed as the leading causes of corruption have been addressed in South Africa, Nigeria and Mauritius cases. These chapters look beyond those traditional arguments at cultural and specific human dimensions accounting for *why* corruption remains so lucrative and deeply entrenched. While it is impossible to quantify the underlying motivations, these chapters bring a new focus to the study of corruption in Africa.

The volume also demonstrates that the notion that corruption is synonymous with African governance is misplaced and condescending.

That notion ignores decades of effort and the evolution of strategies and results achieved by the many African states. In the same light, the argument that corruption is a Western concept alarmingly oversimplifies graft while undermining the fight against it. Undisputedly, corruption remains a global menace undermining governance and effective service delivery for people with low incomes, protection and promotion of fundamental human rights, legitimate and effective state institutions, the rule of law, and checks and balances both necessary and sufficient to reduce abuses of power. As Johnston and Fritzen (2021) note, corruption should not be fought alone; broader issues of justice, fairness, service delivery and human rights should be tackled together with the fight against corruption.

Furthermore, our book emphasises the pressing need to strengthen democratic structures, civil society, media, and think tanks to continue engaging corruption's emerging issues and norms. However, as Johnston and Fritzen put it, the anti-corruption approach has no silver bullet. We further agree with their proposition that it is time in the global anti-corruption movement for introspection about what has worked and what has not, and for a corresponding evolution in theories, strategies and tactics.

We have outlined measures and tools to address corruption issues and reduce kleptocracy and entrenched political monopolies in several African countries. The book accepts that corruption remains a challenge in many countries and will take a holistic, long-term response to its political and socio-economic causes and effects. To that end, we offer the following recommendations:

1. *Contextualised approaches*: Corruption is multidimensional and must be treated as a multidisciplinary issue with several approaches. Moreover, each approach should suit the specific context in which it is applied. No "silver bullet" approach is possible; strategies must depend on the country's broader political and social environment and localised circumstances (Kramer, 2007). As we have emphasised in several chapters, the drive to fight corruption must be homegrown and locally driven. Approaches to fighting corruption have sometimes failed because of perceptions of the continuing influence of neocolonial dominance and control. This narrative must change.

Corrupt actors in the public sector and politicians have exploited this narrative to gain sympathy from the populace and stymie any deterrence imposed by law, perpetuating corruption that benefits only themselves, their families, and their cronies.

The violence and uncertainties accompanying Oligarch and Clan corruption can discourage flourishing anti-corruption reforms. Therefore, reform priorities should create a safe, valued political and economic space where citizens and businesses can articulate, discuss, and defend their interests and needs (Johnston, 2014). Each anti-corruption strategy should be tailored to meet the peculiarities of the country it is meant to be implemented. Localising strategies will provide ownership of the approach and fit the situational background in which strategies are being developed.

2. *Focus on different types of corruption in different sectors*: Different forms appear depending on the country and region. While Koelble discusses levels of state capture in South Africa, Cheromoi et al. describe how political corruption in Uganda, facilitated by informal interactions among political actors, has shaped formal institutions and their corruption tendencies. Post-independence Uganda has seen many political regimes and leaders, yet "a common thread woven through these political regimes is seemingly corrupt behaviour".

Similarly, Marcella Samba-Sesay's chapter on Sierra Leone points to electoral corruption, including vote buying and electoral violence, abuse, harassment, smear campaigns, intimidation and, of particular concern, Violence against Women in Elections (VAWE). These and several other forms of electoral malpractice seem to be well-organised parts of a grand corruption scheme to influence electoral outcomes in local politics. Violence and fraudulent strategies have gradually become unchecked patterns in electoral politics. VAWE was increasingly visible in the 2018 Elections when female aspirants were beaten. It "threatens the integrity of the electoral process and the quality of democracy because it coercively excludes women from having a voice in the political and governance in their country". The causes of this injustice are rooted in deep-seated patriarchal structures manifested in all aspects of life, cultural and traditional practices, and legal, educational and economic inequalities between women and men in Sierra Leone.

As in many regions worldwide, lobbying is mainly unregulated in Africa. Lobbying is not inherently wrong, and it differs from corruption because it is part of the democratic process due to the involvement of citizens and their right to influence political actors. However, if lobbying is unchecked, corrupt activity and networks can arise in forms harmful to democratic rights. Therefore, lobbying requires excellent attention at a very early stage of a country's democratic development. As Barry Solaiman's analysis of the Tunisian case reveals, lobbying remains a garden for the growth of corrupt institutionalised patronage. It undermines the accountability of institutions such as the parliament and judiciary. Corruption led to declining institutional trust, as people were concerned about favouritism and nepotism. Lobbying has influenced the wrongful appointment of persons who lack any meritorious standing. As in Sierra Leone, political intimidation in Tunisia keeps voters away from the polling stations on election day and helps the most corrupt candidates win office. Furthermore, vote buying entrenches kleptocrats who can pay for the vote, denying good candidates with few resources a chance to participate in the electoral competition and taking advantage of voters' poverty while doing nothing to alleviate it. Solaiman's chapter highlights the lack of suitable mechanisms for identifying institutional corruption. While lobbying regulations, including codes of conduct and transparent registers, are relatively common worldwide, the specific rules and mechanisms have yet to be adopted by those on the ground in Tunisia.

3. *Path dependency and historical roots*: African countries have different historical backgrounds and peculiarities, making a one-size-fits-all approach to corruption a recipe for failure. As Koelble describes in his chapter about post-colonial South Africa, the country had a "big bang" moment in 1994, but in the attempt to create a functional post-apartheid democracy, some fundamentals such as the "reorganisation of the state and the legitimisation of its civil services" were overlooked. Questions regarding what a post-colonial democracy should look like, how it should be governed, and whether the Western norms, models and assumptions upon which many post-colonial constitutions are based are even appropriate for implementation have yet to be fully addressed. The South African situation is similar to that of Central and Eastern Europe, which also suffers from high levels of state capture and kleptocratic politics.

As described in the chapter on Uganda written by Cheromoi et al., political corruption is deeply rooted in historical political structures created by state actors whose focus is accumulating wealth and preserving power. The post-independence political history of Uganda and other contextual factors such as ethnicity have given rise to leaders whose behaviours are primarily shaped by those goals. Thus, curbing corruption at the political level requires addressing "the political historical question that influences the behaviours, incentives and sanctions of the formal institutions that are conduits of political corruption". Furthermore, the case of Tunisia shows that if the history of a country and the path dependency of corruption are not considered, important dynamics are neglected. As Solaiman writes in his chapter, Tunisia has often been used as a case study to test theories developed by Western academicians. That process has been hampered by information and power asymmetries between scholars with access to academic journals and other resources and Tunisian citizens who experienced the revolution but do not have access to such resources.

4. *Deep, long-term democratisation approaches*: It is becoming increasingly evident that for the anti-corruption movement to be successful, as Johnston and Fritzen (2021) postulate, there needs to be a deep-seated democratic form of government beyond just the artificial classification of a democratic state. Consolidated democracies tend to have more vital institutions that check corruption and abuse of office. In the same vein, countries with less democratic governments, or no democracy at all, have weaker institutions and less control of power and the abuse thereof. Thus, instituting democracy and strengthening state institutions are essential for fighting corruption. This book has indicated that to curb corruption, societies must institute deep democratisation to further a long-term anti-corruption approach. This

implies that synching with Johnston and Fritzen (2021) and other researchers and practitioners, winning the war against corruption is possible. However, efforts should "focus on justice and fairness, considerable tolerance for political contention, and a willingness to stick with the reform cause over a long process of thoroughgoing, sometimes discontinuous political change". (Johnston and Fritzen 2021). In particular, short-term strategies should be discouraged because only long-term changes in political culture solve an endemic problem in society.

The case of Cameroon, where democracy continues to exist in name only, underscores this point. There, a dictatorship has provided the garden for corruption to flourish. Kwei Haliday Nyingchia describes how state institutions crumble and, due to the absence of political will, the implementation and enactment of productive reforms are minimal. In particular, the judiciary and prosecution services are fragile and ineffective. To control corruption, the independence of the judiciary and other anti-corruption bodies, as well as a potent political opposition, are needed in order to ensure checks and balances and monitor the executive and other institutions without any possibility of interference. Furthermore, criminalisation of conduct such as illicit enrichment, the institution of declaration of assets and severe sanctions for non-declaration are badly needed. This approach is also crucial to increase public trust and political participation. Furthermore, the country still has meagre official salaries, favouritism and systematic impunity.

Corruption remains a significant challenge in Zambia, despite the creation of watchdog institutions and institutional and legal reforms led by governments since independence and the country's transition from a one-party state in the early 1990s. In particular, the public sector has been heavily affected by endemic corruption and misappropriation of public resources, and impunity is common.

Democratic backsliding also occurs in South Africa and Sierra Leone, where electoral fraud damages the quality of elections, and citizens lose trust in institutions and faith in democratic processes. In contrast, however, the South Africa chapter shows how democratic institutions fight back. Still, the state needs committed prosecutors and judges capable of independently assessing case materials. For its part, despite its recent travails, Tunisia still stands apart from North African countries. Such transitions to democracy do not come quickly, and newfound freedoms can be fragile initially before they become entrenched. Overcoming those transitional problems is a critical challenge that Tunisia must navigate in the years and decades. At the same time, the fight against corruption allows countries to design robust checks and balances for their democratic system, such as lobbying regulations. It is difficult enough to design and implement such regulations in countries with established democratic systems that have entrenched mechanisms of governance. Once powerful interests become embedded in transitional situations, they usually resist changes threatening their power.

However, democracy should not only be limited to formal hardware. It must also delve deeper to include fairness, loyalty, legitimacy, and credible and visible accountability – in short, the essential characteristics of high-quality democracy and its implementation. South Africa shows how the fight against corruption cannot depend only on the mere collapse of an old and unjust regime: Koelble explains in Chapter One how corrupt cabals, led by families, have hijacked governance and imposed their dominance in South Africa. Anti-corruption groups and democratising states must build strong state institutions. Additionally, devising and implementing locally rooted and appropriate national anti-corruption strategies is a way to build consensus around minimising corruption. The case of Nigeria demonstrates that although the country has formal institutions and strategies to curb corruption, including three major anti-corruption agencies, corruption remains firmly rooted in the system, as shown by the lack of essential social services and affordable livelihoods. The anti-corruption infrastructure is not applied equally to all Nigerians; instead, it is skewed in favour of ruling party members and sometimes fails to investigate high-profile cases.

5. *Leadership and political will*: The case studies on Nigeria, Sierra Leone, Zambia, Uganda, Cameroon and Mauritius underline the lack of committed leadership willing to minimise, if not eradicate, corruption in these countries. For instance, Uganda has suffered from a leadership crisis since its independence in 1962, resulting in corruption flourishing without nationalistic, patriotic and clean leadership. Uganda's post-independence leaders have failed to respect various laws and constitutions but have exploited citizens' resources, consolidating state power instead of building functioning institutions and pursuing the interests of ordinary people. By focusing on building personal power based on their political parties, families, tribes, friends, and associates, they have turned formal institutions into conduits of corruption.

As Riccardo D'Emidio's chapter reveals, even in the churches of Ghana, there is either no leadership with the know-how needed to strengthen institutions and build systems to minimise corrupting incentives or a total lack of interest in touching the "holy grail" because the leaders benefit from it. Therefore, fighting political corruption requires addressing historical political issues that continue to rotate around the leadership crisis (Mbandlwa, 2020). Cheromoi et al. write that corruption control "requires long-term thinking, strategies, and investments to nurture a new breed of leaders ready to resist our bad political history and stir development for everyone". Political leadership committed to fighting corruption must emerge to mitigate its devastating effects. Leadership and political will must be actively cultivated, not expected to spring up independently. Leadership training in transparency, accountability, and anti-corruption measures must be instituted in schools, colleges, and universities. Professional training for public officials to refresh the ethos and ethics of anti-corruption administration will be essential.

6. *Non-state actors*: By safeguarding democracy, civil society organisations play a crucial role in fighting corruption. However, governments must create and maintain an enabling environment if civil society and the media are to play their watchdog role concerning governance and government institutions. Creating an environment that enables citizens to pursue and defend their interests and empowers them to fight for their rights by political means is critical to amplifying citizens' voices against corruption, abuses, and injustice. For instance, in Sierra Leone, during the elections of 2018, civil society election observers blew the whistle on electoral corruption. Marcella Samba-Sesay shows how an organised, vibrant, and fully functional civil society can support and promote electoral integrity, but also demonstrates the limitations of civil society in addressing issues such as campaign finance and the unregulated use of money.

Koelble also argues that the gap between civil and political society needs to be bridged but shows how that requires adequate infrastructure accessible to all. In addition, the state must build a civil service that impartially provides public goods. He concludes, "Without a commitment to an impartial civil service decoupled from the self-enrichment strategies of politicians, it will be difficult, if not impossible, to develop a transformative development trajectory".

This is also consistent with developments in Nigeria. Kallon's case study shows that coupled with the lack of political will, bureaucratic burdens increase citizens' apathy and reduce their public participation in the fight against corruption. Therefore, the Nigerian government should be more proactive in supporting civil society participation. Creating a legal framework and monitoring budget, planning, and implementation through public hearings and surveys can enable greater public participation. Narrowing the gaps among citizens, civil society organisations, and the government would strengthen the government's response to corruption.

7. *The private sector*: Corruption often occurs when the public and private sectors interact. Therefore, controls only work when the governmental and private sector interface is strictly regulated. Due to its rich natural resources, the African continent remains attractive for foreign companies to invest. However, that has led investors from, for example, India, China, and other countries lacking comprehensive codes of conduct regulating how their investors do business overseas to enter African markets. Despite being a risky investment destination, Djibouti has attracted investors in several sectors. The chapter by Wael Saghir describes how corruption risks become political risks *via* bribery of government officials to admit investors or award contracts.

Such corrupt dealings can discourage honest and efficient competitors from entering the markets. Although Djibouti has criminalised the acceptance of bribes by public officials, the country still requires more robust responses to corruption and better deterrence and implementation mechanisms.

Corruption is not only problematic for investors and multinational corporations; it is also a threat to the host states. Companies can corruptly bypass the host state's environmental, labour force and natural resource protections. Foreign state-owned enterprises can bribe host-state officials to secure business advantages, as with Chinese investments in Djibouti and other African states.

The chapter shows that, on the one hand, the effectiveness of corruption controls depends partly upon changing cultural perceptions of corruption. At the same time, the collaborative approach to combating corruption has resulted in capital-exporting countries imposing rules of engagement for their investors while overseas.

In a similar vein, high-level corruption in Zambia involves both public servants and private entities. Effective anti-corruption action requires active support and participation from all manner of actors in government and the economy.

The chapter by Chisanga et al. identifies the adverse effects of corruption on national development. Corruption reduces economic growth and service provision to people experiencing poverty. In Zambia, it distorts the income distribution, an integral part of economic development, and strongly affects the public's faith in reform efforts. Furthermore, corruption negatively impacts business transparency in procurement bidding on government tenders.

Corporate corruption in development is introduced in the case study of Mauritius written by Sanjeev Narrainen. International development projects represent a fertile ground for corporate corruption, and abuses emanating from the supply side have become pervasive and entrenched in the corporate world. Overlaps of private sector corruption and intricate development projects in the energy sector are explored in this case study. Those problems put tremendous pressure upon the government and undermine anti-corruption actions in two highly volatile sectors that, research has shown, are highly susceptible to corrupt undertakings. The study reveals that contractors and consultants working on development projects can become agents of corruption by facilitating illegal and unethical practices from the supply side, and that external actors bear a great deal of responsibility in their interactions with host countries. Moreover, robust anti-corruption laws are insufficient by themselves to discourage companies from engaging in bribery schemes.

The chapters on Djibouti, Mauritius and Zambia highlight that corruption is not only an internal problem within countries. External actors can also create it. Investing countries – democracies and autocratic states such as

Russia and China – often take advantage of transitional countries, much as they misuse legal loopholes in their systems. Therefore, state capture and robbery can flourish, weakening the country economically and undermining democratic processes. Several chapters highlight the challenging road to development many states must travel and how foreign investors can actively encourage or fight corruption.

8. *Discourses and Narratives*: Riccardo D'Emidio's chapter discusses the role of churches in the fight against corruption in Ghana. Faith, religion and spirituality are deep-seated in citizens' private lives and the state's various functions. Therefore, the government and civil society organisations encourage Ghana's religious leaders to initiate anti-corruption campaigns and awareness-raising initiatives. D'Emidio describes the explosion of the so-called Charismatic movement in Ghana and explores the discursive linkages between the Neo-Pentecostal movement's focus on wealth and prosperity and the overall "corruption complex" in the country. The research indicates that discourses and norms embedded in relationships of power and patronage constrain citizens' engagement and action against corruption. The "corruption complex" is a multifaceted social and political inequality system reproduced by general discourse and elite discourses. There is a significant linkage between the Charismatic quest for wealth and the banalisation, or "the cultural legitimation", of corruption in Ghana. This link is permissive, with ministers giving their blessing and enabling a set of corrupt behaviours feeding into the overall corruption complex. The magnitude and pervasiveness of the Charismatic movement in Ghana raises ethical questions about the effectiveness and impact of anti-corruption awareness campaigns while highlighting social processes, values and expectations that are overlooked in most mainstream anti-corruption scenarios.

Our volume illustrates the urgent need for multidisciplinary and diverse approaches to better understand and conceptualise corruption as an institutionalised practice in African governance. Further, it explains some social issues, like corruption and religion, that are rarely discussed. While this book does not pretend to settle any of those issues once and for all, it is an invitation for fresh thinking and innovative research. Networks of young and established African-oriented researchers now must take hold of the narrative on corruption on the continent.

References

Johnston, M. 2014. *Corruption, Contention, and Reform: The Power of Deep Democratization*. Cambridge and New York: Cambridge University Press.

Johnston, M., and Fritzen, S. 2021. *The Conundrum of corruption: Reform for social justice*. Routledge.

Kramer, W. Michael. 2007. Corruption and Fraud in International Aid Projects. *U4 Brief*, 4. Online: www.cmi.no/publications/file/2752-corruption-and-fraud-in-international-aid-projects.pdf (accessed 10 May 2024).

Mbandlwa, Z. (2020). Challenges of African leadership after the independence. *Solid State Technology*, 63(6), 13241–13254.

INDEX

Note: Page numbers in *italics* indicate a figure and page numbers in **bold** indicate a table on the corresponding page.

ACC *see* Anti-Corruption Commission
Access to Information Authority 113
Acemoglu, D. 201
ADB *see* African Development Bank
Adhidjo, Amadou 92
ADP *see* Alliance Democratic Party
African Development Bank 154–155
African National Congress 13, 17–18, 19
African Union Convention on Preventing and Combating Corruption 95
Agyin-Asare, Charles 189, 190
Alain Hao Thyn Voon 155
Alliance Democratic Party 56
All Peoples Congress 57
All Progressives Congress 43
Alston, P. 59
Amin, Idi 77, 78
Amiri, Khalil 110
Amundsen, I. 71–72
Anand, V. 161
ANC *see* African National Congress
Ani, N. A. 34
ANIF *see* National Agency for Financial Investigation
Anti-Bribery Act of the UK 6
anti-corruption: agenda recommendations 215–222; and the civil society (non-legal) strategy 20, 22–25, 139; and the legal strategy 20–22, 139; misconceptions leading to the failure of 182
Anti-Corruption Commission 8, 203, 207
Apata, G. O. 70
APC *see* All Peoples Congress; All Progressives Congress
Ashford, B. 161
Asiimwe, G. B. 81
Atta Mills, John 192
Authority for Good Governance and the Fight Against Corruption 115, 116, 118

Bacharach, B. 163
'bad apples' perspective of corruption 161
'bad barrel' perspective of corruption 161–162
Baker, W. E. 162
Balachandrudu, K. 77
ballot-stuffing 57–58
Bauhr, Monika 31–32
BEE *see* Black Economic Empowerment policies
Belt and Road Initiative 131
Ben Ali 104, 109

Bernard, T. J. 201–202
Betamax 150–151
Binaisa, Godfrey 79
Birch, S. 59
Biya, Paul 92
Bjarnegard, E. 54
Black Economic Empowerment policies 19–20
"Black First Land First" 16
Blundo, G. 169, 181, 190
Boddewyn, J. 167
Boko Haram 38, 44
Bourgeois, L. J. 162
Bretton Woods Institutions 92–93
BRI *see* Belt and Road Initiative
bribery 107, 134–135, 206; sweetening and grooming process of 160
"Bring Back Our Girls" campaign 38
Bromley, P. 76
Buckley, P. J. 163
Buhari, Muhammadu 45
Burmeister & Wain Scandinavian Contractor 154–155

Caid, Beji 110, 117
Cameroon 5, 88–89; anti-corruption measures and their effects in 89–90; historical causes of corruption in 92–93; impunity and absence of responsibility in 96–98; political establishment and corruption in 90–92; political will to fight corruption in 93–96, 100–101; quality and independence of institutions in 98–100
Cameroon People's Democratic Movement 91
campaign finance 53, 56–57, 66
Canada: lobbying legislation in 118–122, *121*
capitalism 15
capture 164–165
Casson, M. 163
CDA *see* Critical Discourse Analysis
CEB *see* Central Electricity Board
Central Electricity Board 154–155
Chahed, Youssef 104
Challenges of African Leadership after the Independence 83
'Change Habits, Oppose Corruption' Project 95–96
Charismatic Christianity *see* Neo-Pentecostal Christianity

Chatterjee, Partha 23–25
chatwas 151
Cheeseman, N. 51
Chikulo, B. C. 33–34
China 131–132, 137
Chinweuba, G. E. 36
Chipkin, Ivor 14
CHOC Project *see* 'Change Habits, Oppose Corruption' Project
Cingano, F. 159
civil society organizations 22–23, 50–51, 204
Code of Conduct Bureau 44
coercion 135
commercial risk 136
Commission for Human Rights and Administrative Justice 182
complexity theory *see* complex-systems approach
complex-systems approach 74, 75, 76, 82
CONAC *see* National Anti-Corruption Commission
conventional corruption 135
Convention on Combating Bribery of Foreign Public Officials in International Business Transactions 142, 144
corporate corruption 152–154; and allocation of resources and power 162–163; analysis of 159–161; and capture 164–165; case study of 154–159, *157*; challenges of international development projects and 168–171; and corrupt networks 163–164; determinants and attributes of 165–168, **166**, *169*, 171
corruption: combating 20–25, 26, 139–142; as a commercial and political risk 132–137, 143; definition of 14, 33, 132, 198; in development projects 151–153; in economic sector 36, 39–42; effects of the quality and independence of institutions on 98–100; humanitarian sector 44; and impunity 96–98; as an institutionalised practice 182–183, 187; need and greed 31; negative effects of 34–35, 70; political 33, 36, 39; and political lobbying 105–106, 107–108; in political parties 36, 42–43; and political will 93–94; social determinants of 43; theories of 73–75,

80, 182–183, 198–203; using the legal route to combat 20–22, 26
"corruption complex" theory 182–184, 193–194
COVID-19 pandemic 40–42, 99, 109, 150
CPDM *see* Cameroon People's Democratic Movement
Critical Discourse Analysis 186–188, 187; of Ghanaian churches 187–189
CSOs *see* civil society organizations
cybernetic theory 74–75

Dahl, R. A. 162
Daily Maverick 23
dash 133–134, 183
decolonization 19–20
Della Porta 72
democracy 17, 42
Deneulin, S. 194
Djibouti 6; Chinese investment in 131–132, 137–138; combating corruption in 140–141; Foreign Direct Investment in 131–132, 137; investment corruption in 137–139, 143
Doh, J. 167
DP World 138–139
Dye, Thomas 83

ECAs *see* Export Credit Agencies
Economic and Financial Crimes Commission 44, 100
Economic Freedom Fighters 16
economic sector corruption 39–40; and COVID-19 pandemic 40–42
EFCC *see* Economic and Financial Crimes Commission
EFF *see* Economic Freedom Fighters
Elections Management Bodies 55
electoral corruption 39, 43, 50–51; and addressing manipulation through civil societies 64–67; and legal manipulation 53; in 2018 Sierra Leone elections 51–54, 67–68; strategies 54–56; and 'turn-out buying' 58; and vote buying 56–57
electoral fraud *see* electoral corruption
electoral observation strategies 55–56
electoral turnovers 52
electoral violence 50, 54; efforts to address 64; explanation of 58–59; in Sierra Leone 59–61; against women 53–54, 61–64
embezzlement 107
EMBs *see* Elections Management Bodies
Ericsson Egypt LTD 138
ExIm Bank *see* US Export-Import Bank
Export Credit Agencies 142, 144
extortion 135
extractive political corruption 71–72, 81

facilitation payments 135, 138
Fairclough, N. 186
Faulkner, R. R. 162
favouritism 35, 44
FCPA *see* Foreign Corrupt Practices Act
FDI *see* Foreign Direct Investment
#FeesMustFall 16
Foreign Corrupt Practices Act 141, 144
Foreign Direct Investment 131–132; and combating corruption 139–143; and corruption risk 132–137; in Djibouti 131–132, 137–139
fraud 107
Fritzen, S. 215, 217–218

Gbla, Osman 78
Gerould, A. L. 201–202
Ghana 7; anti-corruption framework in 182–184; Critical Discourse Analysis of Neo-Pentecostal Christianity in 187–192; Neo-Pentecostal and Charasmatic movement in 180–181, 184–186
Gifford, P. 181
Golooba-Mutebi, F. 79, 80
Graaf, G. D. 90, 165
Grand Corruption 135
grassroots lobbying 109
greed corruption 31
Gregory, R. 165
guanxi 133
Gupta, Ajay 14–15
Gupta, Atul 14–15
Gupta-Zuma network 14–15, 21, 22
Gyekye, K. 71

Harriman, T. 158
Hermes, Euler 137
Heward-Mills, Dag 189, 190
Heywood, P. M. 209
higher education 208
historical institutionalism 75, 76, 82

Höglund, K. 58
Hope, K. R. 33–34
Huberts, J. 165
humanitarian sector corruption 44

Ijewereme, O. B. 37, 39
Ike, Chinedu Cyril 46–47
illicit enrichment 95
IMF *see* International Monetary Fund
impartiality 14, 19–20, 25
impunity 96–98
INAI *see* Access to Information Authority
Independent Corrupt Practices and Other Related Offences Commission 44
independent media 23
INLUCC *see* Authority for Good Governance and the Fight Against Corruption
institutional corruption theory 90, 105–106, 200–201, 202–203; and political lobbying 107–108; and the regulation of lobbying 116–118
International Central Gospel Church 189
International Chamber of Commerce's Recommendations to Combat Extortion and Bribery in Business Transactions of 1977 143
International Monetary Fund 37
Islam 38
Isopi, A. 152

Jancsics, D. 163
Jávor, I. 163
Johnson, M. 202
Johnston, M. 215, 217–218
Jones, A. 73
Joshi, M. 161
Judicial Service Commission 204
Jugnauth, Pravind 154–155

Karim, M. A. 38
Karoui, Nabil 110, 111, 117
Kasfir, S. L. 78
Kew, D. 158
Khanna, T. 167
Kherigi, Intissar 110
Kingsley, Mua 96
Klaas, B. 51
kola 183
Kpundeh, S. J. 94
Kukutschka, R. M. B. 94

Laakso, L. 59
Lagesse, Bertrand 155
Lawler, E. J. 163
Leana, C. R. 165
Lehoucq, Fabrice 54
Leiren, M. D. 75
Lessig, Lawrence 108, 117
Light House Chapel International 189
Lincoln, Bruce 184
Lindberg, S. I. 52
lobbying *see* political lobbying
Luiz, J. M. 167
Lule, Yusuf 79
Luo, Y. 90, 169

Mackintosh, R. B. 60
MACP *see* Military Aide to Civil Power
Madonsela, Thuli 16
Mail and Guardian 23
Makara, S. 79, 80
Mandela, Nelson 13, 15
Mapolu, H. 78
Marquardt, Niels 92
Martini, Maíra 43
Mattesini, F. 152
Mauritius 6–7, 150; corruption in 150–151, 170–172
Mbabazi, G. 72
Mbaku, J. M. 39, 72
Mbandlwa, Z. 83
Mbeki, Thabo 15
Mbembe, Achille 20
MDBs *see* Multilateral Development Banks
'Menu of Manipulation, The' 55
Merton, R. K. 210
Meyer, B. 185
Michel, Van Hulten 96
Military Aide to Civil Power 61
Ministry of Crime 22
Moehler, D. C. 52
Mukolu, M. O. 38
Mukoon, Shamshir 155
Multilateral Development Banks 152, 158–159
Mungiu-Pippidi, A. 182, 187, 193
Museveni, Yoweri 79–81, **80**, 82
Mutesa, Fredrick 77
Mwenda, Andrew 77, 78, 81

NACAP *see* National Anti-Corruption Action Plan

National Agency for Financial Investigation 100
National Anti-Corruption Action Plan 182, 184
National Anti-Corruption Commission 89, 95, 99
National Election Watch 51, 55, 61, 64–66
National Grand Coalition 56
National Resistance Movement 79–80, 80
need corruption 31
Need or Greed? Conditions for Collective Action against Corruption 31
Nekyon, Adoko 77
neopatrimonialism 72–73
Neo-Pentecostal Christianity 7, 180–181, 184, 193–194; community of 185–186; concepts of wealth and status in 188–192; Critical Discourse Analysis of 187–189; institutions of 186; practices of 185; themes and discourses of 184–185
nepotism 35, 44
NEW *see* National Election Watch
NGC *see* National Grand Coalition
Nichter, S. 58
Nielsen, R. P. 163
Nigeria 3–4, 32–33; and anti-corruption strategies 44–45, 46–47; and Boko Haram 38; corruption risk factors in 33–34; economic sector corruption in 36, 39–42; effects of corruption in 34–35, 46–47; humanitarian sector corruption in 44; political and institutional corruption in 36, 39; political dynamics of 36–38; political party corruption in 36, 42–43; social sector corruption in 36, 43–44
Nigeria: Evidence of corruption and the influence of social norms 43
Nigeria Open Contracting Portal 41
NOCOPO *see* Nigeria Open Contracting Portal
NRM *see* National Resistance Movement
Nwozor, A. 151

Obote, Milton 77, 78–79
Ochieng, Daudi 77
OECD Anti-Bribery Convention *see* Convention on Combating Bribery of Foreign Public Officials in International Business Transactions
OECD Declaration on International Investment and Multinational Enterprises of 1976 143
Ogodor, B. N. 38
OGP *see* Open Government Partnership
Okello, Tito 79
Okonjo-Iweala, Ngozi 35
Olivier de Sardan, J. P. 181, 182–184, 190
Olukoya, Akinwotu 37
Onama, Felix 77
'On the Campaign Trail: documenting women's experiences on the 2018 Elections' 62
Onuh, Paul Ani 46–47
Open Government Partnership 116, 118
'Operation Sparrow Hawk' 89, 91
Otabil, Mensa 188–189, 190–191
over-monetarization 183

PAD & Company Limited 155
Page, Matthew 37, 38, 40, 44
Palepu, K. 167
Parallel Vote Tabulation 65–66
particularism 81
Party Government 42
Passas, N. 161
Paternoster, R. 169
path dependence 75
PDP *see* People's Democratic Party
PDSA *see* Port de Djibouti S.A.
Pentecostalism 180
People's Democratic Party 43
Perez Chapel International 189
periodisation 76
Phil, F. K. 165
Philp, Mark 33
Pillay, S. 70
Pinotti, P. 159
Pinto, J. 165, 169
police 45, 60
political corruption 33, 36, 39; definition of 71–72; and its history in Uganda 77–80, 81–83, 82; theoretical analysis of 73–75
political intervention 132–133
political lobbying 104, 164; definition of 105; and institutional corruption theory 107–108; legislation in Canada 118–122, *121*; regulation of 116–118; in Tunisia 109–112
political party corruption 36, 42–43, 56–57, 59; and lobbying 111

Political Party Registration Commission 53, 55–56
political risk 132, 134, 136
political stability 158, 159
political will 93–94, 100, 206–207
Port de Djibouti S.A. 138–139
power-preserving political corruption 71–72, 81
PPRC *see* Political Party Registration Commission
press freedom 205
principal-agent theory of corruption 73–74, 134, 135
Prunier, G. 78
PSAM *see* Public Service Accountability Monitor
Public Elections Act 2012 56
Public Service Accountability Monitor 23

Rakodi, C. 194
Ramaphosa, Cyril 3, 16, 19
Reimer, I. 75
religion: four domains of 184
resource diversion 35
#RhodesMustFall 16, 20
Robinson, J. 201
Rodrik, Dani 16–17
Rothstein, Bo 16–18; and a "big bang" approach 18–19, 26
Rotondi, V. 81
Rugumamu, Severine 78
"rule of law" 17
"rules of exception" 24–25

Saied, Kais 111
Saint Louis Gate 154–155; case study of 155–156
Sanders, E. 75
Schattschneider, E. E. 42
Schedler, Andreas 54–55, 206
Shadow State: the Politics of State Capture 14
shame 183–184
Shein, E. 51, 54
Sierra Leone 4, 50; corruption of general elections in 51–54, 67–68; efforts to address election violence in 64; and election violence against women 53–54, 61–64; electoral violence in 59–61; National Election Watch efforts in 64–66; smear campaign against the NEC of 55; vote and turn-out buying in 56–58

Sierra Leone's Peoples Party 57
Simpson, S. 169
SLPP *see* Sierra Leone's Peoples Party
SLT *see* Social Learning Theory
Snipes, J. B. 201–202
social capital 43–44
social disorganisation theory 202, 203
social learning theory 201–202
social sector corruption 36, 43–44
South Africa 3; affects of ANC rule on 13–14; analysis of corruption in 16–19, 25–27; legacies from the apartheid regime of 20; and the Zuma regime 14–16
Stanca, L. 81
Stapenhurst, R. 46
state capture 14, 95; and the Gupta-Zuma network 14–16
Stewart, C. 167
Suárez, D. 76
Suleiman, M. N. 38
Sweden 18
Swilling, Mark 14

Tangri, R. 77, 78, 81
think-tanks 111
Thompson, Dennis F. 107, 108
thuggery 60, 64; *see also* electoral violence
Transparency International 8, 41, 43, 45
Trocaire 62
Tunisia 5–6, 104–106; and the Code of Conduct and Ethics of Public Officials 114–115, 118; legal attempts to tackle corruption in 112–114, 115–116; political lobbying in 109–112; regulation of lobbying in 117–118, 122
turn-out buying 58

Uganda 4–5, 70–71; and the Idi Amin Regime (1971-1979) 78; and the Milton Obote Regime (1962-1971) 77–78; and Obote II (1980-1985) and Tito Okello (1985-1986) 78–79; origins of political corruption in 72–73; patterns of political corruption in 81–83, 82; and the Yoweri Museveni Regime (1986-2017) 79–81, 80
Ugoani 94

UK Bribery Act 2010 141
UKEF *see* UK Export Finance
UK Export Finance 142, 144
unconventional corruption 135
unemployment 208
United Nations Convention Against Corruption 89, 95, 140, 141, 182
US Export-Import Bank 142, 144
US Foreign Corrupt Practices Act 6
Uslaner, E. 209
utilitarian-hedonistic approach to corruption 199–200, 202–203

Van Dijk 187, 191
Vannucci, A. 72
VAWE *see* Violence against Women in Elections
Vickery, C. 51, 54
Violence against Women in Elections 54, 61–64
vote buying 50, 56–57

Walton, G. 73
Warburton, J. 74

'Watermelon Politics' 56
western reforms 35
WhatsApp 60
Whistleblowers 21
"Who is Running America?" 83
Whyte, D. 169
Wiener, Mandy 21, 22
Wiener, Norbert 74–75
World Bank Group 41

Ya Maawe, Nyungu 81
Yu, P. 72

Zambia 6, 7–8, 137; anti-corruption agenda in 203–204; causes of corruption in 205–208; consequences of corruption in 208–210; history of corruption in 197–198; theories on corruption in 199–203
zawadi 133–134
Zondo, Raymond 3
Zondo Commission 15, 16
Zuma, Jacob 3, 13–16, 19, 22; *see also* Gupta-Zuma network

Printed in the United States
by Baker & Taylor Publisher Services